# Money

## How to Find It with Astrology

## Lois M. Rodden

First Printing: 1994 by Data News; Editor: Lynn Rodden

Current Printing: 2006

ISBN: 0-86690-564-2

Cover Design: Jack Cipolla

Published by:
American Federation of Astrologers, Inc.
6535 S. Rural Road
Tempe AZ 85283

Published in the United States of America

# Books by Lois M. Rodden

*Modern Transits*

*Mercury Method of Chart Comparison*

*Astro-Data I: Profiles of Women*

*Astro-Data II: American Book of Charts*

*Astro-Data III*

*Astro-Data IV*

*Astro-Data V: Profiles in Crime*

# Index of Horoscopes

# Contents

I do not know what your destiny may be, but I do know that the only ones of you to find happiness will be those who have found a way to serve.—Albert Schweitzer (1875-1965)

# Section I

## Preliminaries

# Chapter 1

# Introduction

**THE GOOD LIFE** is one that is rich with love and companionship, robust health, a growth of spirit, work that gives us a sense of accomplishment and satisfaction, and enough of the creature comforts to bring us pleasure. Because we live in a physical universe, to gain the good life we must deal with the physical as well as the metaphysical. The balance between the two is our finest dance.

*Money: How To Find It With Astrology* does not explore historic or global economics or stock market cycles. It addresses our everyday down-to-earth concerns about work, career and money in our own lives and in the lives of our clients with the hope that it will answer some of the pragmatic questions of how to live a more successful mundane life.

We astrologers have all found that there is no quick answer in the horoscope. We can't look at a chart and say, "You should work for IBM and bring down forty-thou a year by the time you are 30." We can't take our magic marker pen and connect the dots to say, "You are destined to be a plumber—or a movie star—or a professional criminal." Moreover, we are certainly not a finished product at birth. Growth is a process, whether growth of character and integrity or growth of money and success. A horoscope shows us tools and maps, options and signposts along the path of that process. We are working with one of the most sophisticated and complete symbol systems available to describe the human condition but it does not have proper nouns. Michael Munkasey's *Thesaurus Series* is a voluminous collection of keywords associated with the houses, signs and planets, all of which are pictorial. The names that we select for a given situation represent the image, the archetype that the planet symbolizes. For example, the Moon is often called "mother" or "home" because it represents the principle of our need to nest and nurture, both to receive nourishment and unconditional acceptance and to establish a secure, comfortable niche that is the focal point of our capacity to relate to others. *Money: How To Find It With Astrology* **examines the areas of the horoscope in which we may find the prime indicators of our career and income potential as well as a mundane analysis of planetary symbology**

First of all, there is no planet named *Housewife,* or *Cowboy,* or *Street-person* or *Millionaire.*

Second, if it is possible that any of us are destined to a given role without choice, a horoscope does not give us that information; it describes many choices. Not only the chart but our physical heritage, background and present environment must be taken into account; both nature and nurture play their roles. We are born with a given horoscope that outlines our abilities, needs, drives and methods, but the time and place in which we are born, the family to which we are born, the race and sex in which we are born, as well as the variety of external circumstances that we experience and the options that we choose each day, all serve to comprise who we are at each changing moment of the ongoing process.

For the careers and jobs that we choose, we begin with a reflection of our environment. We may not follow exactly the same career as our parents, but most of us stay in the same general area. The children of a farmer grow up to work somewhere in the periphery of an agriculturally-based environment; Hollywood kids look for their first jobs in some level of the entertainment industry; the sons and daughters of professional people receive a good education to prepare them for the professions or they work in the milieu of education or public service occupations. However, history has brought us to a time when we have more options than ever before, especially in the industrial nations. A farmer's son is able to become a rock star, a city girl may return to the land if it calls to her, and a child who is disadvantaged at birth may strive toward a greater vision by working toward academic scholarships.

Third, we can do more than one thing. Those of us who are fortunate enough to be able to read and have books accessible or rich enough to buy books have options limited only by our own interest and capacity. *Money: How To Find It With Astrology* **explores the avenues of the greatest potential in the horoscope and the most fruitful times to pursue alternate choices.** As we examine the planets, signs and houses of astrology in terms of our commercial life, we will discover vocational indicators which point to our most suitable job avenues as well as our prime areas of financial gain, how to guard against financial loss, how to achieve success in our environment and which workplace gives us the greatest satisfaction. As we trace the planets and signs through the mundane houses, their similarities and differences are outlined according to which of the segments of the horoscope they occupy.

We astrologers draw conclusions in much the same way as an economist, a weather forecaster or an anthropologist; from history, documentation of past events, the present climate and trends, as well as the existing environment and status in order to extrapolate an analysis. A horoscope may be interpreted on as many different levels as we find in our lives. The entire chart may be considered a map of the physical and medical condition, it may illustrate our emotional responses and relationships or it may represent a spiritual mandala. The horoscope may also reveal the landscape of the commercial lifestyle, of how we deal with the fiscal realities of our mundane lives.

Major planetary trends influence world conditions. We are all aware of how the great mutations affect our planet, such as the Uranus-Neptune conjunction of 1993 that changed the map of the world. However, different countries, just as different people, have individual patterns. We read that in Japan, for example, a worker may expect a job to last his lifetime, but in the United States jobs last an average of 4.2 years. Americans, in our short history, have demonstrated initiative, mobility and exploration, sometimes to excess; we not only make more job moves but we move our homes and change our relationships more than the population does in most countries.

Life everywhere is always in flux, always in motion. The natal chart  symbolizes who we are at birth but circumstances change, events occur, other people become involved in our lives and we in theirs. Countries jockey for world position, political parties change and the economy fluctuates as well in its cycles. The value of astrology is that it is a study of life's ebb and flow. Astrology outlines the cycles of major patterns in the heavens as they correlate to events in the world and in our own lives, thus providing those of us who study these planetary cycles with a tremendous advantage.

*Money: Haw To Find It With Astrology* uses the birth data of the Rodden series of Data Collections, as well as those of clients, friends and family. **For people given as examples, all data are listed alphabetically with data sources in Chapter 19.** All of the demonstration charts are presented in the tropical zodiac and Koch house system, except when specified otherwise. The difference between Koch and Equal House Systems is discussed in Chapter 3, "House Systems."

When the term *progressed* (PR) is used, it refers to secondary progressions (a day for a year). The term *transit* (TR) refers to daily planetary motion. *Modern Transits* is recommended to accompany *Money: How To Find It With Astrology* as it outlines a pragmatic approach to gain the optimum results in daily situations. *Interposited* refers to the powerful connection of having a house ruled by a planet that is placed in another house. A dual interposition occurs when both houses have the ruler of one posited in the other, such as the ruler of the second house posited in the tenth house and the ruler of the tenth house posited in the second house, which ties the two houses together in interactive situations as surely as though the rulers were conjunct. The partial interposition exists in every chart, that of having the ruler of one house posited in another, which indicates that the affairs of the house where the planet is posited influence or even take precedence over the affairs of the house that the planet rules.

A reference to "hard" planets and aspects refers to Mars, Saturn, Uranus and Pluto, with squares, oppositions, semisquares and sesquisquares. "Soft" planets and aspects refer to the Moon, Venus and Neptune, trines and sextiles. Character, as well as skill and ability, tends to develop under stress accompanied by rewards so it is the balance of "hard" and "soft" indicators that is optimum.

*Money: How To Find It With Astrology* emphasizes certain houses and neglects others. This is because the patterns of the earth houses, two, six and 10 represent our concern with the mundane life while the water houses, four, eight and 12 signify the patterns of wealth. Planetary activity involving the other houses draws our attention to other matters.

There is one point that must be kept in mind with every chapter if not with every page and that is: **The strength and accuracy of every definition is supplemented or depleted by the introduction, reinforcement or inhibition of other factors.** *(Everything depends on everything else.)* As we go through the work, career, success and money indicators, some of them will have one indication and no more, some will be repeated more than once in various ways and some will be counterbalanced by stronger factors. Each definition of *Money: How To Find It With Astrology* must be reinforced by more than one indication to bring it to term as an event or situation. In some older astrology texts this was called "the rule of three," implying that at least three testimonies were requisite. In the charts of people for whom one career choice dominates, we will find that all the indicators synchronize to repeat the theme over and over.

The classical horoscope is used with 10 planets (the Sun, Moon and eight planets) and nine aspects: the conjunction, semisextile, semisquare, sextile, square, trine, sesquisquare, quincunx and opposition. Aspects are discussed in Chapter 4.

For investments which are benefitted by a long range view of market trends, the works of Jeanne Long and of Raymond Merriman are recommended.

- Jeanne Long: International lecturer on Market Timing, author of *The Universal Clock,* a book illustrating how the famous W. D. Gann really traded. Editor in Chief of the *Trader's Astrological Almanac,* specifically written for traders and investors. www.galacticinvestor.com
- Raymond A. Merriman: Founder and Editor of the *MMA Cycles Report* advisory newsletter used by investors and speculators worldwide. Author of *The Annual Forecasts Book, The Gold Book;*
- *The Sun, the Moon and the Silver Market.* www.mmacycles.com

Information may also be obtained from:

- *Crawford Perspectives,* Astronomically Accurate Market Timing. www.crawfordperspectives.com
- *The Fibonacci Market Timer.* www.jigarosoftware.com
- *Gann/Elliott Educators, Inc.* www.bryce-gilmore.com
- *Kasanjian Research.* PO Box 4608, Blue Jay CA 92317

# Chapter 2

# Overview

THE EVALUATION of every chart begins with the overview:

**1. Planets east and west, above and below the horizon, elevated planets, clusters and patterns.** Few of us have extremes in quality or element; a balance of the various factors is customary.

**Planets in the east (or the ASC ruler in the east).** We seek personal awareness and self-expression of our identity. Focusing attention and energy on our introspective world of thought and feeling, we alternate our self-motivated activities with adequate "down time" in order to recharge our batteries. This is particularly obvious when we have planets in the twelfth house, a position that acts as a "circuit-breaker." Exceptionally sensitive to input, we tend to shut down the expression of our twelfth house planets, or withdraw from active participation when they are over-stimulated. An example of someone with planetary emphasis on the east is actress Meryl Street (nine planets), who has an outstanding personality and talent, but withdraws from the public view in pursuit of her own personal interests. Johnny Carson (nine planets) did the same during his many years as host of *The Tonight Show.*

**Planets in the west (or the ASC ruler in the west).** We seek validation from others in an external social and physical environment in order to evaluate our realities and worth. We are not only stimulated, but need and actively seek input, interaction and experience, to be in the center of whatever is going on, and are therefore well equipped to deal with the public on a general basis. Two examples of people with planetary emphasis on the west are humanitarian Dr. Tom Dooley and primitive artist Grandma Moses, both of whom were influenced by the circumstances of their environment and both of whom put the lives of other people before their own.

**Planets above the horizon.** We move into life experience instinctively and without preamble. If we don't start at the top we do at any event make an early start, moving right into the fray to interact with our environment. In our own parameters, whether they are our world, our culture or our neighborhood, everyone knows who we are and we step right out, stage center, to be highly visible. Two examples of people with planetary emphasis on the upper hemisphere are chess champion Bobby Fischer (eight planets) and football player O.J. Simpson (eight planets), both of whom attract public notice.

**Planets below the horizon.** We need to prepare for our public life, often with years of education or training before we feel ready to step before the public. Our time is filled with low-profile activities of maintaining what is essentially a private life. With planets "in the dark" we can still be public figures, or be well known for the matters symbolized by the planet when that planet aspects the MC, a planet in the tenth house, or the ruler of the MC. Two examples of people with planetary emphasis on the lower hemisphere are actress Barbra Streisand (nine planets) and writer Stephen King (nine planets), both of whom maintain a reclusive private life.

**2. Qualities and elements, including a chart signature** (found by combining the dominant element and dominant quality), exemplify our motivation and method of operation. For example, if we have the Sun in Aries with a dominance of planets in water signs and a dominance of planets in cardinal signs, which equates to a signature of Cancer, the emotional and sensitive signature decidedly conflicts with our direct and self-centered Aries Sun. Weigh the signature as one of the major factors in success, as enlarged upon in Chapter 18, "Success." (When counting planets in signs, we include the signs which contain the MC and ASC.)

**Dominant Fire.** We are motivated by the need of goals to look forward to today, this week, this year. We seek stimulation, excitement, challenge. We like to keep our options open to new stimulus and keep our time open to balance work with robust play.

**Dominant Earth.** We are motivated by the need for stability, security, a modest but comfortable financial position and a measure of status. We are inclined to work first, play later and aim toward achieving definitive goals. Though being useful has a high priority, we are product-oriented and seek commercial, tangible rewards.

**Dominant Air.** We are motivated by the need for intellectual and social exchanges that are rational and logical, with communication and games. Play has an important priority, and work is valued that stimulates our creative imagination. With a short threshold on boredom, we are comfortable in situations that require us to develop ideas and concepts.

**Dominant Water.** We are motivated by the need for emotional outlets and strong feeling interactions. We tend to be specific and literal and may take things personally that were not meant as such. At times we may seem overemotional and illogical to rational types, but we know that our feelings are valid whether they make sense to other people or not.

Most of us have element combinations in our charts, such as **Fire-Earth,** with which we are creative and enthusiastic about practical ventures. This is the best money maker combination, with a close second from Earth-Water, *when other chart factors are in agreement.* A contractor who got into a Union fight when he stood up for his people is one example; a metaphysical writer who founded her own organization is another.

**Fire-Air** has intellectual enthusiasms and often has a number of projects going on at the same time. With this combination we can be scattered unless we have some fixity for balance, and are usually in touch with the current "happening scene." An English teacher with this pattern is himself taking two post-grad courses and is coaching his son's little league team. He and his wife recently began learning to line-dance along with a couple of friends.

**Fire-Water** is a passionate combination; our mood swings can easily be drawn into high drama. One example is a street-wise kid who hit the drug scene when he was about fourteen. Later he went back to school to get his degree and went into the police department. As a detective on the vice squad, he has first hand knowledge of all the dramatic stories about the mean streets of the big city. It is a creative, imaginative combination that is not uncommon in the charts of people who make good money.

**Earth-Air** has a practical intellect that works well with the development of ideas into pragmatic results, such as engineering, industry or production. With earth-air, we seek a mundane position about which we can feel good; we value our emotional well-being as well as our status and many of us have a shrewd financial sense. A tech writer with this combination went back to school to take computer classes to expedite the efficiency of her business.

**Earth-Water** combines social and emotional drives in a way that fits us well for dealing with the public as we have a keen perception of human nature. If we get bogged down in details, a periodic "shakeout" of reassessment can clear our priorities. A housewife with this combination dreamed up a new kitchen gadget, patented the prototype and promoted financial backing to go into production. Another example is a successful family services therapist.

**Air-Water** has eclectic interests and examines everything for how it feels and fits. With air-water, we may spend so much time collecting and sorting experiences that we find it hard to focus on one area. We perform best when we have interaction with others while periodically withdrawing for our own self-analysis. The examples include an advertising executive, a columnist and a mathematician, all of whom have a good feel for how their ideas can be implemented.

**Dominant Cardinal Signs** indicate that we are more interested in beginning the project than in the tedious work of completing it, so we need a little balancing help from earth signs or fixed signs in our chart. We are more apt to stay in a long term situation if we are given the opportunity to make many little starts such as a change of headquarters, a new program to expedite, redecorating or renovating.

**With Dominant Fixed Signs,** we have the power of persistence and fidelity of effort but need the balance of some cardinal signs and fire or air to lighten a tendency to heavy-handed inflexibility. It is possible for us to change gears if we have adequate motivation and are given advance notice.

**With Dominant Mutable Signs,** we are always involved in the process; getting our Gemini desk, correspondence or calls caught up, doing our Virgo work preparation, flying off to our new Sagittarius venture and getting our Pisces act together, so we need the balancing accompaniment of a little fixity or earth signs. It is possible for us to get something accomplished if we can learn to set priorities and manage to complete short-term assignments before we lose interest.

**3. Phenomena: stationary or retrograde planets, changes of station, planets with the most and least aspects.**

**Stationary planets** in the birth chart are so powerful they will either mark the life as a whole or we will act them out at some time in a way that influences our lives. When a planet in progressed motion slows down to immobility at station, this puts a marked emphasis on the planet. The change of station, whether direct-to-retrograde or retrograde-to-direct neither represses or releases the expression of that planet, but it concentrates a powerful focus of attention on the matters and house signified.

In one example a woman had Neptune turn stationary/direct in the fifth house and hold an unchanging position for nine years of conjunction to its natal place within five minutes of partile (exact to the minute). There was no other PR aspect to Neptune when her child was kidnaped and never found again, leaving her bewildered and bereft. (A quantity of transit aspects were present to stimulate Neptune.) In a case of a world renowned music group, *The Beach Boys,* Pluto in the second house changed station in Mike Love's chart. The group did not disband or change their musical style but over the stationary period of a half dozen years they did go "underground," one into drugs and another into financial power-plays; one began counseling with a psychiatrist and one became immersed in eastern meditation. The image of the group may have remained the same to the public, but Love's personal experiences of transformation, as well as his interaction with the group made decisive though subtle shifts of priority and direction. With the second house influence, he also went into some investment programs at that time of a diversified nature (Pluto).

Planets that go retrograde, direct and change station are covered more thoroughly by authors of other texts.

**Retrograde planets** in a birth chart are not backwards or delayed but give an interior focus to the usual interpretation. They mark our lives with their influence or impact in much the same way as the stationary planet does. With our retrogrades, we are coming from a different reality; the planet is not active in the customary way but either reverses, rebels or intensifies, perhaps all three. We tend to experience planets in natal retrograde early in our life before we have enough self-awareness or maturity to evaluate the condition or situation, therefore we subordinate that planet's natural expression until we can reach an inner reconciliation in order to act upon it by choice. Thus a planet that is retrograde, stationary or changes station often demonstrates that focus by greater awareness in maturity.

As Uranus, Neptune and Pluto are retrograde approximately five months/direct seven months (retrograde 41 percent, 43 percent and 44 percent respectively), their effect is subtle and often subjective. These three planets can only express consciously on the level and to the degree that we have developed our own conscious awareness of the qualities symbolized by the planet. For this reason their effect has a highly variable spectrum that ranges from the highest to the lowest of human potential. For the most part, with Uranus retrograde, we are more eccentric and independent than we appear to be in the external, conventional position of our lives; with Neptune retrograde we are more sensitive and imaginative than we seem on the surface; and with Pluto retrograde, we are more driven than other people to investigate and transform ourselves and our environment.

Saturn is retrograde for 37 percent of its cycle and indicates that we either go to work when young, have early responsibilities or experience early grief and restrictions. We thereafter resist working "as we are supposed to," and often find our own reasons and goals to develop ambitions for exceptional achievement in maturity. Mercury is retrograde for 19 percent of its cycle, Venus 7.2 percent, Mars 9.5 percent, and Jupiter 30.1 percent. Generally speaking, the more direct planets there are in the chart, what-you-see-is-what-you-get. The more retrograde planets, the more intensity and subtlety we have in our interior lives.

The first time that a client came into the office who had six retrograde planets, he turned out to be a 25-year-old millionaire riding the wave of a new fad. Was it appropriate to tell him that his life was on hold, delayed, inhibited? Not likely. However a decade later he was divorced, bankrupt and wiped out. As he returned to a second peak (retrograde = second chance) it was in a different business; his second success was more deliberate and more solid. (Please do not interpret this to mean that retrograde planets leave us divorced and bankrupt! It more accurately indicates that we have an early surge of effort or experience in an area that is then put on "pause" for a period of inner gestation before its full fruition.)

We see another example of six retrograde planets in the chart of Muhammad Ali as he became World Heavyweight champion in 1964 at age 22. Five years later his career came to an apparent halt (which was actually a pause). His title was declared vacant due to his refusal of his military obligation as a conscientious objector. As a young adult he reevaluated his religion and philosophy, changed his name from Cassius Clay to Muhammad Ali and reentered boxing in 1970.

**A planet that is Dominant** by dint of having the most and/or closest aspects shows the activity that is most obvious in our lives; for example, a dominant Sun indicates that our every move is instinctively geared to the goal of being boss, in command, in charge, an authority figure. A dominant Venus implies that we continually attract social situations and relationships, and may well be before the public in an entertainment field or provide a luxury rather than a necessity in our career position.

One client was a handsome and sybaritic actor with a dominant Venus. After looking at his progressed chart this suggestion was made, "Enjoy your lady, but postpone marriage this year." He got married. On his next visit (after the marriage had dissolved), he was told, "Romance stands out but it's the not the best time to get married." He got married. By his fifth marriage he got the message and since, has had a stream of nubile young women. The older he gets, the younger they get and he loves every one of them. (It was not the dominant Venus that made him a poor marital risk; that was only one factor in the chart as a whole, as well as the options he chose to follow.)

**An Unaspected planet,** that is a planet which does not have any of the planetary big-four: the conjunction, opposition, square or trine, tends to over-react or overcompensate when the planet is activated by a progression. At times we may seem out of control of the matters signified by our unaspected planet, such as working ourselves into a nervous breakdown with an unaspected Saturn or overdosing on food, liquor, sex, drugs, or credit spending with an unaspected Jupiter.

**The Most Elevated planet,** the one closest to the MC, shows qualities that are most obvious. It may or may not relate to the career or public standing; after all we *are* known for other things. The most elevated planet could be—say—Pluto in the eleventh, when we are known as a loyal party member, or Moon in Libra in the eighth when we are seen primarily in our role of parent and partner.

**4. The Character** is shown by the Sun, Moon and Ascendant with planets in the first house plus aspects relating these points to each other and to the chart as a whole. Throughout a lifetime, we generally stay in character. If there is an exceptional trauma or tragedy (such as shown by movement from heavy planets and stressful aspects and situations) our tone drops for a given time, then resettles a little below its former norm. If there is an exceptional win or joy (such as shown by movement with harmonious planets and rewarding aspects and situations), our tone rises for a given time then resettles a little above its former norm. Most of us are fairly well integrated with our charts and the average person who is functional and healthy in our society operates on a generally positive expression of the chart. If we do express some of the negative definitions of the planets and aspects, we do so within socially tolerable limits.

For a more detailed explanation of chart delineation. *The Only Way to Learn Astrology* series by Marion D. March and Joan McEvers is highly recommended.

# Chapter 3

# House Systems

IN VARIOUS house systems, the cusps differ anywhere from minimal when the angles are equinoctial (0 Aries, 0 Cancer, 0 Libra, 0 Capricorn) to changes so extreme that the same sign may fall on two or *more* cusps. The further north that people are born, the greater the variance of house division. When using the Placidian house system, those born above 60 degrees north (Alaska, Russia, Sweden, Finland, Greenland) and even in lesser latitudes have charts in which there may be three or four signs intercepted in one house, and a corresponding three or four houses ruled by one sign.

In the 1980s, we began to hear "Things go better with Koch" as this house system increased in popularity. Where Placidus draws the planets closer to the ASC/DESC, Koch draws the planets closer to the MC/IC. The houses tend to be more evenly divided with Koch making the charts more manageable of people born in extreme latitudes. Other systems are further variations of how to trisect the angles. Some astrologers suggest that one house system appropriately describes our mundane life while another system describes the inner life of character or spiritual growth. Some of us use no house division at all but only the angles of the chart, which remain constant (with a minimal variation) in all systems. However, in the commercial horoscope, houses are an indispensable part of evaluation. With an examination of charts erected on both Koch and Equal House (EQHS) for the study of *Money: How To Find It With Astrology,* the mundane patterns of the life stand out more graphically with EQHS.

To draw an EQHS chart, take the degree and minutes on the ASC and repeat them with each successive sign on the following houses. For example, if the ASC is 20 degrees Virgo 16 minutes, put 20 Libra 16 on the second cusp, 20 Scorpio 16 on the third cusp and so on.

Tropical astrologers accept the Ptolemaic theory that the Vernal Equinox designates the point known as 0 Aries and the 30 degrees which follow are known as Aries; the 30 successive degrees after that are known as Taurus, etc, with the four equinoctial periods each beginning with a cardinal sign, 0 Cancer for the summer equinox, 0 Libra for the autumnal equinox, and 0 Capricorn for the winter solstice. Sidereal astrologers agree that the signs are each 30 degrees in size; however, they differ in their starting point, calculating 0 Aries as a physical location in the constellations that is now some 24 degrees less than the Vernal Equinox due to the precession of the equinoxes.

Astrology is a symbolic system of mythic archetypes describing the human condition. No matter what discipline we follow, we all accept the symbology of 30 degree signs of the zodiac. In physical reality the constellations are not divided into tidy 30 degree segments with a neon stop sign at the demarcation line of each. The zodiac (circle of animals) has constellations that extend anywhere from some 15 to 45 degrees with stars of one constellation overlapping those of the next. In contradiction with our acceptance of signs having 30 degrees, we then begin an endless debate of how to divide the houses into *unequal* degrees, of how to trisect the angles. In various periods of astrological history, either sequentially or simultaneously, the segments of the horoscope have been not only divided equally, but with a dozen different mathematical systems, including one that creates eight houses. The advocates of each system can validate their reasoning with their evidence: "It works."

In the study of *Money: How To Find It With Astrology,* we may keep the house system that we customarily use. If it works, don't fix it. The fact that house systems are extremely flexible is demonstrated by our ability to delineate a horoscope accurately with a variety of techniques. Inasmuch as *Money: How To Find It With Astrology* is not a treatise on house systems, the subject is addressed in this chapter, then referred to only in those cases where the contradiction between the systems makes an appreciable difference in the delineation. For the most part, the body of the text is viable with the Koch discipline. (For people born in the further northern latitudes, the question of any house system other than EQHS is probably already a moot point.)

On the other hand, with intellectual curiosity and the eternal possibility of improvement, it may be suggested that several charts are examined on different house systems, including EQHS, as the mundane definitions unfold in the following chapters. The difference in delineation of the MC and of the tenth cusp is a provocative consideration. The MC is *always included* in EQHS charts; it is a vital point of definition indicating, as it does, the public persona, the garment that is worn before the public. The tenth cusp is more personal as it portrays our dominant lifestyle as well as demonstrating an influence on our career choices. **The MC shows the reputation; the tenth cusp shows the life path.**

Consider a few example charts: Synanon founder Charles E. Dederick has a Sagittarius MC. Before the public he was an inspirational philosopher (with the MC ruler, Jupiter, in Capricorn in the eleventh house) leading the way to freedom from patterns of indulgence with the structured program of his organization. Striking closer to the heart of the man, Dederick's life path (EQHS tenth cusp) is Scorpio, indicating a life in which transformation plays a major role, as well as the demonstration of power to manipulate his environment for either the greater good or for personal dictatorship.

The rulers of Scorpio are Pluto in Gemini in the EQHS fifth house (reaching a group audience or following by way of ideas and education) and Mars in Aquarius in the twelfth house (secretly stockpiling weapons in his million-dollar organizational hideaway). In September 1978, a prosecuting attorney of Synanon found a rattlesnake in his mailbox: Dederick's PR Moon was conjunct his twelfth house Mars. PR Neptune (scandal as well as charisma) is exact-to-the-minute quincunx Mars. When Dederick was arrested, he was found in his Arizona home dead drunk (Mars).

Our reputation is certainly not always limited to our vocation. As pedestrian as it is, Vincent van Gogh may be as well known for cutting off his ear as for being one of history's glorious painters. This amazing chart has seven planets in the tenth house with Pisces on the

MC. Van Gogh has the reputation of a high profile achiever, which we usually find with planetary emphasis on the upper hemisphere, as well as having the Pisces "devotion to the ideal" concept. (For a more detailed analysis of the MC, see Chapter 18, "Success.") The co-rulers of Pisces are Neptune, elevated in Pisces (ninth house) and Jupiter in Sagittarius (fifth house). Van Gogh's vocations ranged from his work with art dealers (ninth house portraying the art agency) to that of a schoolteacher (ninth house associated with education) to his period of Lutheran evangelism (Jupiter in Sagittarius as well as the ninth house symbolizing religion) to his emergence as a serious artist by age 30 (MC in Pisces, Venus elevated in Pisces.)

By EQHS the tenth cusp is Aries; the ruler is Mars, conjunct Venus, certainly a passionate combination. When van Gogh cut off his ear on Christmas Day, 1888, after a day of drinking absinthe with Paul Gauquin and then quarreling, the PR Mars in Aries was within five minutes of trine Jupiter. The two planets are natally in a two-degree square which van Gogh demonstrated with his combustive temper; the trine apparently protected him from bleeding to death or contacting infection. His madness again exploded into violence on July 29, 1890 when he shot himself to death: PR Mars was approaching a conjunction to Mercury.

Note that the arc between van Gogh's MC (22 Pisces 05) and his tenth cusp (21 Aries 09) is 29 degrees, 4 minutes. Translating this arc into an equivalent age, we add 29 years, one month to his birth date, correlating to May 1882. After his work in the ministry, van Gogh stayed with his parents in Etten from April to December 1881, while studying art. In 1882, he moved to the Hague with his model, the prostitute Christien. In effect, he began his career as an artist in the year that is equivalent to the age arc between his MC and his tenth house cusp.

Often the number of degrees between the EQHS tenth cusp and the MC marks a year of career—or life—decisions. A client, Cindy, has the tenth cusp at 27 Virgo and the MC at 23 Libra, an arc of 26 degrees. She began work in a company clerical department (Virgo) and at age 26 moved into the art department (Libra). However, many of us have an MC-EQHS tenth cusp arc that is numerically too early in years for us to identify it with career choices. We may not remember

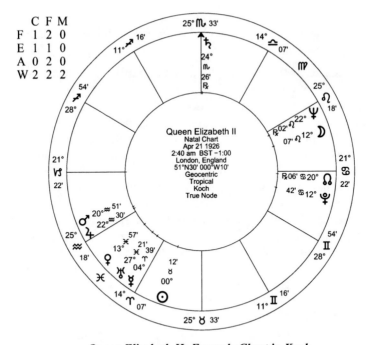

C F M
F 1 2 0
E 1 1 0
A 0 2 0
W 2 2 2

*Queen Elizabeth II: Example Chart in Koch*
*Declinations: ☿ 0N5; ♅ 1S43; ♀ 6S15; ☉ 11N33; ♆ 14N33; ♃ 14S38;*
*♂ 15S54; ♄ 16S34; ☽ 18N59; M 19S9; ⚷ 21N14; A 21S45; ☊ 21N56*

going to work with Daddy at the age of six and being impressed by the
tools of his trade, or even that our friendship with a neighbor when we
were sixteen gave us our first taste of ego satisfaction for some natural
skill we had not yet identified.

England's Queen has a Taurus Sun; she is modest, practical and
unassuming; her Moon in Leo adds a quiet, regal dignity and a natural
love of her role as a gentlewoman with great presence. Capricorn rising indicates a conservative, well-organized monarch. The majority
of her planets are East suggesting that she is one to listen to her own
voice and find her own center of stability before making decisions.
With the element dominance of Water-Fire, her life has always been a
focus of publicity and drama, but with six planets and the MC in fixed
signs she has persistently held to stable traditions, approaching

change with great reservation. The signature of dominant fixed and dominant water equates to Scorpio, which equips the Queen with the capacity to be a powerful influence in her environment.

Queen Elizabeth's MC and Retrograde Saturn are in Scorpio, indicating a reputation of responsibility from an early age with intensity and perseverance for the good of the people, as well as a life of vivid highs and lows. For all other public position she has never received the intimate publicity to which the younger royals are subjected but has always retained a certain autonomy, illustrating the Scorpio discretion. As a ninth house position, Saturn portrays a serious, methodical, (at times even boring) public speaker, one who works hard to present an ethic of sensibility, and whose philosophy and duty are fixed (Scorpio). The MC ruler (Pluto in Cancer, sixth house), suggests that the Queen works as one of a kind within the team, supported by strong family bonds, while the co-ruler (Mars in Aquarius, conjunct Jupiter in the first house) portrays a love of sports, in this case, the hunt; dogs and horses. Scorpio indicates that her life may be influenced by the death of another, and she indeed became queen upon the death of her father, King George VI. Mars (trine the MC) is active, decisive and positive in a stable situation to which she brings a new approach or innovative changes (Aquarius) or which may be subject to unexpected events without notice.

Depicting the difference between the two house systems, Koch and EQHS, the chart of Queen Elizabeth in EQHS shows us six planets that change houses as well as a Scorpio MC and an EQHS Libra tenth cusp. Elizabeth's life path is demonstrated by the more intimate view of her EQHS Libra tenth cusp which shifts the emphasis to her social position as a royal figure, a woman whose life is shaped and colored by her societal role.

The Libra MC implies that she graciously works in partnership with her husband and her peers to maintain peace and harmony. Venus, the ruler, is in Pisces (second house) to suggest that she is not at all heavy-handed but rather, flexible and sympathetic, one who seeks social and financial well-being in her life and in her reign and who is periodically surrounded by drama, confusion or mystery (Pisces). There may even be a touch of mysticism that influences the Queen's life and decisions.

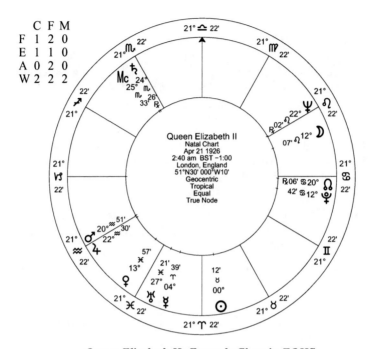

```
      C F M
   F  1 2 0
   E  1 1 0
   A  0 2 0
   W  2 2 2
```

*Queen Elizabeth II: Example Chart in EQHS*

*Declinations: ☿ 0N5; ♅ 1S43; ♀ 6S15; ☉ 11N33; ♆ 14N33; ♃ 14S38;*
*♂ 15S54; ♄ 16S34; ☽ 18N59; M 19S9; ♀ 21N14; A 21S45; ☊ 21N56*

The EQHS tenth cusp Libra, ruler in Pisces, personal life path is in vivid contrast to the Queen's public image of Scorpio-Cancer-Aquarius. (Pluto is approximately one degree trine Venus: **Note the ruler of the tenth cusp trine the ruler of the MC as a favorable indicator of career success.**)

**The arc between the EQHS tenth cusp to the MC** is 34 degrees 10 minutes; at one degree per year age equation this is 34 years, two months: June, 1960. On February 19, 1960, Prince Andrew was born, 10 years after Princess Anne. Some two weeks before the Prince was born, Elizabeth began the steps necessary to restore the name Mountbatten-Windsor to her children. (The name Mountbatten had been removed from the royal family April 9, 1952.) It was noted that Queen Elizabeth suffered post-partum depression after the birth of

Andrew, and the papers skirted around the rumor of a rift in the royal marriage. We don't know if this was a subtle, interior turning point in the career of Queen Elizabeth as we don't always see, in the life of a public figure, which strand in the fabric of time begins a pattern of change. We may not know until the history of this era is completed whether or not the birth of Prince Andrew (or other circumstances at this time) altered the path of his mother or that of a nation.

There are several methods by which to progress the MC. By the Solar Arc Direction Method, the arc traveled by the progressed Sun is added to natal MC and the ASC is then determined from a tables of houses.

By the RA.MS. method (Right Ascension Mean Sun) the mean motion of the Sun is taken in right ascension rather than longitude and added to the natal MC.

By the Classical Method, the chart is recalculated with the same birth time on the progressed date, with one transit day equivalent to one year of life. Say that a person is 10 years old:

count 10 days in the ephemeris and set up the chart with the birth time on that day. This is essentially a quotidian chart, a chart of the day, and varies inappreciably from the RAMS. method. However, the different methods of progressing the chart give results of a progressed MC-ASC that may vary widely, as we shall demonstrate with the dates of the MC conjunct ASC in Queen Elizabeth's chart.

**The arc between Queen Elizabeth's MC to her twelfth cusp** is 25 degrees, 50 minutes, equating in age arc to 25 years, 10 months = February, 1952. King George VI died in his sleep on February 6, 1952: *The King is dead, long live the Queen!* The coronation was held on June 2 of the following year.

**The arc between MC and ASC** is one sign (of 30 degrees) plus 25 degrees and 50 minutes = an age arc of 55 years, 10 months = February 1982. On April 2, 1982, Argentina invaded the Faulkland Islands, a tiny British dependency in the South Atlantic, an aggression that erupted after two decades of dispute. British forces moved swiftly to complete a recapture by June 14. On June 21, 1982, the Prince and Princess of Wales, Charles and Diana, had their first child:

Prince William Philip Arthur Louis was born second in the line of succession after his father. How interesting that Elizabeth became queen with the MC age arc to the twelfth cusp and her heir (after Charles) was born when her MC age arc reached the first cusp.

The year 1982 stood out for Elizabeth for many more reasons. On July 1, she had to go to the hospital for the first time in her life, for dental surgery. Her personal bodyguard. Commander Michael Trestrail, was forced to resign due to blackmail threats by a male homosexual with whom he had been indiscreet. On an early morning in July an intruder broke into her bedroom, an incredible breach of security that she handled coolly enough to avert tragedy, however tragedy did strike close to home when a troop of her personal guards of the Household Cavalry was blown to pieces by an Irish terrorist bomb. The same week an old and dear close friend died suddenly.

**By Solar Arc, the MC joined the ASC** in 1984, partile (exact) in April. The Prime Minister, Margaret Thatcher, continued her program of dismantling a socialized economy, and the 20,000 job cut in the coal-mining industry caused a one year strike that brought costly and often violent confrontations; unemployment in the U.K. was high. Britain broke off diplomatic relations with Libya in April, and on the family scene. Princess Diana gave birth to her second son, Prince Henry Charles Albert David.

**By RA.MS. the MC joined the ASC** in 1988, partile in March. World news had its usual political dynamics; the U.S. was having all the fanfare of its presidential selection of George Bush while Mikhail Gorbachev became president of the U.S.S.R., and Britain and China agreed to the return of Hong Kong to Chinese rule in 1997. The effect of the drop of stock values in October 1987, was felt worldwide, and AIDS was gaining recognition in the heterosexual community. In the royal family, Duchess Sarah and Prince Andrew had a baby girl on August 8, Princess Beatrice. The young royals were beautiful, fashionable, frisky and fun, even though the press was reporting an apparent cold-front between Charles and Diana.

Obviously the Age Arc of MC to ASC was dramatically more meaningful in the life of Queen Elizabeth, but this may not always be the case. PR aspects in all of our lives have greater or lesser impact depending on what else is happening in both our physical and meta-physical worlds.

In a 1992 public address her Royal Highness said, "This was not my favorite year." Windsor, her most cherished castle, was gutted by fire and the British people were grumbling under the strain of economic stress. Her family seemed to be falling apart with the marital separations of her sons, Charles and Andrew, to the tune of overwhelmingly bad press. The public image relating to a Scorpio MC has PR Mars semisquare Mars and sesquisquare Neptune, suggesting the stress and confusion of "what next?", while TR Pluto joined the MC in 1993 and opposed PR Venus and ASC in 1994 to imply a time of reformation for Elizabeth as the symbol of the throne.

On the other hand, PR Venus (ruler of the EQHS tenth cusp, Libra) joined PR ASC in the fourth house, indicating great continued popularity with its trine to the PR MC. That conjunction also made a square to PR Jupiter in the EQHS second to suggest the expenses of redecorating as well as social formalities, and semisquare Pluto in the 6th for indecision and vacillation of how to handle work problems in a cooperative mode while maintaining a power-position. (In this case, note that the ruler of the tenth cusp, Venus, is semisquare the ruler of the MC, Pluto, for a disturbing period of public disapproval.) Life is contradictory, and a ruler may be beloved by her people who, at the same time, are grousing that she should pay her own bloody bills.

Whenever we see a chart that has a different sign on the MC and on the tenth cusp, higher octave planets in the tenth house (or conjunct the MC within 15-20 degrees), or with two or more planets retrograde, we are wise to look at the person again; there is much more here than meets the eye.

# Chapter 4

# Aspects

A PLANETARY aspect is the angle of relationship by a given number of degrees between two planets or between two points of reference in a horoscope. In traditional astrology we consider nine aspects; in experimental work any number of divisions of a 360 degree circle may be considered and studied for obvious and consistent effect. The basic aspects are seven divisions of the circle by twelve, that is, the conjunction at 0 degrees, the semisextile at 30 degrees, the sextile at 60 degrees, the square at 90 degrees, the trine at 120 degrees, the quincunx at 150 degrees and the opposition at 180 degrees, plus two that are divisions of the circle by eight, the semisquare at 45 degrees and the sesquisquare at 135 degrees.

The classical definition of aspects is one with which astrologers basically agree; however, the shading may depend on the school of study and what discipline is followed. We who do professional work for many years begin to fine-tune our definitions of aspects according to our own experience. With the pragmatic viewpoint of *Money: How To Find It With Astrology,* the following definitions are applicable.

The orb of influence of any given aspect varies greatly in different schools of thought. There are astrologers who allow no more than three degrees of orb and others who go to as far as 15 degrees. Each of us must find that which works best in our practice by the response we get from our clients. Many clients validate 10 degrees for the conjunction and opposition, eight degrees for the square and trine, and four to five degrees for the rest of the aspects. The awareness level of the client is also a factor. Some people will respond strongly to the definition of two planets that are 10 degrees apart, where others will not recognize themselves in the description. In all cases, **the closer the aspect, the stronger the influence.**

We all tend to be "planet-sensitive," that is, more keenly aware of the influence of one planet over that of another. One person may be "Saturn-sensitive" where another is "Neptune-sensitive" in that the person responds more quickly and obviously to natal, progressed and transit aspects of and to that planet. This is often the ruler of the Ascendant or MC or a planet that is conjunct an angle in the birth chart. By secondary progression the definition of an aspect may be similar to that of the natal definition or it may have a different connotation. **The first priority is the natal relationship between the two points, which colors the effect of the progressed relationship between the two points.** When a planet progresses to aspect another with which it has no natal dialogue, this is an influence that is generally present for the duration of the aspect; however, it may introduce experiences that were not in the original script.

C. C. Zain in the *Brotherhood of Light* series Volume 2, *Astrological Signatures,* writes that each of the aspects is similar *in nature* to one of the planets. This correspondence is graphic and useful, holding up well after 50 years of astrological exposure. However, the following delineations are not entirely those used by Zain, as the keywords of the opposition and quincunx, as well as the descriptions of the affect of the various aspects have evolved through 30 years experience of private practice.

**The Conjunction.** Two planets that are placed at the same degree are in conjunction. The keyword is *Prominence* and the nature is like that of the Sun in the horoscope in that these two planets are a major influence in both character and life events. Just as the Sun denotes our sense of identity, pride, importance and significance, any two planets in conjunction influence the choice and directions that emerge in life, from vocational goals to home and partnership. No other aspect has so vivid and so encompassing an effect as the conjunction. Dominant patterns are shown: it does not strive toward being, it simply is what it is.

A conjunction that aspects the MC or the ruler of the MC makes a strong statement in regard to career goals. The planets that move into partile of a one degree conjunction in the early years of life, the pre-verbal years, are so important that they make an unconscious imprint that influences future years.

The strongest conjunctions in the chart are those involving the Sun. This is so subjective a focus that the person's sense of self is indistinguishable from the nature of the planet which it joins, in both a motivational and directional sense. The conjunctions of the Sun by secondary progression mark significant years in our lives. When the PR Sun reaches a conjunction to Mercury or PR Mercury reaches the Sun, a "commitment to life" is often made, even when it doesn't reach a conscious level of deliberation. We find ourselves starting or finishing college, starting or leaving major career positions, or entering or leaving a marriage or home.

As an example of the conjunction to the MC, Jon Rodden has Mars approaching a Cancer MC by three degrees from the ninth house. Mars moved to a one-degree conjunction of the MC when he was 14. It turned retrograde to hold the pattern until age 38; a 24-years conjunction that never moves into the tenth house. As a teen he was mildly athletic and had no more than the usual kid scrapes, such as saving up for a motorcycle and, on the first day of ownership, skidding it under a car as he leapt off onto the shoulder of the road. At 20, he joined the army *(You did WHAT?!).*

As an intense Scorpio with Moon in methodical Capricorn, Jon is well equipped to use his MC/Mars opposite Saturn in a dangerous vocation that he handles with cool control, flying helicopters. When Mars changed station at age 27 there was no external break in the sequential flow of his career, but he decided at that time to get a second degree in preparation to teaching math. Insofar as his career is concerned, Mars is a factor in the whole pattern; the Cancer MC and the ruler. Moon in Capricorn, must also be considered along with the second and sixth houses, as given in the following chapters. As to his character. Mars, once more, is a factor in the whole pattern and adds a direct, no-nonsense, straight-shooting determination.

**The Opposition.** Two planets that are placed opposite each other in the same degree are in opposition. The keyword is *Maximum,* and the nature is like that of Saturn in the horoscope in that these two planets demand attention and resolution. Just as Saturn denotes work and responsibility, the planets that are in opposition insist that they must be used, and in so doing, these planets reach the optimum, the maximum of their potential. We often see situations in which we would not use these planets together unless we had to; when forced by circumstances or our own compulsion, we develop our maximum capacity in the affairs symbolized by the two planets.

Both planets require the work of integrating, each with the other. When we try to focus on just one of the two planets in opposition, the one which is easiest and most comfortable, there is a side effect; we become a "victim of circumstance." Situations arise or other people act out the indications of the two planets but not necessarily in a way that we would choose. For example, say that the Sun is opposite Saturn. In order to attain significance in our ambitions for a position of authority, we must develop our maximum organizational capacities. If, for some reason, we want the name without the game, that is, we want to be recognized without accepting work and responsibility, we may find that others are coldly taking control of our lives, or we attract situations of discipline and restriction.

An opposition of Saturn to the MC may show that we are exhaustively thorough in an attempt to gain recognition, and we may feel the weight of the world on our shoulders. The lack of early parental approval can also be a crushing burden to carry. Any opposition in the chart that involves Saturn demands a top priority of attention. We must work to pursue concrete goals of the nature of the planet involved and may never feel that we have done enough or gained enough security to relieve the sense of lack or inadequacy of that planet. The opposition, in the same way as Saturn, demands that we follow the law; the police on the street or the Tao of the universe; if not, the law will restrict us.

The first planets that move into partile of a one-degree opposition in our early years are so important that long into the future we continue to demonstrate a need to work with these planets to insure the stability, safely and security of the matters symbolized. We are also impelled toward fulfilling the maximum capacity of the matters symbolized by planets in natal or progressed opposition. When those oppositions are to the MC, natally or progressed, they exhibit a strong drive of that planet to be noticed and acknowledged but hard work is necessary to achieve the desired recognition. Our peak career development must be built on methodical study when a planet in the third house is opposite the MC or an industrious period of preparation when a planet in the fourth house is opposite the MC.

Betsy Rodden Sells has Uranus opposite the MC by three degrees. Though she demonstrates her unassuming Taurus traits and her practical Capricorn MC, she is the one who was drawn to a different world than the one into which she was born. In her late 20's, she took off with a backpack to explore Europe for six months, and a decade later left a successful job to marry a Brit and with him, open a pub in the English countryside.

**The Square.** Two planets that are 90 degrees apart are in square. The keyword is *Obstacle* and the aspect implies tension and challenge. The nature is like that of Mars in that desire and stress both play a part. The square may be compared to the stick-and-carrot syndrome in that we either want to get out of an uncomfortable situation or we want to reach an impassioned goal. Just as with Mars, the results of the square are constructive or destructive according to our basic nature and the type of effort that we choose to put into the situation. If Mars is not used for positive action it may become a covert shadow, resulting in fights, accidents or surgery; in the same manner, the square must be dealt with vigorously to gain achievement rather than damage. When planets move by progression into a square, it is a cry to change this situation, do something about it, improve it or leave it, but face up to the need for decision and action.

Mars in square aspect is the most assertive and invigorating square in the chart and points to an area in which there certainly is action, projects, production or performance, or else abuse, competition, stress and danger; in both cases involving the dynamics of applied energy to overcome obstacles.

For example, Amy Rodden Hawes has Mars on the ASC one degree, square MC. She is a bass guitarist who has exceptional fingering dexterity on her instrument. Her career often puts her in rough and even dangerous situations; playing with rock groups she may have to load her amps into the car at 3:00 a.m. in the alley behind a bar or night club. Saturn joins closely in this conjunction, adding caution to Amy's calculation of jeopardy. She also has Venus and Jupiter in the fifth house; she loves to perform and draws on the protection of the two benefics while doing so. Remember to look at the whole chart as one position alone will never tell the full story. In Amy's case, there was an accident when she was four years old (March 4, 1954) when the PR MC moved to partile square Mars. She was burned on the chest and arm with scalding water; the years ahead held four plastic surgeries.

**The Trine.** Two planets that are 120 degrees apart are in trine. The keyword is *Luck,* and the nature is like that of Jupiter in the chart in that the rewards come easily and are usually highly beneficial. Just as Jupiter can bring good fortune, the trine always has a compensatory factor that makes it easier to stay in a given situation than leave it. With a trine from the second house to the MC the vocation gives job security; it may pay well enough and have good fringe benefits, or be comfortable and not too stressful, making it easier to stay in that position than to follow a pull to another direction that would take the effort of more education, a move or a risk. When planets move into a trine by progression, the most common reaction is to relax and enjoy our compensations; after all we deserve some ease and rewards. Rather than letting up, this might be the best chance in life to pursue a period of expansion by following the message of the planets indicated, with some observation of discretion and temperance as not to go overboard.

Though Jupiter in trine aspect often shows an area where we are gifted, we tend to give more attention to the oppositions and squares. Jupiter trines give a mundane boost that is most helpful to our financial position; however, at times they may imply too much of a good thing and lead to over-optimism, eating, drinking or spending too much. More than one crime figure with Jupiter trine the MC has gotten away with murder, literally, for years before getting careless with good luck and going too far, to finally end up in prison for life. On the other hand, an educator client with Jupiter trine MC spent a lifetime collecting honors and was known for his generosity and religious faith.

Both a grand trine or a grand square can be equally effective as a "closed system," locking us into a given situation or life style as securely as though all our planets were in fixed signs. With an "exit" planet, one that is outside the pattern but aspects one of the points, we can use that exit planet as the focal point for the dynamics that are locked into the grand trine or grand square.

Betsy Rodden Sells illustrates the point of the trine effect versus that of the opposition as she has Venus in the first house, ruling the second house and trine the MC. She was given merit for her artistic talent from age five and in high school was awarded several small art scholarships. By the age of 19 she became an art director in an ad agency. She was at the right place and time with the talent to gain prestige; she might have stayed there forever were it not for Venus (and Jupiter) opposite Mars, and Uranus opposite the MC, adding the drive to move on.

**The Sextile.** Two planets that are 60 degrees apart are in sextile. The keyword is *Opportunity,* and the nature is like that of Venus in the chart in that it is pleasant but for the most part non-assertive.

Venus brings gratuities. Just as love itself is a gift that is eternally new, the sextile shows opportunities that are presented gently, the window is opened for a certain time, and if the person is insensitive or not paying attention, they may not even know that the chance was there. The sextile is an inconclusive aspect in itself; it is the bridge that leads across or the step that leads to the next step. Often the first experience of the sextile is as inadequate or awkward as standing on one foot; the second step improves the balance. Venus in a sextile progresses nicely as we learn to fit into our social milieu.

A sextile to the MC shows that we can easily work our way up by following the opportunities that arise. Dana Rodden works as a bartender or waiter to support his first love, writing music. He has a sextile of Sun-Mercury to the MC; within a few days after he starts any job he is approached with an offer to go into management (the Sun). As the promotion would take more time than he is willing to give, his answer is, "No, thank you." It's a strange phenomena that the sextile is an opportunity that so often is turned down, and not uncommonly, may be viewed with some regret at a later date. (*Yes, I have often wondered how it might have changed my life if I had taken the op-*

*portunity to go to college when it was offered.*)

With Venus itself sextile the MC a second career may develop that is more enjoyable than the first. Sextiles by progression show a time and place in which to stay alert for every chance that is offered. Even a transit Venus sextile to another planet suggests that one social move may lead to a more pleasurable second, so if we are in the market for playful exchanges, we need not turn down an invitation that is less than perfect; it may lead to something better.

In one example, Emily, a client who was selling her house, had a PR fourth house sextile of Mercury to Mars. It was suggested that there may be an interim move before she relocated. "I've already bought a new condo," she said, "and I am **not** moving twice." When escrow closed on her house sale, the construction on the condominium was not finished; she had to spend a month in a rental with her household in storage before she could move in.

**The Semisextile.** Two planets that are 30 degrees apart are in semisextile. The keyword is *Growth,* and the nature is like that of the Moon in that it waxes and wanes. Just as the Moon relates to impulse and "feel," the semisextile relies on instinct more than education. The more that is put into the situation the more it develops; however, it does not maintain a steady rate of growth but alternates with periods in the dark. Nor are the two planets equal partners; one always takes dominion over the other, sometimes alternately, and it is hard to find the time to take care of the lesser planet.

In real estate the descriptive word is "appreciation," showing the growth of property value. With a semisextile to the career MC/tenth or to the second house of income, there is a natural growth in an alternating current, or pulse, with a feel for the time and place of progress. A semisextile by progression shows matters that begin with no fanfare or even much notice, but that gradually develop into something more substantial.

As an example, Robert, a client, had been struggling for three years to establish his business against a tough economy and tight money. When his PR Mars (ruling his second house and placed in the sixth house) made a four-year semisextile to Jupiter, he gradually inched forward, month by month, expanding the variety of his inventory (sixth house) in tandem with the profit margin that began to accrue in his account books.

The Moon in a semisextile learns in natural and gradual steps to absorb the qualities signified by the other planet. With Moon semisextile the MC the career has waxing and waning periods. Some of us with this aspect demonstrate a successful career when we are young and gradually in mid-life phase into another area where we feel more at home.

**The Semisquare.** Two planets that are 45 degrees apart are in semisquare. The keyword is *Friction,* and the nature is like Mercury in that the affairs denoted are highly responsive to the learning experience. These two planets do not initially have a clue of how to act together, nor do they have any understanding of how to communicate that difficulty until, like Mercury, they have the education of experience. A semisquare in the natal chart shows an area where we vacillate from one stance to another, trying a number of approaches before we find one that works. Mercury semisquare the MC indicates on-the-job-training or learning by trial and error.

There may be some ambivalence about the career. (*How do I know if I'll like it until I try it?*)

A semisquare by progression shows indecision that is an irritating worry as we don't know whether to follow this planet or that, to buy-or-sell, move-or-stay, do this-or-that; we simply do not have enough information to make an informed decision. Even though indecision can weaken our position, we must be sure to get all the facts and figures before making the move ahead. In some cases, the passage of time and experience may hold the only possible answer.

Mercury in a semisquare shows fluctuation in work skills or even job changing, learning with each new experience. In some charts the judgment is flawed or the individual is verbally indiscreet.

One client came to the office who had twelve semisquares in his natal chart! Not only that but he was a Gemini who, by the age of 34 had worked in sixteen different jobs after dropping out of high school, with nearly as many residential changes. This certainly demonstrates that the semisquare, which is generally considered a minor aspect, can be as much of a handicap in the life as the "big bad aspects" we usually consider difficult.

**The Sesquisquare.** Two planets that are 135 degrees apart are in sesquisquare (or biquintile). The keyword is *Disruption,* and the nature is like that of Uranus in that the affairs denoted tend to suddenly break-up and reform in a new compound. If both planets are in the same element, the effect is not as agitating as when they are in contradictory elements, such as earth and air, or air and water. Sesquisquares are notable in the charts of adventurers, astronauts, and other examples of people who travel uncharted waters or blaze new trails.

A sesquisquare by progression can indicate sudden disruptions, such as abrupt job moves or relationship changes, unexpected detours where we have to backtrack and approach from a different direction. The end result is often remarkable, not that which is expected but nonetheless rewarding if we are able to remain flexible and roll with the punches. After the dust clears and things once more stabilize, conditions never go entirely back to where they were before.

Uranus in sesquisquare to the MC can range anywhere from totally unstable and eccentric to highly creative and unique. With this aspect, we certainly take the path less traveled and often contributes something exceptional to our field.

Lynn Rodden has a Venus-MC sesquisquare in fire and earth signs. She began her career working as a model, an unstable vocation at best, and supplemented her income by working in office capacities in the entertainment industry. This choice did not satisfy the requirements of the MC, its ruler, the second house or the potential other chart. As Venus moved through the sixth house, Lynn was absorbed with the work of personal and emotional development while PR Saturn opposite Mercury took over the role as star player, demanding that she develop her maximum ability of clerical skills in organizational roles. Eventually Lynn became a professional woman working out of her home (EQHS second cusp ruler, Jupiter, in the fourth house conjunct the ruler of her MC and the Sun); she acted out the role of her sesquisquare-trail-blazing Venus to become certified in the practice of SHEN (Specific Human Energy Nexus), a new school of energy-based bodywork designed to remove a client's emotional blocks.

**The Quincunx.** Two planets that are 150 degrees apart are in quincunx (or inconjunct). The keyword is *Adjustment,* and the nature is like that of Neptune in that the affairs denoted tend to be nebulous, with a spectrum as subtle as the shades of a rainbow. Consider, for example, that there is a matter to which we have become comfortably adjusted when suddenly the calibration is different with a crisis that must be resolved. Actually the situation has been building for some time but the quincunx, when activated, brings it into sharp focus with a sense of urgency. When health matters arise during the experience of the quincunx, they are best handled with immediate attention.

Conversely, it may seem to be a spontaneous gift or opportunity. As an example, Venus in quincunx may result in "love at first sight." Whether this is a crisis or a gift depends on a whole schematic of other considerations both in life and in the chart. By progression the outcome depends largely on the nature of the natal relationship between the two planets. In the same manner as Neptune, the quincunx may appear as an ideal situation or it may generate anguished confusion.

Neptune in a quincunx may appear well adjusted on the surface while simmering a growing discontent for years before a spontaneous situation focuses all the attention on a need for resolution. With this aspect, we may have an area of creative brilliance but we are at the same time considered more than a little weird. With any quincunx to the MC, we may continue in a career position because of job security but we are on automatic pilot; our interest is elsewhere.

A client came into the office who had Mars progressed into the tenth house (natally in the ninth house) quincunx Neptune in the fourth house. The two planets were in opposition natally. Under questioning he said, "No, there has been no recent job move. No, I don't travel with my work. No, I am not moving nor do I plan to." (*Total denial from a client is so disconcerting!*) It was suggested that a dynamic (Mars) job move (tenth house) involving a change of location (fourth house) and more travel (ninth house) was a possibility, but if so, to consider the stability of the proposal (Neptune), as it may start out as a spontaneous, exceptional situation that would require adjustment (quincunx), with the chance that later it would not deliver all that it promised (Neptune natal opposition). Four days later the client called in great excitement, "I've just been offered the position of East

Coast Rep for the company; it would mean moving my family to New York State and it sounds perfect!" It was perfect—for a year—but the New York office had competitive undercurrents and criticisms that were uncomfortable (Mars-Neptune), the travel was wearing (Mars in the ninth) and the family missed California (fourth house).

**The parallels of declination** may also be considered. Though based on a different coordinate system, that of planets which are north or south of the zodiacal ecliptic, they add so much *Intensity* to planetary pairs at the same degree of declination that they are valuable enough to merit a full study. The parallels are considered to have an influence that is similar to that of Pluto for their dynamics and subtle undercurrents. Of Pluto in aspect to the MC (or ASC) it may be said that still waters run deep; the person may have a double life or at the least a profound inner life. What we see is the tip of the iceberg.

**Consider the aspects by the example of a household situation.** Say that the living room carpet is shabby and needs replacement. A conjunction represents buying wall-to-wall carpeting for the whole house. An opposition represents a necessity that leads to maximum achievement; we can either get wall-to-wall carpet, a room-size carpet, or have the floors refinished with no carpet but we simply *have to do something* about that living room. We finally decide on one or the other and the result is stunning. The conjunction and the opposition may have very similar results though the motivation and the method of reaching those results varies.

A square represents a dilemma. We definitely want to get rid of the old carpet and improve the room, and just as definitely we want a certain color and a certain size. The first store does not have the right color, the next does not have the right size and the third has prices that are ridiculous. We finally find exactly what we want after putting a great deal of effort into overcoming the obstacles, and we are delighted because *we did it!*

With a trine, our mother-in-law gives us a carpet. It may not be the color we had in mind, or the texture or size that we like best, but we can't beat the price. As time goes on we learn to appreciate it more than we did originally.

With the "big four," the conjunction, opposition, square and trine, the entire house (life) is under consideration. With the remaining aspects, certain areas of the house (life) require attention at specific times.

A sextile represents a small rug in the entry hall. It leads into the living room on one side and the bedroom hall on the other, so always implies that there is a choice of direction in which to go. We may try one before we decide that we like another better. A semisextile is the welcome mat on the front step. A semisquare is indecisive, we don't know whether to buy a carpet or not because we don't know if we are going to stay in this house or move, or whether we should stick to beige or try out something different, perhaps a wild orange. (*What if I lose my job, or what if my mate gets transferred? Maybe I should wait a while and see what happens. What if I make a decision and it's a mistake?*) It's a tough call that leaves us in limbo until we get all the information necessary to make an informed decision.

With a sesquisquare, we buy a carpet for a room and then find that the color is wrong for the north window light. We return it for another and find the size is wrong, change our mind and have linoleum tile laid instead. Or we buy the carpet and then sell the house and the new people tear it out. We reach a conclusion and gain a result but then conditions change; it was not what we had in mind originally. With a quincunx we didn't even think about a new carpet until we got the news that the most important people on the *planet* are coming to visit next month, and we'd better get this place fixed up. Now.

No matter what the aspect is between two (or more) planets, that aspect is of less importance than the nature of the planets that are in dialogue natally. If these two planets are complimentary to each other by nature or by sign and placement, even a stressful aspect can be resolved constructively. If these two planets are uncomplimentary to each other by nature or by sign and placement, even a favorable aspect can result in difficulties. **Of all the considerations in drawing a conclusion, the foremost is the question of how we are using our chart and living our life. What is our past track record, how healthy is our personal integration, what is our natural attitude toward each of the planets and how do we customarily use our opportunities and resolve our difficulties?**

# Section 2

## Work

# Chapter 5

# Employment

*In order that people may be happy in their work,*
*these three things are needed: they must be fit for it.*
*They must not do too much of it. And they must have*
*a sense of success in it.—John Ruskin (1819-1900)*

THE AVERAGE American worker changes jobs seven times in a lifetime. To find that work for which we are fit and to have some sense of success in it, we usually have to go through a process of trial and error before finding the area that is most comfortable. The first-time job hunter who is uneducated and untrained, usually a student or graduate, or one who was formerly an unpaid worker (such as a homemaker), tends to look for local entry-level employment. In astrological terms most of us can look back at our first job and find it described by whatever planets were in progressed aspect at the time, along with a sixth house aspect.

As we gain experience and maturity, we generally find that in order to compete in the job market and land that position in a more desirable field or location, additional education or job training is necessary. Those of us who choose to progress in our vocation through a prescribed curriculum of specialized courses are those who have aspects between the ninth house to the sixth or second houses. In later job hunts we find ourselves competing with others who are in the same field or who may be just entering the field and willing to take less money, or we ourselves may want a career change. A job hunt typically lasts from eight to twenty-three weeks or more, depending on the state of the economy, our age and qualifications, any local currently held prejudice against our color, gender or sexual preference, and how high we aim. At any event, not only our natal chart but our progressed planets as well give us excellent indications of where and how to go about our job search.

**A resume** is a chronological record of jobs, titles and accomplishments. Though it is customarily written in favor of self interest, we are wise to not go too far with creative journalism; a prospective employer who checks the references does not want to find fiction. On the first page, we put our name, age, address and phone number. If we don't have a typewriter (or word processor), we might borrow one from a friend or go to the local library to rent one by the hour. We then state our education and subject specialties. To apply for a specific position in the company we give our qualifications for that position. We then list our prior positions in reverse order, that is, the most recently held job first, the prior one next and so on, listing the years we were there. We include any special role, experience or awards we may have garnered in that position. For our resume packet, we include copies of letters of recommendation. If we have a business-like photo, that may be included.

**The five most effective methods of finding a job, according to various surveys, are:**

1. Apply directly and *in person* to the desired place of employment. During an interview, be attentive and make eye contact, lean forward to show interest and speak when spoken to. Pick a day with strong transits involving both Saturn and Jupiter if possible, though Jupiter is more important at this point, such as a TR Sun aspect to our natal Jupiter to help the good impression that we wish to make. "Easy" aspects are not as valuable as *quantify* of aspects to the MC and 10th house ruler for the attention we want, to Jupiter or Venus for approval and to the Sun for recognition. If Mercury is retrograde, call the prospective employer back a day or two before it goes direct.

2. Ask friends for job leads. The more competition there is for the desired job, the more advantageous it is to have eleventh house connections. A good word from someone already established at the firm

is a big plus.

3. Ask relatives for job leads. If any of our kin are employed in a place where we would like to work, find out the name of the personnel director or supervisor to make an appointment for an interview. Consider aspects to the third, fourth or tenth houses as good indicators for helpful family contacts.

4. Use a job placement service. Whether this comes from our school or college or from an agency, it is most effective when our ninth house is active.

5. If that new job is just not happening, investigate further options by reading Richard Nelson Bolles, *What Color is Your Parachute? A Practical Manual for Job Hunters and Career Changers.* When we are unemployed at the time of a Neptune aspect it may be tempting to resign ourselves to this minor "retirement." Sidestep the possibility of slipping into apathy by laying out a plan of attack and scheduling appointments when there is as much activity as possible from TR Mars and Jupiter.

Those of us who are employed by others have natal Sun aspects to the second and/or sixth houses plus Mercury aspects to the second and sixth houses, second and tenth houses or sixth and tenth houses. We also have a greater frequency of Venus, Neptune and Moon in angular houses or conjunct the angles. When we have interposited relationships between the sixth and twelfth houses (ruler of the sixth in the twelfth house or vice versa) we lean toward subordinate positions.

As the natural ruler of the sixth house. Mercury tells us a great deal about the type of work that is most appropriate for our natural inclinations and skills. Any aspect between Mercury and a planet constitutes a dialogue; the closer the aspect the more vivid the statement. Generally speaking, the hard aspects (conjunction, opposition, square) have the strongest voice, the trine and sextile speak gently, and the lesser aspects are inconsistent.

**Mercury-Sun aspects:** As Mercury is never more than 28 degrees from the Sun, the conjunction will occur in approximately one chart out of four; the semisextile is rare. The Sun-Mercury aspect or lack of aspect is not a factor in high or low intelligence but it gives its own type of thought process. Any planet conjunct the Sun becomes more subjective and those of us with Mercury conjunct the Sun have a more personal reality than those without the aspect; we are more apt to say, "This is true in my experience, so this is Truth." We may even be suspicious or dismissive of other people's views. *(That's not the way I do it so it must be wrong.)* When Mercury is placed further away from the Sun, either dexter or sinister, we are more lenient, or perhaps indifferent, when other's views differ from ours. When Mercury is retrograde, either natally or by progression, the process of mental assimilation requires review in several stages.

**Mercury-Moon aspects:** With these contacts, a practical, perceptive mind is shown that is suitable for academic fields. We are attracted to contact with the general public, often in nurturing or service-oriented jobs, commodities or goods, or in some cases specifically in a domestic setting. We have a natural feel for the public pulse and for the needs of people. Our best work is developed with a team, our partner, our kin or a support group. We are seldom far from an entourage, with family, clients, students, audience or patrons; we may have a staff or band of coworkers. With the hard aspects between Moon and Mercury, the positions held are less consistent and may even show erratic job changes.

**Mercury-Venus aspects:** The conjunction suggests an unpretentious, easy-going mental attitude and a disinterest in responding to the world's demands until we have satisfied our priority of establishing personal relationships. Once we have gained satisfaction in our social and emotional bonding, we are prepared to work in areas where people and peer interaction are present. With a sensitivity to social and cultural mores, we seek out pleasant surroundings. Our work approach tends to be easy-going rather than markedly ambitious unless this is contradicted by a strong Saturn. We want the satisfaction of approval for our efforts and we are usually helpful and appreciative of others. We do not operate well under stress as we depend more on charm than muscle, but we certainly do well in any vocation where graciousness and courtesy are a requirement. The semisextile, semisquare and sextile require a period of learning how to fit in with others and a less intense focus on seeking a partner than seen with the conjunction.

**Mercury-Mars aspects:** These aspects indicate a restless, virile, satirical mind that is easily bored without a tough challenge to combat and we are impatient with others who are slower or not as skilled. Pragmatic and realistic, we work well with facts and figures and with the mental challenge of objective, tangible problems. We exhibit a competitive, definitive approach to the development of polemics and expertise. If other aspects indicate aesthetic or abstract capacities, the concept is taken a step further into the production of solid results. Among writers, even the poets and mystics have Mercury-Mars contacts either natally or by progression at the time of production. Our mental abilities include a taste for mathematics, mechanistic skills and handling machinery or equipment, fields that require craftsmanship and the ability to focus for long hours. There can even be a touch of danger or enmity in the work and certainly performance demands as well as deadline stress.

**Mercury-Jupiter aspects:** Formal training geared to professional fields is a marked success factor when we have these two planets in dialogue. The aspect by itself does not guarantee an education but it does indicate that a formal degree makes the career choices accessible for which we are best suited. Without the proper education our abilities may fall short of our aspirations. Professional fields are most appropriate, along with self-employment or working for large corporations; we have a sense of propriety and aptness. Many of us seem to have either a good money sense or money-luck. If not from an advantaged background, we manage to marry well or have a remarkable "windfall" at some time in our lives. We think big, either in a fiscal and mundane sense or in philosophical scope, and there's usually a career break or good fortune at some point along the way. However, success may only be a short burst of acclaim if it is not supported by a solid foundation of work and commitment.

**Mercury-Saturn aspects:** With these two planets in contact, we display a mind well fitted for detail work that takes time and patience; practical, capable and efficient. We often go to work when we are young, especially with the hard aspects or retrograde Saturn. Mercury-Saturn aspects imply that we were the obedient child who took responsibility during adolescence by our own volition, if not by necessity. We have better relationships with older people during our youth than with our peer group and often have a lonely adolescence. As adults, we gain a sense of security and great satisfaction from order and discipline; we are thorough and conscientious with an aptitude for applied precision. Though the marked need for solitude endures, for a happier balance we must learn to include the lighter satisfactions of life. When we are so conscientious that we turn the smallest task into an endless chore, we frequently become overburdened to the point of exhaustion, if not depression.

**Mercury-Uranus aspects:** Though these contacts are reputed to be the mark of genius, this is not substantiated in documented studies; they are found in the same amount and degree in the charts of people who have high, low and average I.Q. What it does add is an ability to think in original terms, to be unwilling to follow the crowd, to hear the beat of a different drum. It shows atypical work environments, frequent breaks in routine, unstructured hours and often free-lance work or self employment. If we work for another, our position must be unique in our field or our specific tasks not subject to someone else's orders. We work well with sophisticated equipment, high technology or innovative methods. If we go into conventional jobs, we are apt to move from one job to another until we find a work environment that allows mobility or independence.

**Mercury-Neptune aspects:** Mercury is found more frequently in a relationship with Neptune than with Uranus in the charts of high I.Q. people (along with Sun-Neptune), but may also be linked with the underachiever. This is not due to lack of ability, but rather to a vision that is unrealistic in the practical mundane world as it is. We can imagine a goal or image, an ideal to which we strive but find that either our capacity to reach that goal is handicapped or the basic premise is flawed. We may be the artist or designer, writer or musician whose output falls short of our own aspirations, or the inventor or promoter whose work is called Utopian by those who do not comprehend our dream.

We are attracted to reclusive work environments and modest positions, doing well in service occupations where we can fit into a compliant or subordinate role. When we do receive recognition, it is more apt to be our product, performance or image that is spotlighted than our personal identity. In some few cases we do make that quantum leap of a creative genius that surpasses anything done before, and on the opposite end of the spectrum, some of us are unrealistic to the point of being nonfunctional, or get caught in a web of confusion, deception or incompetence.

**Mercury-Pluto aspects:** With these planets in aspect, we display a mind capable of handling multiple levels simultaneously, while at the same time focusing intently on one subject or activity. At our best we make presentations to a mass media or shape public opinion with our area of expertise. When absorbed in a subject, we have the capacity to concentrate and gain a momentum that can sweep others along with our viewpoint. However, it is all too easy for us to get into group situations where there are factions or political jockeying for position, particularly when we demonstrate a need to be in control or "right."

When we have the hard aspects, there seems to be a need for us to conform to certain standards and codes of conduct which we find difficult. Often we are not "one of the gang" among our coworkers but take either a singular role or we isolate ourselves in our work activity. We take a different role than others in our work environment and often have a feeling of solitude or isolation from the rest of the group. At times we are subject to prejudice or even exclusion so we learn early to keep our own counsel and go along with the program.

Neptune and Pluto are sextile from 1940 to 2000 and Pluto's orbit is inside that of Neptune from 1979-1999. Three generations of people have the possibility of Mercury in aspect to Neptune and Pluto simultaneously. Those of us born during these years can express the full human spectrum of inherent need, all the way from a desire for unity for the good of our group, our nation, our world, and a hope for a more ideal society where we each contribute our share voluntarily, to violent overthrows and breakdowns of power structures that dissolve all semblance of order in our opportunistic steps of succession. With each generation we attack and expose various societal taboos inherent to our time in history to the light of examination and renovation. Our experiments with drug use show our attempt to deal with an imperfect world, not only recreational drugs but a variety of medications that increase in sophistication each decade with the seductive promise of an ability to alter consciousness, mood and intelligence by influencing brain patterns.

When we express the highest ideals of being part of mankind, we seek to cooperate with others (Pluto) to gain a more perfect union (Neptune) politically or personally. Group interaction, whether between races, nations or families during this sixty year period of mass population growth must eventually be renovated with negotiated cooperation for mutual agreements that better the planet, rather than destructive power-struggles that bring everything, including hope for the future, to an impasse of chaos.

**The Job Outlook.** Since Pluto went through Virgo (1957-1971), the fastest growing occupations are those where the workers have higher levels of education, particularly in new technologies. This does not mean that we have to have a four-year college degree, but it does mean that we get additional education or training (ninth house) or specialized courses to fit us with specific skills for a greater chance of advancement and increased income. Those with less than a high-school education have little opportunity of doing more than menial labor in today's job market.

*The 1993 Information Please Almanac* lists over 50 of the most rapidly growing, best employment opportunities of the latter 20th century, most of which reflect the increased population among the aged along with a growing birth rate, as well as more advanced technologies, especially in medical fields and in computers.

Among the most promising medical fields: EEG, respiratory and radiology technologists, podiatrists, health service managers and aides for home health care as well as nursing facilities, medical assistants, nursing aides and psychiatric aides, occupational therapists, physical therapists, surgical technologists and registered nurses. At least one planet in Virgo and/or Pisces, appropriate Mercury skills and sixth house aspects are necessary, twelfth house aspects if work is in a hospital or clinic.

Educational fields: Kindergarten and elementary school teachers, secondary school teachers, pre-school workers and teacher's aides. Mercury, fifth house and third house aspects are valuable.

Computer fields: Programmers, systems analysts, operations research analysts. Uranus aspects to the Sun, Mercury or the angles are helpful as well as ninth house aspects for special training.

Food and beverage service workers: Chefs, cooks and other kitchen workers, hotel managers and assistants, janitors and cleaners. Examine Mars, the Moon position and Cancer, with careful consideration of the sixth house.

Marketing: Accounting and auditors, adjusters, investigators and bill collectors, cashiers, clerical supervisors and managers, general managers and executives, general office clerks, management analysts and consultants, manufacturing and wholesale sales representatives, marketing, advertising and public relations managers, retail sales workers, secretaries, service sales representatives, stock clerks, travel agents, paralegals, receptionist and information clerks. Mercury is important; consider the eighth house, sixth house and ninth houses. Jupiter helps in our social formalities of dealing with the public, as does the Venus courtesies; the eleventh house for influence, and planets on the west of the chart. The Moon in aspect to the outer planets, especially Uranus, may attract us to contact with the general public (unless the Moon is limited by self-absorption in personal development).

**How do we deal with the boss who is a jerk?** First of all, we look at our tenth house. Mars in the tenth (or ruling the MC) attracts a boss who has the impertinence to want to run his business his own way. To our best advantage, we may use our Mars in decisive action, take a straightforward role when challenged without being confrontational and stand up for our own position. We need to control our temper in career situations.

With Neptune in the tenth house we find it best to avoid office gossip or we ourselves may be drawn into collusion. If we should feel that we are "the victim," it may be time to talk the situation over realistically with a good Saturn-type friend before we exaggerate the whole mess.

Mercury problems with the tenth house may show a boss who can't get the point across; perhaps we can lead the way by initiating clarity in communication. Check instructions to make sure that the objective is definitive. If the boss or a co-worker steals our ideas, put them in writing before presentation.

If we suspect that moral or ethical issues are at stake, perhaps we should examine our own Jupiter for honesty and our Sun for integrity. If our gut reaction says, "This is wrong," we may trust the instinct of our Moon and see if the boss has his priorities straight. And if we do. With Pluto in our tenth house, our boss believes in supply and demand. We supply, he demands. To avoid coercion, we may examine our own belt-line of how much we can compromise without losing pride in ourselves and our work, and go no further than what we consider fair. We are not in a position to give ultimatums, and if the boss plays that game, we have to be prepared to call his bluff.

We need to be consistent with our Venus dialogue in the tenth house as courtesy is always a winner. If the boss is vacillating or avoids making decisions, we might make suggestions that are to the company's advantage. If we have the Sun relating to the tenth house and the boss is bragging (at the time that we'd like a little credit), we can create a win-win situation by acknowledging his Sun (Good job, Mr. Big) and then pointing out our own contribution. If we can't drag approval out of the boss no matter how well we organize our Saturn, be assured that somewhere down the line our hard work will pay off; this is the promise that Saturn makes. If the result does not come through, our Uranus will sooner or later kick in and we may tell the boss to go jump in the lake while we are off to a new field or to start a business for ourselves.

**To delineate a chart for our mundane life, follow the twelve-step program that is illustrated in the following example.**

For major patterns consider the Big-Four (the conjunction, opposition, square and trine) as all other aspects refer to specific situations, given areas or definitive times in the life. For an extra clue in delineating each planet, look at the dispositor, *the first dispositor only.* Always watch for indicators that reinforce a theme by repeating it in different ways. (For a more detailed analysis, review the appropriate chapters as we go through the twelve steps. The first four steps are covered in Chapter 2, "Overview.")

## Example Chart of Employment

**1. Planets east/west, above/below.** As we can see in the example chart on the following page, Rex Hall has eight planets east, six

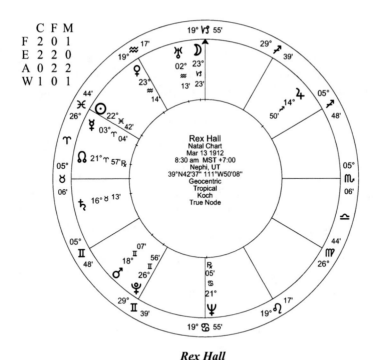

**Rex Hall**

***Declinations:*** *☿ 0N56; ☉ 2S54; ☊ 8N34; ♂ 13N14; ♀ 14S29; ♄ 14N43;*
  *♀ 17N7; ♅ 20S12; Ψ 21N15; ♃ 21S48; M 21S58; ♂ 24N56; ☽ 26S33*

above. His interests are self motivated, he makes his own opportunities in life and seeks the fulfillment of his own validation. He meets people with openness and a friendly attitude (Aquarius and eleventh house) and initiates his public involvement at an early age (Moon elevated).

**2. Qualities and elements.** With a predominance of four earth and four air signs, including the MC and ASC, the signature indicates a practical mind motivated by ideas for which Hall seeks results. The qualities are balanced.

**3. Phenomena.** Neptune is retrograde in the fourth house. Hall's early dreams were put on "hold" when he settled into a marriage at age 20. At his Saturn return he left home, seeking more out of life than a small-town rut. It was 15 years before he bought his next home with the financial help of his second wife. Pluto is Stationary, a position which places a powerful focus on his ability to cooperate with others for his livelihood (second house) as well as a drive to exercise power in his earning capacity. The elevated Moon represents fluctuation and variety in his career. The Sun is dominant by dint of having the majority of aspects, an indicator that repeats Hall's drive to be his own boss or be in control of his own directions.

**4. Character.** The Sun is in Pisces (mutable water, the fishes, ruled by Jupiter-Neptune). Hall is adaptable and emotionally responsive to situations and environments with a natural sense of faith in the ultimate order and possessed of the vision of a better life. He has the dual capacity of metaphysical awareness and mundane ambition. He can find his significance in eleventh house matters as a sympathetic leader in community affairs. With the dispositor, Neptune, in Cancer in the fourth house, his vision encompasses the perfect home base from which to operate, and with Jupiter in Sagittarius in the eighth house, he optimistically aims for expansion in his business and financial position.

The Moon is in Capricorn (mutable earth, the goat, ruled by Saturn), symbolizing a natural instinct toward initiating practical, expedient ambitions to advance his goal of upward mobility. Though his nature is conservative, his approach is innovative. He would feel natural and "at home" before the public (tenth house Moon). The dispositor, Saturn, is in the 1st house; Hall's security is linked with his personal ability to take control.

The ASC is Taurus (fixed earth, the bull, ruled by Venus). Hall's personal manner is slow and steady, easy-going and laid-back. He is a big, gruff man, seldom angry or disgruntled, with great stamina and perseverance in a set course. The dispositor is Venus in Aquarius, eleventh house; Hall is surrounded by friends and extremely well liked in his local clubs and organizations.

**5. Employment.** Hall's Sun is square the second house planets, with no aspect to the 6th house; however, Mercury rules the second and the sixth houses and is sextile the tenth house Uranus, connections that are seen in the charts of those who are employed. Mercury is semisquare Saturn, an indication of applied precision once Hall learns how to take responsibility for his own ambitions. Mercury is sextile Uranus; he works well with technological equipment and is suited to abrupt changes of schedule on the job or in career moves that create progressive opportunities. Mercury square Pluto depicts a need to develop his ability to handle several jobs while fitting into work roles that require cooperation with different factions.

**6. Self-employment.** We note a dominant Sun, as well as Uranus in the tenth house, disclosing Hall's desire to be in business for himself. Saturn in the first house demonstrates a hard worker with self-directed ambition, but the contradictory Neptune on the angle is not helpful. It mirrors the vision but not the necessary drive and with a trine to the Sun, the question rises of whether or not Hall finds it too easy to rest on past laurels. Mars is conjunct Pluto, a plus factor even though succedent. Their opposition to Jupiter and T-square to the Sun add optimism and passion but Hall's timing or judgment may be impulsive. The three succedent positions enervate the impact of the T-square, which would be much more effective on angles with the Neptune trine away from the angle.

**7. Planets in the sixth house.** The sixth house is ruled by Mercury, posited in the twelfth. This implies a retiring, reclusive, obscure position at work. Whereas Hall has a "visible" chart with the Moon and Uranus elevated, his actual work is not well known or has hidden factors. Mercury is sextile Uranus in the tenth house so his best work environment is to follow a sequence of opportunities that develop innovative progress into advanced or high-tech fields. Mercury's dispositor is Mars in Gemini (second house), adding to the testimony that Hall's work is due to financial necessity.

**8. Financial attitude.** The Moon is in Capricorn to portray a tight money manager who knows how to follow a rigid budget, often from necessity. Venus in Aquarius may describe contradictions in his finances as Hall could be conservative one day and indifferent the next, according to the changing winds of his hopes and wishes. His Sun in Pisces repeats this indication by its very nature as well as its eleventh house position.

**9. Vocational Indicators.** Due to its dialogue with the tenth house, Mars in the second house is a vocational indicator. Appropriate areas of livelihood for Hall are construction, working with tools, instruments or equipment; in Gemini, work with his hands, his mind or wits in transportation or communication fields. The close quincunx of Mars to the MC depicts his initial response of eagerness to the challenge of a new job position. The aspect of Mars sesquisquare Uranus indicates that he can blaze trails in innovative ways; however, abrupt changes of career could be detrimental to his income. Pluto in the second is quincunx the Moon: Hall could work in major power-organizations as the only one capable of handling this particular job. The two quincunx aspects leading from the second house into the MC imply that Hall may stay on a job for financial security but his interest could wane if he stayed for long. This theme is repeated by the Moon in the tenth house.

The two planets in the second house, Pluto and Mars, co-rule Scorpio, the seventh cusp. Hall's financial position is directly involved with his partner, either in business or personally and the T-square implies areas of conflict in this partnership. To work out mutually equitable (Pluto) contracts (Gemini) and legal agreements (Jupiter in Sagittarius), the blend of dual priorities (Pisces) must be based on honorable (Sun) agreements.

The ruler of the second house cusp and dispositor of the second house planets is Mercury in the twelfth. Hall either works behind the scenes, has periods of unemployment, or retires from work because he has attained great wealth. Which shall it be?

**10. Wealth.** The ruler of the second and sixth houses (Mercury for both) is in the twelfth, making no aspect to the eighth house. The eighth house Jupiter is quincunx Saturn, the ruler of the MC, not a major aspect. We do not have adequate indications to suggest wealth.

**11. Success.** The MC in Capricorn reveals Hall's practical initiative in career ambitions. To be successful in his field, he would work his way up, step by patient and hardworking step. He would take personal responsibility and direct his most ambitious goals toward civic welfare. The ruler, Saturn, is in Taurus, repeating the theme of a long apprenticeship to reach his peak, sticking to a game plan with practical stability. The Moon, on the other hand, seldom stays consistently before the public but must alternate exposure with periods of privacy.

The fluctuation of Hall's career in a two-to-three year pulse is a handicap to the Capricorn-Taurus indicators of success. Uranus in the tenth house adds another dimension, that of vivid individuality that impels Hall toward sudden, unconventional changes of direction in his career.

The MC is trine Saturn, its own ruler, in the first house. This is a prime indicator of Hall's strength of character, that he takes responsibility for his own actions in a way that gives him a peace of mind that goes beyond the world's rewards. The MC also opposes Neptune; though Hall may reach for and touch the ultimate, his achievement could never match the extent of his vision.

The chart strongly indicates that Hall would like to be self-employed or in business for himself; however, there are enough contradictions with the sixth, the second and eighth houses that it is not advisable. It may be suggested that Hall seek employment in a major construction or production field in which he is given free reign to handle middle management and personnel.

**12. The Life Path.** In Hall's chart, the EQHS tenth cusp is 5 degrees Aquarius and the ruler, Uranus becomes the most elevated planet. This presents the possibility of a life subject to sudden changes, remarkable departures from the world into which he was born and independent decisions that show the mark of originality. It leans toward a free-lance career in which Hall is never the standard representative of his field.

Rex Hall's first job was in a lumber mill. He became an apprentice carpenter and very quickly, a skilled cabinetmaker. At 29, he left his small town and never looked back.

In 1942, Hall remarried. It was war time and the factories were booming. He applied for a job in an aircraft factory, claiming for himself an engineering degree. He said that for the first few months he watched and listened while reading every manual available, and his performance skills were so remarkable that he was promoted to chief engineer of the BPY5A flying boat within a year.

Hall stayed in the company for 12 years; the fluctuation of the Moon was reflected in his change of department every few years.

Mercury was expressed in his major assignment of writing technical instruction manuals (sextile Uranus). When Hall left the factory, it was to go into his own business, a dream he had entertained for years. In 1954, when PR Venus made a trine to Jupiter, he obtained financial backing from a dozen investors to manufacture a new invention, an appliance (which has since then been successfully improved). Within two years the aspect moved out, there was no activity involving the eighth house and the business went broke. PR ASC joined Pluto to symbolize the extreme. Hall went back to the aircraft factory and spent the next 15 years paying back his investors. When asked, "Why didn't you declare bankruptcy?" he answered simply, "My investors were my friends; they believed in me."

After his second heart attack, Hall took an early retirement. With the rulers of the Pisces twelfth house posited in the eighth and the fourth houses he did have financial protection for a modest life style. For the last decade of his life, he used his early skills of carpentry to remodel much of his home as well as explore his artistic gifts in oil painting. He was active in the Chamber of Commerce and in his men's club. Though not successful by the world's measure of fame and money, he was highly successful as a husband and father and a member of the community. Rex Hall died of a massive coronary on January 17, 1984.

# Chapter 6

# Self Employment

*When you get the entrepreneurial urge, visit someone who has his own business. It may cure you.*—Richard A. Moran

WHEN WE are self employed, the Sun, Mars, Pluto, Saturn and Uranus are seen more frequently in angular houses or conjunct the angles and in strong aspects to other planets (within one or two degrees of orb), testifying to our willingness to take the driver's seat in our lives. Our self-motivation is aided by a positive attitude, a healthy ego drive and self-esteem (Sun), a feel for the public pulse or how to reach our market (Moon) and receptivity toward input as well as eagerness to learn (Mercury).

Whether employed or self employed, we demonstrate Uranus aspects to the tenth and sixth houses; however, we who are self employed have close Uranus aspects to the Sun more frequently. Uranus square the MC also indicates activities that are either independent or unconventional. As the eleventh house gives an indication of our civic position or our place in our societal group, the ruler of the eleventh cusp is angular twice as often when we are self employed as when we are employed by another.

All the sign qualities represent factors which aid business success: a self-motivated ability to instigate effort (cardinal signs), focus, persistence and determination (fixed signs), and the flexibility necessary to shift with the commercial tides (mutable signs).

**Business** owners have a special drive of self determinism and independence. We are the people who will work 16 hours a day for ourselves so we don't have to work eight hours a day for someone else, longer hours for less money, sometimes for years, in order to get established. According to experts, our home-based businesses earn 70 percent of the amount of take-home pay that we would earn working for someone else, and 65 percent of new businesses fail in the first five years. This means that we must either have someone else to cover basic living expenses and pay the bills during our formative period, hold down an income-producing job during that stage or have a financial cushion to carry us past the time of a negative cash flow.

We are prudent to outline a plan of action and worst-case-scenario budget before we start and give ourselves a deadline of two or three years, whatever time that we can invest before our loss consumes more than the value of that time amount. For example, suppose that we have worked for 10 years to buy a home, then mortgage the home to start a business. If the business is unable, in a year or two, to make the house payments, the loss of our home represents a loss of our prior 10-year investment. In this case the investment is too high.

We need to evaluate the lifestyle that we are willing to follow during the time span that it takes to start generating a profit margin. We may calculate how much income we need on a monthly basis and how much business is required to generate that income. Those of us who like to sleep late and turn off the phone during business hours, who do not actively pursue a purchasing market every day, who are unwilling to give up weekly recreations or cut expenses to the bone are obviously not the ones who should start our own business. Health insurance or medical coverage must be considered, as this is an appreciable fringe benefit of employment.

Mars-Saturn aspects contribute to our ability to put in extra hours under tough conditions as well as demonstrate a skill for calculating jeopardy, unless we use our Mars in a reckless way to burn bridges behind us in rashly impulsive action. We exhibit prudent judgment when we evaluate the risk of being confrontational during those times when a hard Mars-Saturn contacts our chart and unjust imposition seems prevalent.

Jupiter-Saturn aspects are helpful for a fine sense of expansion versus stabilization, or expense that stimulates equitable return when they are used in balance. C. E. O. Carter spoke of these two planets in aspect as "great results with hard work." In an average chart they are more apt to have an effect of win-a-few, lose-a-few; we bring in a $100 sale at the same time that a $100 invoice comes due. We pay a high price for extravagance with Jupiter-Saturn aspects, but slow, conservative work toward growth creates steady progress and often outstanding results. Jupiter and Saturn do effectively describe periods in which to expand or stabilize according to their aspects to other points in the chart.

Saturn in hard aspects denotes a keen awareness of restrictions and limitations and in the worst case scenario may be involved in job loss or inability to meet the payroll or expenses. In soft aspects it highlights the best times to organize and stabilize conditions for the achievement of security. Jupiter in hard aspects implies excess and over-optimism that leads to inflated expense; in soft aspects, Jupiter is advantageous to sales at a peak price, job promotions that increase the income, and the benefit of education and experience.

Obviously those of us who are self employed value job satisfaction and independence above salary, at least initially to stick with our period of establishment. We must have a high level of self-motivation, such as indicated by a dynamic Mars, vivid Uranus statements and some degree of cardinal signs for self initiative. The dictionary defines an entrepreneur as "the one who organizes, manages and assumes the risks of a business or enterprise." Risk is a key word here; the pirates and adventurers of yesterday are the movers and shakers in the business world of today who find the challenge irresistible and the achievement highly rewarding.

Business is "the employment, trade, profession." In a sense we are all in business, we who earn a living and pay our bills. The financial necessity of physical existence requires daily commercial transactions in order to build a good life. However, to be more specific, a business person is one who is in command of a unit of commerce, and business success is measured in terms of monetary return. Business failure is the loss of that control. The Sun in active position and aspect denotes the ability to control circumstances or control other people, to be the boss, to be in a position of authority.

Consider some of the following examples in a study of 500 people in successful business control. For many, the Sun was not at all outstanding by quantity and closeness of aspects; however, in half the cases the Sun was natally on an angle. In many of the remaining example charts the Sun moved to the angular house by the time people were in adolescence. In the majority of the example charts the Sun was either in aspect to the MC or tenth house ruler, or posited or ruler of the tenth house. This is usually a close aspect but not necessarily a harmonious one. In other cases the Sun moved into a relationship with the tenth house at the time of going into business. Even in job seeking, a progressed aspect involving the Sun is a decided advantage toward being in control of our own life.

In *all* the example charts of business owners the Sun had a relationship to the fourth house as it was either posited, ruling, in aspect to a planet in the fourth house or in aspect to the ruler. As the fourth house designates factory, store or home, that which is known legally as real property, this dialogue suggests the control of fixed holdings. No other houses were consistently aspected by the Sun. If the business is at home, the fourth house in a dialogue with the second house is appropriate.

Saturn or a planet in Capricorn was in strong aspect to the first house in 90 percent of the charts. In most of the charts the Moon was in aspect to Jupiter or Saturn, or Jupiter held an aspect to Saturn. The Moon was in an angular house position in a fourth of the charts, less than the average expectancy: Neptune also had angular positions that were fewer than average. Mercury was on an angle in half of the charts, and Mars, Uranus and Pluto above average in angular positions. Venus held the least count of angularity, by a scant one fourth of the charts; in those charts where Venus was angular the businesses in the study were a toy store, cosmetic and hair salons, motels and resorts and entertainment fields.

Counting Sun, Moon and Ascendant signs, the masculine signs (fire and air) predominated by 30 percent over the expected average. This is of course part of the culture; traits that are successful in accomplishment are those which are labeled "masculine," such as directness, decisiveness, assertiveness, outgoing competence. The balance of power is still primarily in the hands of men; a woman doing the same work is paid some 30-40 percent less. In the late 20th century, women are taking more positive executive roles while striving to gain economic parity with men in the market place.

For the chart overview, angular houses had 20 percent more occupancy by planets, with the upper east quadrant outstanding along with the second and fourth houses. In 80 percent of the charts, the MC or tenth house ruler was conjunct or trine the sixth house ruler, or there was an interposition (such as the ruler of the tenth house in the sixth house and/or the ruler of the sixth house in the tenth house). The remaining 20 percent had some other relationship of the MC or tenth house to the sixth house. In 70 percent of the charts, the MC or its house ruler was conjunct, trine, or interposited to the eighth house. Two-thirds of the remaining examples had a dialogue of some kind between the tenth house and the eighth house. The final 10 percent fell in the charts of people who had bankruptcy or business failure or were struggling under severe handicaps.

In 94 percent of the cases studied there was a strong and usually favorable aspect between the tenth house and the second house. **In summation, to become a business owner, it is advantageous, if not requisite, to have the MC or its ruler in dialogue with the second house, the sixth house, and the eighth house.** The fifth house has the connotation of adding pleasure or creative satisfaction in one's work by its dialogue with the first, second, or sixth houses, as well as representing the clientele.

The overall aspects in the charts of those who are involved in activities of venture capital illustrate a point of which astrologers are keenly aware—that hard aspects are more indicative of accomplishment than soft aspects. All the charts had close squares, most had oppositions. One of the most fruitful aspects noted is the conciliation pattern. That is, two planets in opposition engage a third planet that is trine the planet at one end of the opposition and sextile the planet at the other end. The demand of resolution (of the opposition) is aided by the outlet of opportunities (sextile) that can be turned to great advantage (trine). J. Paul Getty, for example, has Jupiter opposite Saturn, conciliated by Mercury. Henry Ford has Sun-Mercury opposite

Moon, conciliated by Neptune. Neptune itself is opposite Saturn and receives a conciliation by the Sun on one side and the Moon on the other, an awesome double conciliation pattern. Howard Hughes has five planets in the fourth house, most of which oppose Pluto in the tenth, with Mars-Saturn conciliating from the sixth house.

Of course good luck is an advantage. The greatest talent, the greatest desire, and the greatest perseverance cannot overcome conditions that are totally inhibitive of fruition. However it is interesting to note that 80 percent of the entrepreneurial charts have a T-square, while only 20 percent have a grand trine.

Chapter 14, "Business Wealth," continues the discussion of the entrepreneurial giant with example charts.

## Example Chart of Self Employment

1. **Planets east/west, above/below.** George Murphy has eight planets west and seven above. There is a strong need to interact with others and be where the action is. He is highly visible, personable and well known within the perimeters of his field.

2. **Qualities and elements.** Including the MC and ASC, Murphy has a count of five mutable signs and five fixed signs to imply extreme adaptability and perseverance. (He said jokingly of himself, "I am inflexibly indecisive.") With four air signs the need for social and intellectual exchanges is repeated. The signature comes to movable-air and fixed-air, Libra-Aquarius. As this repeats the elements of his Sun, Moon and ASC signs. Murphy knows who he is and what he is about. He is not searching for hidden meanings or to "find himself."

3. **Phenomena.** Saturn is retrograde, representing the drive to work for his own reasons, not those of another. Pluto is dominant and elevated, conjunct the MC and ruling the second house, designating it as the prime candidate for the vocational indicator. Pluto represents Murphy's power to influence public opinion and the affairs of others, as well as control his environment through teamwork and cooperation, or coercion and manipulation. (The means of exercising power through Pluto is discussed farther in Chapter 14, "Business Wealth.")

4. **Character.** The Sun is in Gemini (mutable air, the twins, ruled by Mercury). Murphy is intellectual, versatile, restless, mobile and

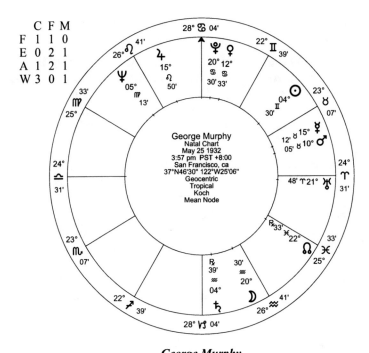

**George Murphy**

*Declinations:* ♌ 2S39; ♅ 7N57; A 9S31; ♆ 10N20; ☿ 14N21; ♂ 14N22;
♃ 16N58; ☽ 17S15; ♄ 19S24; M 20N33; ☉ 21N3; ⚷ 22N31; ♀ 25N57

changeable, drawn to verbal and social exchanges. He can find significance in eighth house matters, dealing with business or public financial affairs. This is reinforced by the dispositor in Taurus, a money
sign, as well as Scorpio on the second cusp. The Taurus dispositor sta-
bilizes his Gemini traits and adds practical expediency.

The Moon is in Aquarius (fixed air, the water-bearer, ruled by
Uranus and Saturn), repeating the theme of mental interaction with an
interest in people and ideas. The co-dispositor, Saturn, also in Aquarius, reflects a sense of responsibility and a natural efficiency in working with technology as well as in handling people. The dispositor,
Uranus in Aries, is opposite the ASC, which can suggest conflict, not
because of the opposition but because Murphy seeks relationship to
balance his Libra ASC (and with the ruler, Venus in Cancer, the un-

conditional acceptance of family), while he is influenced by his Uranus to demand freedom and independence.

The ASC is in Libra (cardinal air, justice, ruled by Venus). In his personal manner, Murphy is genteel, poised, thoughtful and interested in others. The dispositor, Venus in Cancer, is conjunct Pluto, depicting his ability to facilitate negotiations with persuasive appeal; he is also a skillful performer in speaking before any public presentation media.

5. **Employment.** The Sun has a midpoint semisquare to both the sixth and second house rulers, Uranus and Pluto; Mercury is conjunct the second ruler but in a T-square to the tenth and fourth houses, not the aspects we see commonly for those who are employed by another. Uranus as well makes a distinct statement with its opposition to the ASC. Mercury conjunct Mars portrays Murphy's quick mind, well fitted for polemics, hard facts and figures. Mars square Saturn indicates that he is a disciplined worker who is on the job long after others have left. Saturn trine the Sun in air signs adds to his natural organizational skills.

6. **Self-employment.** Pluto is conjunct the MC, Saturn the IC and Uranus the DESC. Venus and Neptune are in positions which are discreetly away from vocational points. There are cardinal angles, the Sun is trine the fourth house Saturn, and the Moon is opposite Jupiter in the tenth house. The second house ruler, Pluto, is conjunct the MC and the eighth house contains the Sun. Murphy's chart points strongly toward self-employment in his own business.

7. **Planets in the sixth house.** The best performance of Uranus involves an inconsistent schedule, an indication that repeats Murphy's Gemini need of mobility, as well as being appropriate for the use of sophisticated technology or equipment. The rulers of the Pisces cusp are Neptune, which makes no aspect to the MC, and Jupiter in the tenth house, work in the public view, work that gains public attention, or professional work.

8. **Financial attitude.** With the Moon in Aquarius, the instinctive approach is, "I did it my way," and Venus in Cancer mirrors a personal comfort level in making money grow.

9. **Vocational indicators.** Scorpio is on the second house cusp, Pluto is conjunct the MC. The ruler of the second house posited in the ninth house indicates that an education is required to gain expertise on a given specific subject; Mars in the seventh house implies one-to-one exchanges or competitions. Pluto is conjunct Venus for the ability to sway and promote others through charm and courtesy in public functions and formalities; however it is T-square the ASC-Uranus, suggesting that cooperation issues can rapidly reach an impasse, at which time Uranus and the Aquarius Moon team up to make a declaration of detached independence. This is a combination that is more conducive to free-lance employment than taking orders. The dominant Pluto along with Mars in the seventh depicts Murphy's ability to work in a power-position with a series of individuals sequentially as well as simultaneously.

10. **Wealth.** The rulers of the second house (Mars) and twelfth house (Mercury) are conjunct in the seventh house, and the co-ruler of the fourth house (Saturn) is posited in the fourth house trine the eighth house and square the second house. The interpositions that are seen in the charts of great wealth are not present, however the indicators have enough quantity and strength for a successful business that this goal may be recommended.

11. **Success.** The MC is Cancer, showing the need to work with the family or a partner in a field that responds to the needs of the people. The ruler, Moon in Aquarius, implies that Murphy would not be the standard representative of his field but would add his own innovation. The Moon in the fourth house indicates the possibility of a family business or even working in the home. Jupiter in the tenth house describes Murphy's public position as prestigious, honorable and successful. He may take life in large bites, even to the point of more than he can chew at times. With its opposition to the Moon, T-square Mars-Mercury, in expansion or his drive for freedom, his judgment may occasionally be questionable.

The requisites of financial and mundane success of the MC/tenth house interactive with the second, sixth and eighth houses are met: the second house ruler is conjunct the MC, the sixth house ruler is posited in the tenth house and, with Leo intercepted in the tenth house, the ruler (Sun) is posited in the eighth house. (With EQHS there is no interception and the MC is ruled solely by the Moon, with Jupiter still posited in the tenth house. In this case the relationship between the eighth and tenth houses is weak, with Venus semisextile Jupiter and the Sun sesquisquare the Moon. This is more descriptive of gradual growth with intermittent disruptions and implies that a successful financial position would take longer, not reaching an optimum until after age 58, when the Sun moves into the tenth house.)

12. **The Life Path.** In Murphy's chart the EQHS 10th cusp is the same sign as the MC with only 3 degrees 33 minutes difference. At age 3½, Murphy's widowed father left the boy in a foster home while he relocated to another city, the city that Murphy later chose for his adult home. The MC reached the EQHS eleventh cusp when Murphy was age 26 years 5½ months = November 10, 1958. He married June 12, 1958 and received his Masters in Business Administration, Accounting specialty, from UCLA in 1959.

Please note that the 12 steps describe the theme and compare them to the facts: George Murphy is a Certified Public Accountant with his own business in his own building. He is not a Donald Trump or a Bill Gates but he is a successful businessman in a metropolitan area doing what he chooses to do. He has all of his business on computers and has a staff that is skilled in electronic equipment; he himself travels over several states to see clients. He has appeared on television and is an entertaining public speaker. Murphy's father was an accountant and his son has also worked in his office as an accountant. Both of his wives have worked in his office. He has had financial setbacks at various times but his growth has been, for the most part, consistent.

Does this chart mean that Murphy was "destined" to be a C.P.A. or that there were no other choices? Certainly not. Follow the 12 steps and consider the possible vocations of teaching, writing, the legal profession, even politics. A case could be made for each of those fields.

# Chapter 7

# Unemployment

*Give a man a fish and you feed him for a day. Teach a man to fish and you feed him for a lifetime.*—Chinese proverb

HISTORICALLY the last segment of the horoscope has gotten the reputation of housing the indigent, vagrants, parasites and criminals, the physically and mentally handicapped or disabled, and, on a more personal and individual level, our unconscious blocks to achievement or satisfaction, classically known as "self-undoing." This seems a rather harsh definition for the natural ruler, as Jupiter embodies the sanctuary of the twelfth house, suggesting the comfort and protection which makes it a safe haven to withdraw into the bliss of worldly renunciation. Neptune, with all its mystery and ambiguity, was allotted the rulership of Pisces and its association with the twelfth house only after its discovery in 1845.

The twelfth house is the house of retirement, of unemployment. Criminals or the handicapped fall under the twelfth house jurisdiction if they are in prison, an institution or in some other place of confinement or retirement. This protects not only the person but society. When we withdraw into a hospital at the time of physical illness or injury there is a total relinquishment of self; our body, our very life is given over to the care of others, which can be a great relief at the time.

**Who are the unemployed?** Those of us who are too young or too old to work, who are preoccupied with other activities such as childbearing, home-making, parenting or care-taking in other unpaid capacities, plus those who are unable or unwilling to enter paid service are among the unemployed. There are also times when we are temporarily out of a job, either by choice or by circumstances.

Whereas planets in the sixth house are subordinate in the sense of having to work or do labor with the matters signified, planets in the twelfth house are subordinate only in the sense that their motivation is not worldly. The financial reward is neither the reason nor goal of twelfth house activity. Certainly entrepreneurial types have active planets in or ruling the twelfth house, but these planets contribute to other hidden agendas, not to the drive for business accomplishment and fiscal achievement.

In the charts of performers such as actors, musicians, dancers and other entertainers, producers and directors, writers and artists, the twelfth house creates a venue which allows the time and place to polish and develop their craft before taking their act on the road. The twelfth house provides a "down time" preparatory to the public presentation.

C. C. Zain, in the *Church of Light* series, wrote that planets in cadent houses which conjunct the angles within 15 degrees are powerful indicators of angularity. The work of Michel and Francoise Gauquelin has further documented the twelfth house (as well as the ninth, and to a lesser degree, the third and sixth houses) as powerful positions for Mars in the charts of athletes, Saturn in the charts of scientists, Jupiter in the charts of politicians and actors, and the Moon in the charts of writers. The drive symbolized by each of these planets is for its own fulfillment; the incentive to be rich and famous is not the motivation. When this result occurs it is a fringe benefit.

For average people, twelfth house planets are strongly motivational but not usually as vocational significators; we are more apt to express these planets as private hobbies or interests in either a minor environment or solitude. In all cases, with twelfth house planets, we require privacy as well as time alone, time apart, time to withdraw from the stress of interaction. The eleventh, twelfth and first houses are all "self motivated; the eleventh to seek our own truth, whatever that may be; the twelfth to seek our own vision, however Utopian it may be; and the first to seek our own identity, whoever and whatever we may come to realize as self.

In the early 1990s, a four-year study of literacy in America was very sobering, as it found that nearly half of the nation's 191 million adults were not proficient enough in English to write a letter or calculate the answers to simple everyday problems such as a bus schedule. These are people who are engaged in menial labor, or they are among the unemployed and must be protected and provided for by their family or the state. Unemployment from the work force is essentially a phenomena of economics organized on a capitalistic basis. It was not until 1935 that the United States established a national insurance scheme as a result of the depression of the 1930s. This was the worst time in history for worldwide unemployment as it reached as high as 30 percent in some areas.

Before the last Pluto-in-Scorpio period, the mid-18th century, the primary world economy was agriculturally based. Cottage industry turned out utensils and dishes, tools and weapons from farm forges, while textiles and garments were hand manufactured in homes. Unemployment was not a government issue; when workers left their military or government service or the mines and mills, they returned to the land to feed themselves and their families from their farms or home villages. Unmarried women, with little status, lived with their kin as household members, as did the aged. With the industrial revolution, cities burgeoned. Steel mills, construction, publishing, commerce, transportation and factories all boomed in expansion, and farming became another business rather than a way of life for the general population.

In the 20th century, labor unions and the governments of most nations formed various kinds of protection for their population, some type of support and welfare for their young, their aged, the infirm and the unemployed. In an economic society, employment cycles become a predictable part of the nation's economy. There have been nine recessions since World War II. Welfare is a great boon for the needy—but it can insidiously erode a person's pride and the structure of society itself when it encourages dependency. Most nations require that people make some contribution of labor to the state when the state supports them, just as they must contribute labor to any employer who pays their hire. When the government supports a large percentage of its population who are able-bodied without any commensurate effort on their part, they are enervating the vitality of their nation and cultivating a ghetto culture.

When we are among the unemployed, the extent and variety of our Neptune aspects is remarkable. C. E. O. Carter wrote that Moon-Neptune is often "cloistered," that is to say monastic, secluded, obscured, retiring. This is not always the case; when placed in the chart of a high-profile achiever it is capable of expression that ranges from the role of active idealist (activist) to that of a scheming confidence-crook.

However, Neptune aspecting any planet will show an area or a time in the life when the focus leads away from the nine-to-five commitment of the mundane marketplace. People with close Neptune aspects dream of having "that little place in the country" or other ways to satisfy their inner hunger to withdraw into their own mystical well of solitude. Even vacations away from work are accompanied by Neptune transits, and progressed Neptune aspects may well dog our footsteps when we "just can't get a job anywhere." Other people use their close Neptune aspects in other areas of escape, or in other areas of creative imagination.

During the 1940-2000 Neptune-Pluto sextile, the two planets moved in and out of a one degree contact through 1948-1989. Many individuals born in this time window, from self-undoing, are subject to the various breakdowns attributable to drug or alcohol abuse, as well as medical disability due to AIDS. Neptune (in the earth sign Capricorn) sextile Pluto is also a factor in industrial debility and recession, layoffs and unemployment, where alternate opportunities (sextile) and life styles must be cultivated.

When we are fired from a job, aspects from TR Saturn to Sun or even the two-day TR Sun to Saturn, particularly the square, may well show the fall of the ax. The opposition is more apt to indicate a demand of more work with less reward. Hard aspects of Mercury-Saturn tend to indicate periods when we "tighten the belt," cutting our budget due to feeling poor. PR Moon aspects to Saturn often indicate that we would like to fix up our homestead but funds are limited or lacking; it is an appropriate time to pay attention to fences and landscaping, cement and glass work, all foundations that in the long run improve our property value.

Saturn transiting its own angles (conjunction, opening square, opposition, closing square) or transiting the tenth house is well known for presenting a bill to pay our dues; we don't get anything we have not worked for, but what we work for, we get and keep. If duty and propriety have not been observed or if there are financial or moral debts outstanding, this is the time that is subject to downfall. Years of observation not only validate this tradition, but suggest another area of difficulty; when transit Saturn goes through the eighth house, that which is not built on a firm foundation is subject to breakdown.

Bobby is one of many young men and women who moved back home in the 1990s when jobs were scarce. His second house ruler, Jupiter, was semisextile Neptune in the twelfth house during the few years prior when he had been in school, working part time, and was exact the year that he collected unemployment. Jupiter-Neptune rule his Pisces fourth cusp for the protection and benefit found at home. He also picked up cash with handyman jobs, using his sixth house Mars constructively. A bare-bones Saturn ruling and posited in the 8th house was not helpful for him to build up a credit cushion. **Remember, poverty is not hard aspects, it is the lack of aspects, along with enervating soft planets, particularly Neptune.**

## Example Chart of Temporary Unemployment

David Elliot's job history demonstrates his Capricorn MC for methodical discipline in organizational fields interspersed with periods of restriction or slow progress. The MC ruler, Saturn, is strongly aspected in a containment between Pluto and Mars and grand trine the elevated Moon and the ASC to imply that he would achieve a fortunate and comfortable career position.

Elliot's birth was difficult and his infancy sickly; in childhood there were abusive periods in Juvenile Hall and foster homes when his single mother was unable to take care of him. When he was 18 his mother remarried and for the first time, it seemed that there was actually a home to represent stability. Saturn turned retrograde that year.

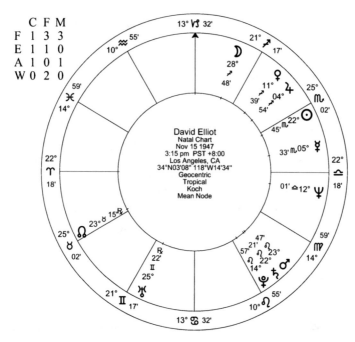

**David Elliot**

**Declinations:** ♆ *3S23;* A *8N41;* ☿ *11S17;* ♄ *14N59;* ♂ *15N25;* ☉ *18S28;* ☊ *18N38;* ♃ *20S32;* ♀ *22S45;* M *22S46;* ♀ *23N9;* ♅ *23N30;* ☽ *26S32*

Considering the 12-step delineation, we find:

1. **Planets east/west, above/below.** Nine planets are west. Elliot has a great drive to interact with others. He knows enough about the ins and outs of the music business to write a book and can pick up a phone to call unlisted numbers of some of the top superstars. The balance is five above/five below, but note that the personal planets are above and the higher octave planets below. This portrays Elliot's ability to interact on personal levels while keeping his most profound, intense feelings and realities private.

2. **Qualities and Elements.** There are seven fire and five fixed signs, giving a signature of Leo. The three planets posited in Leo are also dominant by quantity of aspects, symbolizing power (Pluto) control (Saturn) and drive (Mars); the dispositor is the Sun in Scorpio.

The chart exhibits a strong, dynamic character with deep loyalties and integrity. Elliot's enthusiasms endure, he is a generous friend and a passionately proud and caring parent.

3. **Phenomena.** Uranus is retrograde, signifying the early changes in Elliot's life, sudden changes that represent the instability that can be so shattering to a child; actually, he felt that he never had a childhood. His early education was not from books as much as from the streets to give him a different viewpoint from traditional conventions. Pluto is on the station-retrograde to emphasize his ability to reach within deep reservoirs and transmute the pain of difficult beginnings into a grasp of some of the imponderable meanings of life. He had nothing on which to base an evaluation of belonging to any peer group; his childhood experiences of powerlessness were those which should not happen to any youngster.

As a teenager in the 1960s he embraced the patterns of his generation of peace, love and rock 'n roll, finding acceptance with the flower children, but it was not until Elliot reached his '40s that he realized his center. He said, "With all I've done, or all that I might do in this life, I know now that there will never be anything more important than my kids."

The Moon is elevated to within 15 degrees of the MC, illustrating his reputation of being a parent (Moon) as well as a homespun philosopher who likes to visit and talk with people and who has a personal phone book the size of Toledo.

4. **Character.** Sun in Scorpio (fixed water, the scorpion, co-ruled by Pluto and Mars). Elliot has a natural sense of reserve; he wants to know all about everyone else but keeps his own counsel. He has strong likes and dislikes and intense feelings. A good part of his significance is found in his marriage to Ruth (Sun in the seventh house). He is proud of her role as an all-encompassing mother to their family as well as her art career: Ruth is one of the team of cartoonists awarded an Emmy for *The Simpsons,* a TV series. The dispositors of the Sun are both in Leo in the fifth house; their seven children compose the core and substance of value in Elliot's life.

The Moon is in Sagittarius (mutable fire, the archer, ruled by Jupiter). Elliot can talk about a range of subjects; his interests are broad and varied. Sagittarius adds lightness and humor to leaven the prior indications of intensity, and the dispositor, Jupiter, also in Sagittarius, assists his philosophical ability to let go of things when it's time instead of holding on. As the Moon shows our level of empathy for others, and in Elliot's chart is posited in Sagittarius along with a quantity of west-side planets and Jupiter in the eighth house, he exhibits a generosity of spirit; he habitually has little gifts, calls and thoughtful messages for others.

The ASC is Aries (cardinal fire, the ram, ruled by Mars). Elliot's personal manner is direct and without pretense. He initiates calls, conversation, social invitations and work projects. (This is modified to some extent by the fixed signs, including the dispositor of the ASC, Mars in Leo).

5. **Employment.** The Sun is square Saturn-Mars by one degree, with Saturn ruling the MC. The Sun has no interaction with the fourth house. Mercury, ruling the sixth house, is not strongly aspected but its dispositors go back to the same focus, Pluto-Saturn-Mars. These three planets are repeated again and again as a focal point in the chart.

6. **Self-employment.** There are cardinal angles, the three planets in Leo are dominant; however, they are not close to angles. The Leo-Scorpio signature implies that Elliot may well carry authority in a strong role of command or control but the position is not inclined toward his own business.

7. **Planets in the sixth house.** Neptune is 10 degrees away from the seventh cusp. The close square that it makes to the MC suggests obstacles in work that are elusive or jobs that dissolve or disappear as well as work that can be dramatic or extraordinary. Could this suggest an inability or disinclination to work? Not with the strong Saturn.

8. **Financial attitude.** The Moon and Venus are both in Sagittarius to disclose a philosophical attitude toward money, knowing that "something will always come through."

9. **Vocational indicators.** Taurus is on the second house cusp and the ruler, Venus, is posited in the eighth house, semisextile the MC, sextile Neptune in the sixth house. The livelihood roles are indicated as those of working with other people's money or possessions (eighth

house), handling business administration (Capricorn MC), being involved in the entertainment media (Venus, a strong fifth house) and in advertising or public representation (Sagittarius, ninth house); all in gradual and uneven development (semisextile).

10. **Wealth.** The second house ruler has a minor aspect to the MC, a semisextile. The eighth house rulers, Mars and Pluto contain Saturn, the ruler of the tenth house, and are posited in the fifth house. Elliot's personal income is indicated to not be as strong as the monies that are represented by his employers (MC ruler), and later, by his children.

11. **Success.** The MC in Capricorn shows initiative in a practical career in which Elliot works his way up by effort and application. Material realities take first priority and hard work gains respect. The ruler, Saturn, is in Leo in the fifth house to depict a singular role of authority; it also implies that his reputation and career is influenced by his parenting role and children, as well as the possibility that he could gain a reputation through the acclaim gained by one (or more) of the children.

12. **The Life Path.** The MC and tenth cusp are both Capricorn, 8 degrees, 45 minutes apart. By an age arc of eight years, nine months the MC crossed the tenth cusp; all that Elliot recalls is throat surgery that year. Adding 30 years of age arc to symbolize 30 degrees of the full successive sign, in August, 1986, at age 38, the MC crossed the eleventh EQHS cusp; David moved his family to the metropolis to pursue greater ambitions.

To review Elliot's career history, we find that, as a young man, he had a variety of jobs in the periphery of the music industry. On August 8, 1973 he started work for Mike Love of the *Beach Boys* as personal manager and property development manager of Love's estate, living on the property, as well as the acting liaison for *Brother Records*. PR Venus, ruler of the second house, was ten minutes past partile conjunction of the MC. PR Jupiter was conjunct Venus for a decade and he was in the milieu of money and fame, meeting top music people as an everyday matter of course.

When Elliot left Love's employ after five years, he explored his Scorpio skills by working as a private investigator. Within a few years this dovetailed into bill collections. In 1987 he took the role of promoter of a new type of music equipment, working in partnership with the inventor, exemplifying Neptune in the sixth house as well as the P.R. skills of Sagittarius. On May 22, 1989 he began work with a major financial institution in the collections department. The PR MC was opposite Saturn and Mars and PR ASC was separating from a trine to Neptune.

This resume demonstrates a smooth transition, which was not always the case. There were several times when Elliot's career moves seemed to hit nebulous obstacles. He left Mike Love expecting to move into a Public Rep position in the music industry. The PR MC was trine Neptune, which sounds wonderful, right? Wrong. The two points are in a natal square. Elliot floundered through several jobs which seemed to dissolve from one day to the next before he began working as a private eye, and then in 1987 as a promoter.

In early 1989 the financial backing dried up for the prototype of the inventor's product that Elliot was representing. PR ASC was trine Neptune—over a wide natal opposition. Nothing seemed clear cut or tangible. Jobs were tight and his Capricorn MC kept him keenly aware that he had a family to support.

There are three lessons to point out in Elliot's chart. One, the MC shows the optimum conduct that is requisite to gain and hold a successful mundane position. Two, the second house ruler symbolizes the means of livelihood (that is supplemented but not replaced by other considerations), and three, always check out Neptune promises with a healthy dose of Saturn caution. Our appraisal easily tends to over-or-under estimation with Neptune.

**The handicapped or disabled** often have very "fortunate" patterns such as grand trines, or Venus, Jupiter or Neptune well aspected in the twelfth house or in water houses. For example. Dusty has spinal tumors and lives on disability; he has a grand trine involving MC, ASC and Venus, the ruler of his twelfth house. Pluto conjunct natal Sun holds a lifetime semisquare to Venus.

## Example Chart of Disability Welfare

Karen Clark was brain damaged at birth due to lack of oxygen; her twelfth house ruler, the Sun, is posited in the eighth house in a yod to

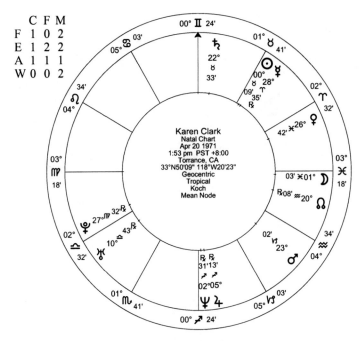

**Karen Clark**

*Declinations: ♀ 2S39; ♅ 3S35; ☽ 10S16; A 10N17; ⊙ 11N32; ☿ 12N20; ☊ 14S28; ♀ 16N 3; ♄ 16N33; ♆ 18S59; ♃ 20S10; M 20N15; ♂ 22S30*

Pluto and Neptune; Mars-Saturn-Pluto are in a grand trine. In August, 1987, when she was 16, her mother, Geneva, put her in a group home. The PR MC was semisextile PR Sun and semisquare natal Sun. When Geneva brought her home in May, 1992, PR Jupiter conjunct Neptune, both retrograde in the fourth house, were joined by the Moon. Karen died quietly and unexpectedly of a seizure on the morning of September 29, 1993, Landers, California.

## Example Chart of Disability Welfare

Kristy Clark, who is autistic, has a twelfth house ruled by retrograde Mercury in the tenth house which began to receive a one-degree opposition from progressed Uranus when she was 13; this aspect will last her lifetime. Sun-Moon-Neptune are in a close grand trine, with Neptune opposite Saturn (one-degree from 1991 to

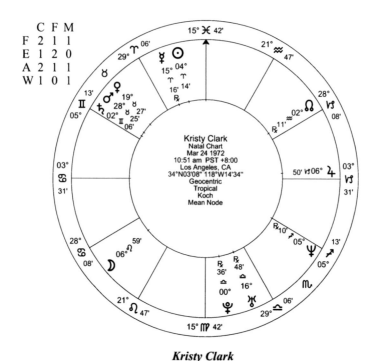

**Kristy Clark**

**Declinations:** ⊙ *1N41; M 5S38; ♅ 5S58; ☿ 9N12; ♀ 15N6; ☽ 18N14;*
*♄ 18N55; ☊ 19S22; ♆ 19S31; ♀ 19N54; ♂ 20N46; ♃ 22S57; A 23N24*

2023). (By EQHS this opposition is between the sixth to twelfth
houses rather than the fifth to eleventh houses). Saturn also rules
the eighth house and is in a trine to Pluto in the fourth house, the astrological indicators that are requisite for public welfare assistance. Note the close Neptune aspects for both girls; for Karen the
Moon in Pisces is opposite the ASC in a square to Neptune, cloistered, so to speak. In October 1989, her mother put Kristy into the
group home. PR MC and PR Mercury were conjunct natal Sun,
with all three trine Neptune. In May 1992, Geneva brought both
girls home. Kristy had a new Moon in Aries and PR Mercury was
on the station-direct.

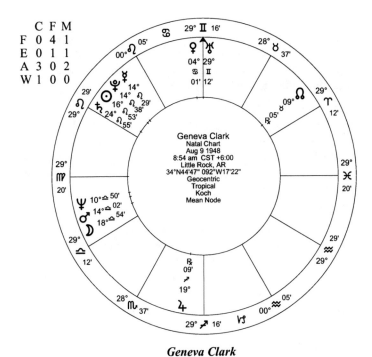

| | C | F | M |
|---|---|---|---|
| F | 0 | 4 | 1 |
| E | 0 | 1 | 1 |
| A | 3 | 0 | 2 |
| W | 1 | 0 | 0 |

*Geneva Clark*

*Declinations: A 0N16; ♆ 2S53; ♂ 5S30; ☽ 5S49; ♄ 14N22; ☊ 14N23;*
*⊙ 15N47; ☿ 18N6; ♀ 18N37; ♃ 22S43; ♀ 23N20; M 23N27; ♅ 23N37*

## Example Chart of Welfare

Does Geneva Clark's chart suggest contentment to live on welfare with her daughters' disability support? In review of the 12-step program of delineation we find nine planets east with strongly tenanted eleventh and first houses, showing self-directed interests in personal development. With dominant fire-air, Clark is eager to pursue ideas and actions which stimulate her interest and involvement.

Clark's first vocational goal was to be a child psychologist, reflecting the MC ruler. Mercury, conjunct Pluto (psychology) in the eleventh house (counseling). With Jupiter retrograde in the third house, her early academic desires ,were not considered appropriate or encouraged by her family. She began the study of astrology at nineteen, but all educational aspirations took a back seat when she had two handicapped daughters. (She also had a son in 1977, Kevin, who is mentally gifted). Her studies began to expand over the years to philosophically grasp the meanings of her life's experiences, as well as a deepening other interest in astrology.

Uranus and Venus contain the MC to describe unexpected changes when the page closes on one chapter to begin another, as well as her nurturing domestic role. Venus in the tenth house in Cancer is appropriate for dark's light, homey manner and her sweet "earth mother" nurturing to her family but she also has an intensely deep and responsible Mercury-Pluto-Sun-Saturn stellium in Leo.

Clark's first job was with computers, doing data processing (Uranus). During the children's early years, they were a full time job (Uranus ruling the fifth house and crossing the MC). Saturn rules the fifth house with either Koch (Aquarius fifth cusp) or EQHS (Capricorn fifth cusp); it made minor aspects when the girls were born and moved into the twelfth house when they were babies. During the years the girls were institutionalized, PR Saturn was semisextile the ASC, sextile the MC. Throughout Clark's adult life, until 1992, the PR Sun moved through the twelfth house.

The ruler of Clark's second house (Venus) is posited in the tenth house, suggesting that she ease into self-employment. In 1985, she began a business at home, selling fresh-baked goods to local restaurants. By 1989, Mars was in the second house and she began a home production of rubber stamps. Mercury rules the MC and is placed in the eleventh house; she also worked for a year as an instructional aide with handicapped children. Her chart is a remarkable example of the flexibility of the tenth and second houses in choosing a career as Clark illustrated the symbology of Uranus, Venus, Cancer, Gemini, Mercury in the eleventh house and PR Mars in the second house, all while working under the handicap of caring for retarded children!

The Sun moved into Clark's first house in 1992, squaring the MC and Uranus. She was distressed by the care her girls were getting and assumed conservatorship; she brought them home in May 1992. Their disability payments cost the government less in welfare to her as their mother than it cost to keep them in an institution. When Karen died,

PR Venus was conjunct Pluto within one minute with both semisquare PR Uranus; PR Saturn was sextile PR Uranus within one minute.

Venus and Neptune are in angular positions, which does not usually portray a strong career drive, but these indicators have contradictions. Clark also has Uranus angular and Neptune is conjunct Mars and Moon. By 1994, the disability money was barely enough for subsistence, living with two dependent children, one a handicapped young adult. What, then, is the optimum vocational indicator? Our key points are Uranus (the sixth house ruler) in the tenth house along with the second house ruler; appropriate positions for self-employment. Venus has moved into the strong eleventh house.

As Venus moves through progressed aspects it can indicate free-lance work in counseling, social work or civic affairs through computers, perhaps along a computer-net line of a business that is geared to family assistance (Cancer), to community welfare or self-help programs (eleventh house), research of family benefits (Pluto-Sun, with Sun ruling the twelfth), or even central coordination (Saturn) of missing children (Cancer, Pluto, twelfth house).

**Retirement** is referred to as "the golden years." This is the ideal of the twelfth and fourth houses, completing our time span in a familiar, comfortable, safe environment. However, Neptune, as the natural ruler of the twelfth house, may very well stimulate an ideal and a reality that differ as widely as the grand canyon. The rewards of retirement depend on several factors. Just as our extent of net worth (eighth house) depends on how well our money is managed (second house), the benefits of our retirement (twelfth house) depend on how well our work (sixth house) has been managed.

The quality of life, whether in our own home (fourth house) or in a retirement village or convalescent home (twelfth house) depends to a great extent on how healthy our daily habits of diet, rest and exercise have been (sixth house). *(If I'd known I was going to live this long I would have taken better care of myself.)* The natural pattern of the water houses is a grand trine, testifying to the model of retirement (twelfth house), the end of life (fourth house) and death (eighth house) as a process that is meant to flow in natural and comfortable interaction. During the working years, it is physically and emotionally healthy to cultivate friendships, hobbies and interests, not only for balance, rest and recreation, but to have a full, integrated life that is not based on one area alone, work or business or family.

## Example Charts of Retirement

Mary Alice and Web Parker operated their pharmacy business together for many years. Web is a calm, warm Leo who is a passionate golfer as well as an active member of the Lion's Club. Mary Alice is a bright, curious Gemini who loves lectures and classes and seriously writes poetry. They are both involved in their family affairs and both participate in a social group which meets for a variety of activities.

In their mid to late 60s, they sold both the business and their home, moving into a condominium and a new life style. Their lives are full and active and they are young enough to enjoy their retirement. When they moved, Mary Alice had her twelfth house ruler, Mercury, trine the 4th house ruler, Saturn, and she was delighted to have more time to organize her many interests. With natal Mercury (twelfth house ruler) semisquare Neptune (sixth house ruler), she took care of some health worries with a successful surgery. Mercury is one-degree semisextile Venus (eighth house ruler), portraying the accruement of retirement benefits, plus benevolent Jupiter has progressed into the 8th house from where it will sextile Mercury for the rest of her life.

Web had PR Mercury conjunct Saturn when they sold; it took six months to turn over the business to the new owners as he stayed on in an advisory capacity. His four Leo planets are natally in the eighth house, and two of them trine his twelfth house Moon within a few degrees. At the year of his retirement, PR MC in the twelfth house made a trine to Neptune *(how appropriate!)*

With Mary Alice and Web as an example, we may evaluate our retirement according to the twelfth and fourth houses, particularly in their relationship to the eighth house. *If the indications are not natally suitable, change them.* For example, if there is no aspect between the eighth and twelfth houses, calculate the time in the future when the

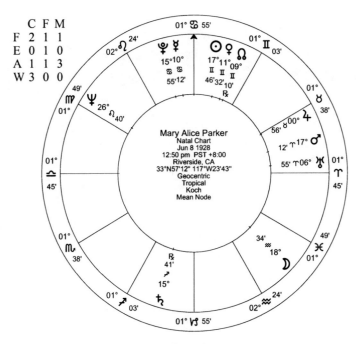

**Mary Alice Parker**

*Declinations: A 0S43; ♅ 2N6; ♂ 5N19; ♃ 10N45; ♆ 13N8; ☽ 19S57; ♄*
*21S1; ♀ 21N40; ♀ 21N51; ♃1 21N53; ☉ 22N53, M 23N26; ☿ 23N40*

appropriate planets move into a relationship and act upon it for the desired results, such as starting a retirement account or making sure that medical and disability insurance is covered. When the eighth and fourth houses are active, if at all possible, buy a home, even at the cost of living for a dozen years on a limited budget. Those of us who do not own property and retire on a fixed, minimal Social Security income often find our golden years to be severely tarnished. Prudently, we may look ahead to the end of life (fourth house) to evaluate our options when we are no longer able bodied, and discuss with our mate or family what course we would like them to take on our behalf if we are not able to speak for ourselves.

We have a lifetime in which to become the person we want to be, in the position that we want to have for our later years. Money is an

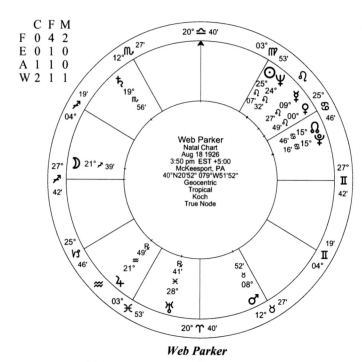

**Web Parker**

*Declinations:* ♅ 1S14; M 8S5; ♂ 11N40; ☉ 13N9; ♆ 13N44; ♃ 15S17; ☿ 15N34; ♄ 15S43; ♀ 20N15; ☽ 21S5; ♀ 21N6; ☊ 22N31; A 23S26

important part of living in a physical world, but not to the extent that the price is too high. Our balance is best served when we work also for that which makes our hearts happy, so that our retirement gives us peace within ourselves as well as continued activities of interest.

# Chapter 8

# Planets in the Sixth House

*It's hard to soar with eagles when you work with a bunch of turkeys.*—Anon

THOUGH we soar with eagles in the tenth house, in the 6th house we work with a bunch of turkeys. This is essentially a subordinate area of the chart, associated with service occupations, blue-collar work, civil servants, domestic help and the healing and helping professions. With planets posited in the sixth house, we not only do not seek the limelight but actively withdraw from fame and glory. The work performance and getting the job done is the ethic, not the acclaim or awards; these come from other areas of the chart. The sixth house indicates the workaday capacities of problem solving and dealing with daily mundane realities.

In those minimum cases when a planet in the sixth house is the vocational indicator, it tends to be an "everyday" occupation rather than a leader in the field. For example, with Mercury in the sixth house we may write for a living but this position seldom occurs in the charts of famed novelists. Neptune in the sixth house may portray a steady working actor but seldom denotes that we are acclaimed for our great dramatic talent. As with all astrological delineation, consider all the factors before making a judgment call. Consider the relative strength of the sixth house planets and the position of the planet ruling the cusp as well as all aspects to key vocational points such as the second house, the tenth house and the MC.

Traditionally, military service is associated with the sixth house. To this it may be added that the twelfth house is also involved; in the lower ranks of the military, a young man or woman is told what to eat, where to sleep, where to go, what work to do and when; military service is, in effect, indentured bondage. In example charts, aspects to Neptune synchronize with the time of joining the military. The dialogues of Neptune also add to the camaraderie of blending into the unit. (Pluto demands the distinction of being *singular* within the whole).

Other factors that come into play for military service include Mars and Saturn aspects which are appropriate for the good physical condition that comes with military training. Venus-Mars interactions are not uncommon, as well as Mars-Jupiter, for rowdy good fun, or perhaps for an unaccustomed liberty to seek sexual adventures and freedom not present in the home environment.

For those who stay in the military as a career, Mars is either in aspect to Saturn or they both make strong statements to indicate an ability to fit into a disciplined life style as well as respond to a stringent performance demand. Saturn-Pluto is also frequently evident. Mars-Uranus is possible for certain unusual assignments of peril, such as found in the Rangers or Green Berets, but only if there is a strong Saturn in the chart at the same time to contain and direct that explosive energy. In military charts, Venus-Jupiter aspects represent a handsome uniform with a chest full of ribbons and medals, and imply honors and formalities such as those which accompany advancements in position. The natural fire houses are also prominent, especially the ninth house, not only for changes of location but for the pomp and circumstance of military rituals.

As we examine planets posited in the sixth house, we may also consider the planet that rules the sign on the cusp of the sixth house. However, when the planet that rules the sixth house cusp is placed in another sign, its influence is modified and colored by that sign and house and therefore does not have the clarity of definition that is suggested by the planet posited. Say that we have Leo on the sixth cusp, for example, and the Sun is in Taurus in the third house. We may read the delineation of "Sun in the sixth house" but the description will be modified by the actual position of the Sun (in the third house) and by the sign in which it is placed (Taurus).

**Sun in the sixth house.** Though seldom business owners with this position, we are highly capable of carrying authority in problem-solving capacities that call for expertise and craftsmanship. We are not basically team players but do better in employment where a certain amount of autonomy is maintained, where we are given an assignment and allowed to do it in our own time and our own way. Free-lance employment is favored as well, where we can set our own schedule. We frequently have an attitude of criticism or dissatisfaction with the higher echelon at work as we can see what's needed and feel that if we were the head of the company we could operate it better than the present management. These ideas are usually sound, but the implementation is not. We are more capable in handling a segment of middle management than in coordinating an overview of the entire operation.

With the Sun in the sixth house, we tend to stay in a position where we have to report to a higher authority or to someone in greater command. When attracted to service occupations, we often improve social standards or working conditions in our area of expertise. If our Sun is square the MC, we may fight city hall to improve the world, or at least our corner of it. We have an active concern for moral and ethical issues in our field.

To gain a sense of purpose in life, we must have long-range goals, life-goals, something *worthwhile.* Our own health and well-being may be affected if we are not comfortable in our daily work patterns.

With fixed Sun signs in the sixth house, we exhibit endurance in our career goals (particularly when the fixed sign is also on the DESC); with a mutable Sun sign we must have flexibility in our daily work or we get bored (more so when the seventh cusp is also mutable), and with a cardinal Sun sign in the sixth house (reinforced by a cardinal seventh house cusp), we must be free to initiate work projects either on the job or in our personal work areas of home or hobby.

**Moon in the sixth house.** We are not only good with teamwork, it seems to be requisite to our daily sense of well-being, either on the job or in our private family or support group. We have an instinctive feel for the public pulse and work well in nurturing fields, in the home environment or with items of domestic trade, that is, supplies to fill the needs of the home, family, or general public. Our work and working environment involves many small units, items, supplies; we may be gadget junkies who have to resist the urge to over-inventory by stocking up on everything in the stationary store, the hardware store or the five-and-dime variety store.

We need that support group to do our best productive work. As we easily feel emotional climates, we are subject to shyness, timidity or insecurity, and if not given approval and comfort by our family or team we become discouraged and feel unwanted. Solitude is optimum at times but not consistently or we tend to become apathetic, closing off into a shell or at the most extreme, turn to the artificial stimulants of food or substance abuse. With a sixth house Moon, we are more capable and better adjusted when nourished by bonding environments.

Our work fluctuates in time, tune, mood and tempo. Work patterns are never entirely even but wax and wane, with surges of activity followed by fallow periods. We are not comfortable with work situations that have a consistent routine but perform best when we can meet the public and deal with others for a given time followed by an introspective span of withdrawal. Our popularity, in the same way, is cyclic. During the waxing period we are drawn to people en masse; during the waning period we need to be alone to renew from within.

Talents or gifts are often present in our early youth but we have no idea what to do with them and must learn to integrate life experience before we find our most secure and comfortable work areas. For some of us, youthful marriages or family problems, or even a physical or health handicap, may take all of our attention to resolve before we establish ourselves in fruitful work patterns.

**Mercury in the sixth house.** The work we seek involves the use of the mind and voice, such as teaching, writing, acting, singing and speaking. Service fields, clerical and academic fields, technical training, or the activity of transportation or motion is indicated, such as the use of vehicles or instruments, sports or labor which requires mobility or dexterity. The work environment must be flexible. Mercury in this position does not lead to career changing and frequent job moves as much as it does to day-to-day variety in the work itself. We may also, at one time or more in the life, hold two or more jobs simultaneously, or have dual job roles.

This is not notable as a stressful position; we are highly capable of rational problem-solving in methods and procedures. There seems to always be a necessity of decisions, choices and alternatives to consider. *(Should I move or stay, go to this school or that, take this role or the other, object or adapt?)* We usually speak up on issues, and in an emotional climate may represent the voice of reason.

Either Mercury or the Moon in the sixth house often indicates that we have a good mind (when these planets aspect the angles) but it may not be fully utilized. With Mercury in the sixth house, the mental output tends to be modest. The written work is generally polemic or technical or falls into a routine variety. Public figures whose career is symbolized by Mercury in the sixth, such as writers or sports figures, are moderately known and are seldom noted for having remarkable lives. In the cases where we do achieve fame, it can be traced to factors other than the 6th house position.

**Venus in the sixth house.** We *must* feel appreciated for work to be pleasurable. Validation by approbation makes it all worthwhile, as work itself, in the sense of long hours and hard labor, or even the weekly pay check regardless of how hefty, is not the prime goal. The end purpose of work is to gain beauty, comfort, ease, pleasure and approval. Harmony and pleasant surroundings in the work place, as well as appreciation for the service that we give, are essential for our sense of well-being and satisfaction. If there is strife among coworkers we bend over backwards to make peace, or else close off in polite silence and mute misery.

We want to love and be loved as all people do, but we may fall short of expressing our emotions or empathy for others. Sometimes love itself is the problem; a mate or family member causes heartache that interferes with our serenity in daily work. At times we "love not wisely but too well." It seems difficult to get our love life into a position of balance; it is either lacking in fulfillment or suddenly becomes a major distraction. It is possible with this placement of Venus that without love, work has no meaning. Perhaps we have to reconcile ourselves to the extent or limitation of our need for emotional satisfactions before we can give our work the priority that it calls for. In some examples, personal love is sublimated to the "greater love" of God, mankind, peace, beauty or art.

In other cases there are fine marriages, where a supportive mate shares our concerns; when this is the case we can safely and freely make a song of our work day. Social exchange and friendships in the work place are highly enjoyable, and in the charts of many of us, the work output itself gives pleasure, comfort or entertainment to others.

**Mars in the sixth house.** The need here is for our work to be vigorous, active, competitive and often physical. We are drawn to business aggression and can attract hostility from coworkers or even unwelcome sexual attention in the workplace. The job itself may involve tools, mechanistic equipment, instruments, alcohol or places where alcohol is produced or served.

We are well equipped to tackle tough challenges or even danger in the work environment, as with the military, sports, or critical political positions. We must take care, however, to avoid on-the-job accidents or undue stress. The actors with this placement are cast in rowdy, macho, tough hero (or antihero) roles, the athletes run headlong into injuries and the performers have stringent tours in which they are involved with heavy equipment and rough conditions.

We spend long hours wrestling and combating the physical world and sometimes take up crusades fueled by our anger at being used unfairly or by "fate." It often seems difficult for us to specify precisely what personal affront it is that makes us angry but some general situation arouses us to resistance and objection. The action taken in resolution may be constructive or destructive according to our nature and how we use the aspects to our Mars. Many times we show no visible signs of temper but display petty or critical complaints about the job or coworkers, taking the role of the company grouch. Covert anger tends to turn inward, perhaps in substance abuse, social rebellion or medical complaints.

**Jupiter in the sixth house.** For the most part, Jupiter in the sixth demonstrates remarkable examples of publicity or notoriety in bright, brief flashes. We are award winners in the public view for a few seasons, such as an actor who is a hot property or a sports champion who is in the limelight for a decade, more or less, before fading into routine life. We stand out with our receipt of awards or with being prestigious in our organization or community, but this is seldom a position for consistent public notice; we are more apt to be the televised "Queen For A Day." For some of us, the outstanding popularity or publicity keeps growing when other indicators repeat the theme of major success, or if Jupiter is conjunct the DESC within some ten to fifteen degrees.

Many times our work involves education, publishing, advertising, the law, or long distance travel. Few of us are in sales, which is surprising as Jupiter is associated with sales. Our own education is important to those of us who aim for the professional fields, not only for the original academic degree but for continued courses to update our expertise. As employees, we tend to work for big financial institutions or in expensive work environments, a plush office or headquarters where the company has the best of quality equipment.

If not educated, we may dream of honors and riches and of an extravagant life of fame and glory that is not as easy to come by as we might wish. Exhibitions of self indulgence or lack of modesty in our life style can bring problems. Perhaps we gain attention so easily or are given so many accolades that we find it difficult to remain unassuming. To counteract the extremes of Jupiter, those of us who have earth signs to keep our feet modestly on the ground fare better than those who are by nature more flamboyant. Sometimes our moral or ethical honesty is questioned; usually we are exonerated and maintain a highly respected position in the community. If we do get into a law suit, it becomes an endless hassle of redundant red tape before it is resolved.

**Saturn in the sixth house.** The work ethic is so important to us that we take our work home with us, or keep on the job long after office hours; we easily become the chronic workaholics. Too often we are the unsung heroes who hold the entire organization together without getting adequate credit and never reaching the pinnacle of our own ambitions. Perfectionists on the work assignment, we perform with perseverance and attention to detail. Often our post is obscure and our tasks repetitively routine. Highly respected by our coworkers, we are acknowledged by our superiors with a pat on the back for being conscientious at the same time that we are being imposed upon with the extra load to carry, while someone else with more flair than substance gets the longed-for promotion.

If those of us with Saturn in the sixth house do not work, or attempt to live a leisurely life style, we court the possibility of mental or medical breakdowns that limit our capacities to a frugal routine. Conversely, we must learn to set aside some time for ourselves so as not to become overburdened. Our balance is better served when we learn to play, to have hobbies, to have quiet times to enjoy simple pleasures. We must be careful to not take on the heavy responsibility of another person's problems, debts or worries. This is particularly noticeable when Saturn is close to the angle or moves into the seventh house. A work partnership can be a wonderful way to share an ambition in common as long as both parties share the yoke equally, but we who have Saturn in the sixth house are often all too ready to carry more than our share.

**Uranus in the sixth house.** The need to work independently of routine will attract us to free-lance employment or to establish our own business or vocation. In standard fields we manage to stand out as "different." In a nine-to-five job we do best when keeping our own time and space as an atypical employee. When we are unable to escape a strictly conventional work environment, we develop nervous complaints and may exhibit erratic behavior or even experience nervous breakdowns. A constructive outlet is demonstrated when we take our eccentricities into areas of private pursuit or have hobbies for our spare time that satisfy unconventional interests. It is quite possible in some cases for our avocational pursuit to develop into full-time work.

We perform well with sophisticated equipment or unusual props as well as in work environments or conditions that are subject to sudden changes at a moment's notice. We don't simply have problems at work, we have *crises* and abrupt changes of direction that make wonderful anecdotes. Split-second problem-solving may be necessary on the job to solve radical or unexpected dilemmas. At optimum, we contribute innovations to our field that show ingenuity and originality.

**Neptune in the sixth house.** Our work gives us something perfectly suited to our needs, wants and capabilities, but that image of perfection may be an illusion. There is some area of anxiety or dissatisfaction with the job condition, the coworkers or the boss that may be exaggerated to an unrealistic degree. Or perhaps it was not an exaggeration after all; sometimes the job simply dissolves; one day it's not there any more and the dream turns to ashes. It is not uncommon for us to have periods when it is difficult to find employment in our chosen field.

We may work for the vision of some ideal, the hope of some grand philanthropy, of service and caring for others, or the dream may be that of personal creative glory, fame and fortune. We can draw on our psychic instinct or insight into human character. When Neptune is close to the DESC, that Utopian vision may not be too realistic, or our psychic hunches may be colored by personal prejudice that leaves us bewildered and confused. There is often some drama in the work, inefficiency or a touch of mystery or intrigue. We certainly know the secrets of others and could crack open a Pandora's box of scandal if we chose. If we are not strictly honest ourselves, we can be pulled into deception and muddle with a long train of disorder. Though job conflicts tend to be elusive and hard to grasp on a solid footing, problem solving is best handled with by-the-book integrity.

At optimum, we give a service to the world that is greater than ourselves of truth and beauty that stems from our oneness with the universe.

**Pluto in the sixth house.** Our work involves a series of single units, each complete in itself, but which together make up a polished product or project. We often work under the auspices of coercion in the sense that certain cultural rules, standards and policies must be met, such as those of the Board of Health, the Board of Examiners, the Party Policy, Editor's Guidelines, Company Protocol. We fit comfortably enough in our group but our work is not usually on a peer level, it is more apt to be singular in that we are the only one who does our specific task.

We manage to keep a subordinate role in the group and may even actively avoid the politics of manipulating for position. At some junction we rebel against the need to conform to life's necessity and withdraw into a cocoon to get away from the demands of the workplace.

Psychological or medical problems can consume our interest for a period of metamorphosis after which we return to our work on a deeper level of performance. The work itself is regenerative. At optimum, we take our work to a greater depth of commitment that sets standards for our field.

In the charts of those of us who are actively pursuing our success factors (as discussed in Chapter 18), sixth house planets gain more credit with use. The effort that has been put into learning our craft under stringent conditions gives us a cutting edge in dealing with our colleagues, peers and competitors. We are the people who "pull ourselves up by our bootstraps," who work to improve our lot and who transform subordinate efforts into superior abilities.

# Section 3

Money: How to Find it with Astrology

# Chapter 9

# The Medium of Exchange

*Money may not buy happiness but it can sure rent some great substitutes.*—Anon

FOR THOUSANDS of years throughout the different cultures of the world, the barter system worked well and even today there are places where cattle can be traded for a wife. The problem with barter, however, is in trying to fix a fair trade for both parties, so rather than trading my goat for your plow, we both agreed to a *medium of exchange.* As it quickly became too cumbersome and even dangerous to carry about our salt, shells, jewelry or whatever it was we decided was valuable in our culture, we devised a currency of coins, then paper to serve as that medium. Thus money became the middleman.

It is believed that the Chinese were trading with gold cubes as early as 2000 B.C. and with paper money as early as A.D. 1300. By the middle ages the European cultures were basing their currency on a given standard, that of gold which gradually was supplemented with paper money, standing as a symbol for the heavy and precious metal that was stored in lending houses.

Around the time that Pluto was last in Scorpio (1737-1748) a series of mechanical inventions took the hand-production of goods out of the cottages and villages as the Industrial Revolution evolved. Iron works, textile weaving, the steam engine, railways and engineering created a new world. In 1776, when Pluto was in practical Capricorn trine Neptune in sensible Virgo and Uranus was in curious Gemini, the Scottish philosophy professor Adam Smith proposed his revolutionary thesis: that the source of a nation's wealth was not gold and silver but in the ability of an educated citizenry to produce goods and services.

In the United States the first paper money issued by the Government was printed in 1861 to finance the Civil War. Prior to that, 8,000 separate banks were printing 8,000 different kinds of money. We did not finally leave the gold standard until the height of the Great Depression in the 1930s. When Franklin Delano Roosevelt (1882-1945) became President in 1932, he followed the economic policies of John Maynard Keynes (1883-1946), whose most important work was published in 1936, *The General Theory of Employment, Interest and Money.* Keynes' theories still dominate economic policy in most of the free world, favoring production above the metal standard.

In the 1920s and 1930s, especially during World War II, another remarkable factor entered the picture; women left the home in emerging independence to join the work force. Pluto was in Cancer (home and family) square Uranus in Aries (pioneering self-initiative), a square that was operative from 1928 for nearly a decade instigating a liberation that boomed along with production and consumption in the 1940s.

Today the Federal Reserve System acts as a broker between the government and our local banks. Through the FRS the government manipulates a money supply that is supposed to insure non-inflationary prices, full employment and continued growth of the production of goods and services. It's no secret to any of us that this does not always work, whichever political party is in office.

In the early 1930s a Russian economist named Nikolai Kondratieff stated that there are vast tides in human affairs, greater and lesser cycles that measure the pulse of the universe. Founding his wave theory, Kondratieff described a 60-year period in the fiscal patterns of the industrial nations.

A graph of the United States gross national product outlines an upswing of 25 years, 1789-1814, and a decline of 35 years, 1814-1849. The second wave rose for 24 years, 1849-1873, with a decline of 23 years, 1873-1896, a wave-total of 47 years. The upward movement of the third wave lasted 24 years, from 1896-1920, then there was a two-year drop before the not uncommon rally of 1922-29, at which time the stock market dropped and the economy plummeted. The government, under F.D. Roosevelt, began printing money not backed by the treasury, beginning a pattern of deficit spending, and with this placebo the downward spiral was banked in a short 13 years in its descent, until 1940, a down cycle of 20 years. The wave-cycle totaled 44 years.

The next wave rose with an incredible upswing that began in 1942; with the military budget and increased production of World War II the average family income doubled in the leading world nations. In the ensuing 30-year upswing we cultivated our Pluto-in-Leo generation as one of the wealthiest youth cultures in history, resulting in the self-absorbed "me" generation of the 1970s. The peak period faltered in the 1970s, but the customary vigorous rally occurred in the late 1980s before an abrupt drop in real estate and industry. If the down cycle is rounded off at an average, it may be expected to last until approximately 1996.

The trough, or down point, has in every case been less definitive in planetary positions and timing, however the low point focuses in 1989-1996 with Uranus and Neptune traveling together in Capricorn. During the four previous lows Neptune was in earth signs; at all the prior high points Pluto has been in earth or water. Although the world economy has been in a recession in the last decade of the nineteenth century, Pluto in Scorpio has taken the world monetary unit to unheard of extremes of wealth in many industries, and tragic extremes of poverty for other people, even to the extent of mass starvation. Pluto finally leaves Scorpio to go into Sagittarius in 1996 as Neptune and Uranus leave Capricorn for Aquarius in 1996 and 1998 respectively.

The two graphs on the next page show the U.S. GNP for the last two centuries and the stylized graph of the Kondratieff wave theory for your comparison.

The economists who discount the wave theory regard it as "little better than astrology," a short-sighted view from those who attach no meaning to cycles. Other economists have developed the theme, such

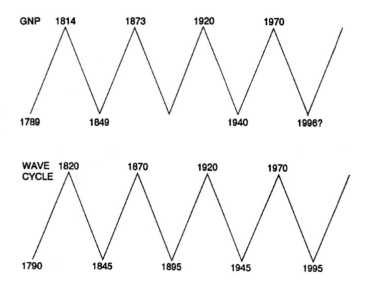

as the late, great Joseph Schumpeter. He believed in a 40-month cycle and superimposed on it an eight-year Juglar cycle, and superimposed on that a long 50-year Kondratieff cycle. The reason the 1930s Depression was so bad, according to him, was that all these cycles hit their low point simultaneously.

What is the future of money? It is very likely that we will eventually move into a monetary system devoid of currency other than pocket change to buy an ice cream cone, with an international identification as intimate as a fingerprint to handle all of our records and transactions. Our paycheck will go into the same computer that records all our purchases. As it is, cash comprises only a quarter of the money supply; the rest is in figures on ledgers that are rapidly being integrated by electronic impulses into computer memory. Paper money takes a leap of faith at any event; that piece of printed and colored paper has no intrinsic value whatsoever. It is a merely a symbol of the operating system.

This overview is no more than a sketch, as work is available from more qualified astrologers on the study of economic cycles as they correlate to astronomical flux. However, the nature and motion of the planets is the language of astrologers. In our personal lives, and in the life of our nation and our world, we look at the natural cycles, mutations and phenomena of the universe with wonder as we recognize that not only the heavens but we ourselves move in rhythm, in a patterned dance that even in chaos has it's own order. For every dark night, light returns with the new day and for every long day's journey, there is night ahead for rest.

# Chapter 10

# Financial Attitude

*There are no adults; I think an adult is just a child who owes money.*—Kenneth Branaugh

HOW DO we feel about money? To answer that question with the horoscope we begin with Venus and the Moon, then consider the Ascendant and Sun signs. Venus, as the natural ruler of the second house shows the emotional connotation of money with pleasure, comfort, ease and gifts, with good feelings of being attractive and likable. Many of us, when we get the blues, can ease that feeling by getting dressed up in finery or going out to buy something for ourselves.

Years ago, a friend was widowed after having one of the world's good marriages. This did not change his economic position; on the contrary it was costly to hire a full time housekeeper to care for his two young sons, so his behavior was astonishing when, with hollow eyes and drawn face, he went on a spending spree. He bought a new TV, new household and kitchen goods, even a new car. A psychologist friend explained that he was trying to comfort himself with goods as "things" are often associated with rewards.

Love itself is one of life's greatest gifts, as new and perennial as springtime, and the association of Venus with gratuities is shown by the lover's desire to shower gifts upon the beloved. The pleasure of the lover is in pleasing the beloved. As the initial glow subsides, the handling of finances may, in fact, become one of the major emotional battlegrounds of a relationship. Money can be used as a weapon, as a compensation for inadequacies or as a means of holding on to another as well as a promise, reward or appeasement. Half of the couples that go to Family Service Agencies for counseling report severe problems with money, yet it is actually a small proportion who are in difficulty because of inadequate income or unusual financial needs. The money they are arguing about often represents a mundane symbol of their areas of deeper emotional strife, as well as any unrealistic attitudes they may have about their own or shared resources.

Advertisers are well aware, and encourage the sale of everything from toothpaste to motorcycles by emphasizing the natural drive of Venus for attention, approval and love. About 20 percent of our television viewing time consists of ads which encourage the viewer toward instant gratification. When we need to be the big spender who picks up the check, buys excessive and costly clothes and supplies, or needs the ego-bolstering of expensive toys to impress people, we might well learn to come to terms with the emotional needs of our Venus, and Moon as well, in more intimate ways. Spending, or it's inverse coin, being miserly, seldom satisfies the emotional demands of our inner child. Many times, money problems can be dealt with satisfactorily when we recognize that the difficulties are often not questions of dollars and cents but of our attitudes and feelings. All the budgeting in the world can't compensate for ignorance of these hidden meanings of money.

The Moon is the second indicator of our financial attitude. Our urge for acquisition begins with prehensile behavior. When an infant instinctively reaches for an object to grasp it, then hands it to mother, then reaches for it again, the Moon is in a process of healthy development. If the infant does not trust the receiver to give the object back, if the world is filled with harshness and denial, if there are no toys or training objects, if there is not the security of unconditional acceptance, we learn to feel in a certain way as symbolized by our Moon, that is later reflected in our money attitudes. The Moon shows our unconscious level of security that begins with our need for nourishment. When a pattern of inability to delay gratification continues into adulthood, it is an infantile Moon syndrome, a cry from the inner child, "Feed me."

Habits and feelings about possessions are shown in large part by the Moon's position and aspects. In the charts of those of us who are able to accumulate goods and possessions, we are aided by a trine or close sextile involving the Moon. A childhood that has a foundation of stability in a safe environment is one of the greatest gifts that we can give to our children. The sense of self, the assurance that we are deserving of the aims we seek, and the ability to put our house in order (our lives) rests on a safe childhood. The damaged child may spend a lifetime trying to satisfy a hungry Moon.

The following definitions are for normal, healthy signs. If the Moon or Venus are not well placed by sign or house or severely debilitated, the effect is either muted or, some cases, warped. To a lesser extent, the ASC and Sun are also considered.

**Moon or Venus in Aries.** Those of us with an Aries Moon or Venus have a pragmatic money sense. Even if born to money or benefitted by marriage or luck we want to make our own mark, make our own money, keep an impetus, keep the flow of money moving. We make money with initiative, instigation, pursuit; we eagerly seek challenges to overcome and obstacles to conquer, and we can spend with equal zest. We work our way up and seldom stay in poor circumstances.

**Moon or Venus in Taurus.** Conscientious about our financial responsibilities, we are usually good managers, aware of fiscal realities and certainly practical, sometimes materialistic. We hang onto our money and work toward comfort carefully and shrewdly, mindful of expense while purchasing quality goods. Our security need is to gain tangible results and we appreciate property, goods, equipment, collections and the finest of possessions.

**Moon or Venus in Gemini.** We have more fiscal ups-and-downs than stable money sense. With our Gemini Venus or Moon, we vacillate between various profit plans and crazy schemes (or even questionable practices). We can gain from lucky breaks and lose from gullible persuasion. Our need for variety can lead us to career changes that may or may not help our financial picture. Fortunately, we gain a little more stability with our financial realities in maturity than we had in youth. We can prosper by investment but are not good at saving; we are better managers of other people's money than our own cash flow.

**Moon or Venus in Cancer.** We generally hold onto money and make it grow, always finding fertile ways to "turn a buck." Money assistance comes from family or marriage, or we have more emphasis and incentive after we marry. We are drawn to interact with the public and know naturally how to appeal to the public tastes, the needs of women and children, real estate or property, foods, commodities and business. Our earning capacity fluctuates in time, tempo and quantity. We spend for family and home and are subject to impulse and mood spending.

**Moon or Venus in Leo.** With a need for a prestigious position of dignity, we like to display a grand generosity. We are often dramatically giving even when we can't afford it, putting on a good show. However, we are also discreet; our net worth is not open to discussion. We have a natural feel for managerial fields where we can express expertise and authority, in business or some area that is our own kingdom. At times we can be gamblers. We are proud of our ability to manage well but want to be known for a broader area than that of commerce.

**Moon or Venus in Virgo.** We are modest about money and its sources, and even apologetic at any displays of wealth, such as an expensive car. We are good at handling fiscal details and are often in charge of accounts and bills, handling our own and others' records, papers, expenses and/or incidental commercial reports. We are not uncommonly "penny-wise, pound-foolish." We love to get a bargain and can operate well in economical circumstances. The "inclination is not to spend freely and at times other people consider us "cheap." In work we are better at implementing the operation than as boss, though minor executive posts are comfortable.

**Moon or Venus in Libra.** The balance is always necessary with our Libra Venus or Moon; because we adore having nice things and being able to buy them, we must pursue the crass business of making money. Of course it's much nicer to be given presents! In some cases we find a life of ease more important than the stress of pursuing a living. We tend to spend freely on toys (which we can justify as life's necessities) and buy attractive possessions such as clothes, car, furnishings, et al, but if low on funds or in modest circumstances we are capable of keeping a reserve. We have a measure of luck or support from family, mate or friends and often choose a field of activity that involves a product or service that pleases the public and gains approval; we "soft-sell" with charm, or work with an interest in others that is pleasing.

**Moon or Venus in Scorpio.** Though we appear to be open about money, we usually keep an undeclared reserve or even a hidden income source. We can also be a beneficiary of the goods or labor of others through marriage, loans, the mate's resources, family business or undercover deals. Some of us let others pick up the check or pay the rent, and even get into "sharp" practices that could not stand too much legal scrutiny. Wanting to control our environment, we may do so through holding the purse strings. Shrewd managers of our own funds, we are not notably generous and whether rich or poor, always know where every penny is.

**Moon or Venus in Sagittarius.** With this position, money-luck is evident; we can fall back on someone or something as help always comes through even if it is at the last minute. We usually marry well, receive an estate or gifts, have affluent friends or work with or for well-to-do people. We spend generously in a big way when the money is there; however, we are not notably good managers as we don't count the cost reasonably. Some of us are indulgent and extravagant, elegant, even ostentatious, running up bills and living well beyond our means; we think big, want big, and expect to be rich. If poor, we dream, plan, scheme and look forward to the day when our ship will come in. We are not people who save money well as we just can't grasp the "rainy day" concept, even when it's pouring.

**Moon or Venus in Capricorn.** Tight financial managers, we can pinch pennies and account for every expense. Most of us have some period of time when we either know poverty or have a rigid budget, teaching us the importance of money. When we make purchases we spend for quality and show and we want our money's worth. Some of us shade our business transactions to our own benefit but for the most part our accounting is accurate because we would be shamed if caught cheating. As we want to be important we translate money into terms of position and status; for basic security we like property and first class quality possessions.

**Moon or Venus in Aquarius.** There are contradictions in our finances, often extremes in our lifetime of big wins and drastic losses. We may be materialistic and shrewd in business, even brilliant, or we may not care a fig about what anyone thinks and do what we feel is important. We will spend for the hobby or private interest before paying for clothes or groceries and will leave a job or field if we hear the siren song of change. Though indifferent managers of a budget, we always seem to have something on which to fall back. Our attitude toward money is mainly that of, "Let someone else worry about it; I'm busy doing my own thing."

**Moon or Venus in Pisces.** For the most part we are none too realistic about money but operate on feelings and hunches that are often surprisingly accurate. In some cases, we have a business genius in responding to the public taste or in providing a service or product that catches the public imagination in popularity; other times we sell a concept, the image or aura, something intangible. Financial confusion or evasion is possible that ranges from undercover schemes to mismanagement. When money is there, we spend easily and are extremely generous and devoted to philanthropy. We lean to artistic and aesthetic fields, and not uncommonly, long to give our gifts freely to improve the universal welfare.

# Chapter 11

# Houses of the Commercial Horoscope

## The First House

*I may not be totally perfect but parts of me are excellent.*—Ashleigh Brilliant

LIKE IT or not, we are judged by our looks. That first impression is vitally important so make it a good one. Remember what mother said, "Stand up straight."

In the charts of successful people we find a strong 1st house by way of planets posited or strong positive aspects involving the ASC. A gifted first house gives one an edge, but we can all learn to hone and develop our first house to its best advantage; the first commodity we market in any situation is ourselves. Whatever our appearance and style, and whatever our rising sign, the ASC, planets in the first house and the ASC ruler present the first picture we exhibit to others; this is how we define ourselves. Personal hygiene and good grooming, cleanliness and a neat appearance are more appropriate to the professional life than making a statement with extreme fashions or inappropriate behavior.

As our planets progress to new aspects, as our Ascendant changes signs and as transits move through the 1st house, we can take advantage of this constant stream of opportunities to develop personal skills and talents. TR Saturn-Mercury contacts or Saturn-Pluto dialogues give us excellent timing for self improvement programs or for breaking unwanted habits. Venus aspects suggest the best time to cosmetically improve our appearance while Mars aspects direct us toward exercise, dance or aerobics to get into shape. Each of the planets by progression and transit have their own message.

The Ascendant, or rising sign, is one of the prime indicators of our personal interests and abilities. We demonstrate the conduct and personal behavior represented by the ASC in our attempts to influence our environment. During our adolescence most of us make all the blunders associated with our rising sign as we try out the various ways to interact suggested by that sign and its ruler. We not only gain more capacity and awareness of the ASC qualities with the experience of years but we add the dimension of each of the signs, decanates and duads through which the ASC progresses and its dialogue with everything else in the chart.

As the ASC (or any planet) moves into successive signs and houses, it does not change who we are but adds more and different experiences to influence the process of our growth..

The ASC and first house planets are major indicators of whether we have a temperament that is pragmatic, intellectual or aesthetic. For those of us who are oriented to the mundane life the 1st house has a strong dialogue with public houses (the MC and planets above the horizon) and assertive planets (Sun, Mars, Saturn, Uranus, Pluto) by rulership or aspect.

## The Second House

*O money, money, money, I'm not necessarily one of those who think thee holy,*
*But I often stop to wonder how thou canst go out so fast when thou comest in so slowly.*—Ogden Nash, Hymn to the Thing That Makes the Wolf Go (Jan. 1934)

How do we make a living? Look to the second house. The MC tells us about Status and awards, about success, about that which gives us credit or discredit. The second house represents the importance of material things in our lives and the worth of the dollar in our time and place, as well as qualities which we consider valuable. It does not show our self-worth, as that is the sum of the composite whole called the self, our total integrity (integration). However, planets in the 2nd house and the planet ruling the cusp are evidential in our personal value system, along with our Sun, Moon, ASC and the ninth house of our philosophy. **For our own economics, or those of our nation, to be in order, our values must first be in order.**

Our attitudes about money are largely described by the positions of the Moon and Venus, but the second house, planets posited, the sign on the cusp and its ruler, exemplify the symbolic indicators in the chart of how we actually meet the mundane necessity. It represents our material goods, how we attain them, how we handle them and what we do with them.

The second house is our cash flow, the bird-in-the-hand, the coins in our purse or pocket or our personal checking account with which we handle the commercial transactions of everyday life. It covers collectibles and personal possession of jewelry, art, clothing, but not real property. It is the income potential on the present-time market, the ability to make money and the general indicator of how and where money may be made. The second house shows the attention given to the mundane affairs of life; it is not indicative of wealth by itself. Generally we pay cash for food, entertainment, incidental clothing, supplies and transportation, most of the daily essentials and sundries. This is the cash flow of the second house. As life progresses and the ASC and first house planets move into the second house, the income potential is favored accordingly.

With many planets in the second house, a sense of self-assurance is evident, along with a practical approach to the mundane affairs of life. With this stellium we are not too competitive but we do tend to be pragmatic, adjusting to things as they are. We enjoy a gradual rate of progress toward our goal of the comfortable life rather than the drive of the tenth house for acclaim. We tend to stay with one career direction, gradually improving uncomfortable situations or limitations. We are seldom improvident and there is a tendency to collect or amass possessions, with an attachment for our home, property or valuables.

Whatever our position there is a great deal of time and attention paid to the commercial transactions of material survival. With a cardinal stellium in the second house, the judgment and financial timing is not as keen as with the fixed signs, which generally show a materialistic bent. With a mutable stellium, we have a relaxed financial approach and more flexibility in trying different fields.

## The Third House

*We are coming to realize . . . that there is a certain sterility in economic monuments that stand alone in a sea of illiteracy. Conquest of illiteracy comes first.*—John Kenneth Galbraith, Economic Development (1964)

For the ability to read and write, be thankful; education is a great gift. A library that is free and available is a remarkable privilege. Studies document more promotions to higher positions in our jobs for those of us who have an articulate vocabulary.

The third house, with planets posited, the sign on the cusp and its ruler symbolize bookkeeping, mailings, communication, news and information, transport of goods and services and the cost of these matters. It covers papers, magazines and journals, that monthly staggering phone bill, trucking and shipping, mail-order sales or purchases. In publishing we need both third and ninth house activity, and in mail-order businesses a dialogue between the third and seventh houses to reach our market.

An automobile may be a toy, a status symbol or a possession but, whatever value we assign to it, the upkeep and overhead of our car or any other means of transportation is shown by the third house, as well as the distance or convenience of daily travel to and from work or other destinations. When we are in business with our kin, or when brothers and sisters influence our income, this is also shown by third house aspects.

Much of modern life is transacted on the telephone. The phone company coined the phrase, "Let your fingers do the walking"; finding business contacts by thumbing through the advertising section of the phone book is a time-saving approach in an overbooked busy day. When we are talking on the phone, it is not the time to eat, drink, smoke, chew anything or mumble. Even if handling (or making) a complaint, a pleasant tone gets the best results. It alienates people to put them on "hold" or talk to someone else while we are on the phone. Lock all children in the closet; they may be adorable at three but only a grandmother appreciates hearing them answer the phone.

For our answering machine, recording a *brief* message is appropriate. If we take business calls on our phone, make that a *businesslike brief* message. In all cases record some type of identification in the message. There is little that is more annoying than making a business call and getting a message that is long and "cute" from someone who is nameless and whose voice we don't recognize; when we dutifully leave our name and number we wonder for days if we reached the right number. Whether our daily communication is in person, by fax, modem or phone, remember that courtesy is important.

## The Fourth House

*The first man who, having fenced in a piece of land, said, "This is mine," and found other people naive enough to believe him, that man was the true founder of civil society.*—Jean Jacques Rousseau, Discours sur l'Origine et le Fondement de l'Inegalite parmi les Hommes (1754)

Fixed wealth, legally called "real property," falls within the dominion of the fourth house, planets posited, the sign on the cusp and its ruler. This area of the horoscope represents the earth and agriculture, and the possession of home, land, farm, factory, store or business location under property ownership. People with wealth own property. Even a large income and a solid bank account does not create the substance in the commercial world that property does.

The prima mobile of most species is two-fold and interlacing, status and territory; these drives are so powerful that they even supersede the mating game. Where do we find our niche? In what condition and environment are we most nurtured and "at home?" To build a stable and secure base of operations we must first establish unity in our own home. To recognize a family of man we must first practice tolerance with our own family.

The residence is always the fourth house. If we are either a renter or the landlord, the sixth house is also considered. When property is bought or sold, the eighth house must come into play. Long range moves involve the ninth house, short range moves the third house.

For buying and selling property, look to Jupiter and Saturn by progression and/or transit for an overview of favorable times for expanding or conserving. Consider the eighth house for how we fit into the national economy. The eighth house is also crucial for the transfer of title; the second house may or may not be involved depending on whether or not cash money changes hands.

When choosing a real estate broker, find favorable aspects to the eleventh house; our broker is our advisor and counselor, as is our legal counsel. (When we, ourselves, are the agent or broker, the service we perform is signified by the third house; the agency is denoted by the ninth house. The eleventh house represents advisory capacities.) Advertising is shown by the ninth house plus favorable Jupiter or Moon aspects. The TR Moon in a fire sign is excellent, and always choose an increasing TR Moon when publicity is desired.

When Mercury is retrograde, it is a good time to make repairs and research the market by talking to different brokers or property appraisers, but avoid the Mercury retrograde period when possible for listing the house or signing contracts. If it is unavoidable, consider the aspects that Mercury makes to the chart during its retrograde period and try to focus on the more favorable of the choices available. If we must sign contracts and agreements during a Mercury retrograde, remember that later modifications and codicils are possible. Even on binding contracts the paper work gets misplaced or needs another signature, the loan officer is out to lunch and forgets to return our call or the escrow department delays the transfer of funds for some reason.

Success or failure never rests on one factor alone; consider the other planets as well for favorable days. Pay attention to transits that aspect the seventh house planet or ruler when a purchase offer is made as the seventh house represents the buying party; we also consider Pluto for our own power position in negotiations.

In business, permanent capital, the stock that is not subject to dividend but stays in corporate ownership, is basic to the fourth house.

# The Fifth House

*Buy old masters. They bring better prices than young mistresses.*—Lord Beaverbrook (1879-1964)

Speculation, that is purchase of stock goods or commercial transaction out of the regular order of trade for future sale at an enhanced price, is represented by the fifth house, with planets posited, the sign on the cusp and its ruler. Negotiable funds in our own name and possession are shown by the second house; however, corporate securities are signified by the eighth house whether we are the person drawing dividends or the corporation paying dividends to the stockholders. Therefore, bonds do not fall under fifth house rulership unless they are purely speculative. Business entertainment and the expense account are included in this area as well as any business that adds entertainment or pleasure rather than necessity, including toy stores, boutiques, art galleries, show rooms or displays.

Children and their care, feeding, education and maintenance are one of the biggest expenses in the lives of those of us who are parents. With fifth and sixth house interpositions, or with fifth house planets moving into the 6th house, we may also actively work with our children in both the caretaker sense and in a co-worker capacity.

If not parents, the expense of the fifth house is shown by our toys. Our CD player, tape deck, VCR, video-camera, board games, golf clubs, tennis rackets and bowling balls, jogging shoes, workout fashions and all the tools and trappings of fun are shown here. Recreation and entertainment includes sporting events, as both participant and observer. When planets progress from the fifth to the sixth house we may move into a pattern of "healthy toys" and activities such as trampoline, rowing machine, swimming or other sports, or "useful toys" such as computers complete with ever-more-complex games, music synthesizers and equipment and various high-tech products, or enjoyable pastimes such as arts and crafts or gardening.

Courtship and/or sex games can also be an area of expense, and when fifth house planets move into the sixth house, we must guard against medical expenses such as abortions from unwanted pregnancies or medical treatment because of sexually transmitted infections.

Creative endeavors and a vested interest in our own image is portrayed by the fifth house. Associated with the MC or the career indicators, it portrays our audience or following. This is an important factor for politicians, entertainers, writers, speakers or teachers, psychologists or doctors, as well as to those of us who have such service related professions as auto mechanics and cosmetology, because our clientele follows us through shop moves.

## The Sixth House

*I like work; it fascinates me. I can sit and look at it for hours.*—Jerome K. Jerome (1859-1927)

The sixth house, planets posited, the sign on the cusp and its ruler depict the areas pertinent to business in regard to our co-workers, the work crew, sales staff, the office or work quarters and conditions, equipment, maintenance, supplies and overhead expenses. It covers all the details of systems, methods and procedures. When we are the employer it is our employees, workman's compensation, medical overhead and social security payments, and it is also employee theft. (Mars involvement or aspects to the sixth house are remarkably common in the charts of business owners who have problems with internal product loss.) The sixth house represents our product supply, the raw goods or wholesale market availability and as such, is a vital core to our business success. Retained earnings, or surplus not distributed to stockholders that is tied up in inventory and equipment is signified by the 6th house (that which is tied up in real estate is shown by the fourth house).

To create harmony in our daily work life, we must treat our co-workers with dignity, whether we (or they) are in the janitorial or presidential position. In our private lives, we may consider the expenses of the 6th house to include our water bill, heating and electricity, the street cleaner and trash pickup service, our mechanic and plumber as well as more intimate "employees" such as our beautician or barber, dry-cleaner and shoemaker. In our home or job location, we consider all of our tools and equipment and their maintenance as falling under the jurisdiction of the 6th house, including supplies, typewriter and computer upkeep, the Xerox and fax machine and the nice little local shops where incidental purchases are made.

## The Seventh House

*Marry money.*—Max Schulman's advice to aspiring authors

If our professional life holds any contact with people at all, the message of the seventh house is abundantly clear. Acknowledge others, make eye contact, offer a firm handshake, state our own name and **remember** the other person's name. Pay attention, show an interest, listen to the other person. We don't have to wait for someone else to initiate contact as we ourselves can act upon the most positive message of our seventh house. Whenever the natural ruler, Venus, is operative, we may hone and cultivate social skills. Being pleasant and attentive and remaining open to input are the most successful traits in dealing with the public, let alone in dealing with a significant other.

Those of us with an active seventh house, as seen by planets posited, the sign on the cusp and its ruler seek external stimulation, interaction, feedback, input. We need "the other," the partner or adversary, often in competition in order to balance and measure our own worth and reality. Equitable relationships and partnerships are shown by the seventh house, whether personal or business. It is associated with reciprocity, mergers, agreements and arbitration. When posited planets move into the eighth house the business climate as well as the economic relationship of shared resources becomes a focal point of our personal disputes or agreements. If we are a wholesaler, the seventh house describes our retail market; to a retailer it depicts the buying public; it is also the other corporate entity. In the event of a law suit it is the suing party, the "open enemy" (as compared to the twelfth house, which is hidden).

## The Eighth House

*He who controls the money controls the country.*—Baron Rothschild (1744-1812)

Money that goes into a savings account is in the possession of the bank or trust company, which pays interest. Any item that is a credit purchase is charged interest and the deed of ownership is in the hands of the seller until purchase is completed. All eighth house monies are in one way or another jointly held resources. We may also consider the eighth house, with planets posited, the sign on the cusp and its ruler for how well we fit into the national economy.

Major purchases, the house, car, ledgers and bills of lading, debts receivable, mortgage deeds, promissory notes and all credit buying and selling are eighth house matters. Banking, flooring, factoring, taxes, insurance, equity, trust deeds, fiduciaries, corporate funds, the partner's income, joint accounts, stock equity where dividends are paid out of profits: all fall under the jurisdiction of our eighth house. Big business is not done on cash terms. Any and every business transaction larger than a lemonade stand requires eighth house action. As a matter of fact, the product supply of the lemonade stand was probably started with venture capital via Mom.

The bottom line is, what are we worth when we are dead? Do we leave an estate or any bequests? If we go down to a bank or lending institution *today* to fill out a credit statement, what is our net worth? How much of a credit line are we able to floor? **Though cash flow and earning power are represented by the second house, our financial worth is shown by the eighth house.**

People in high income brackets whose lifestyle exceeds the maximum of their income without a compensatory funding in business, property, equity or investment may have a strong second house and a relatively weak eighth house. On the other hand, a strong eighth house with a relatively weak second house can mean that we are active in handling the matters listed above without much personal spending clout. It is not a balance of equal power between the two houses that we need to evaluate but a consideration of the second and eighth house aspects that are working, by way of their dialogue with other planets and houses.

Aspects between the second and eighth houses are helpful to fiscal skills, but **aspects between both the second and eighth house to the MC/tenth are essential for financial success in business.** If the eighth house contacts the MC and the second house does not, we may be dealing with money (as in banking or other eighth house matters) or working with very expensive productions or equipment that belong to other people. If the ruler of the second house is in the eighth house, our income rises and falls along with the economy of the buying public.

The most expensive commodity that we can buy is money. When purchasing is done with credit cards, the cost of any item may be as much as 20 percent above retail. Bankruptcy is an eighth house crisis that often follows a long period of "easy" aspects to the eighth house at the same time as minimum aspects to the second house. This is one of the most seductive ploys of modern life, "Buy now, pay later." The loan companies get rich, the system is injured and the gullible are wasted.

## The Ninth House

*In life it is training rather than birth that counts.* –Ihara Saikaku (1642-1693)

Of all the people who get educational degrees, only 20 percent remain in the field that was their major. The most efficient use of the ninth house, planets posited, the sign on the cusp and its ruler is specific training to gain competence in a given area. When the ninth house aspects the mundane houses, two, six and 10, it indicates a more appropriate choice of educational majors than following interests that are not productive on the job market.

For example, a Capricorn who gets a masters in business administration, with both Saturn and a ninth house interaction to mundane houses, or a Libran who majors in fine art along with a Venus aspect and the ninth house in dialogue with mundane houses are both following appropriate leads toward success. A Sagittarian who takes archery in junior college or an Aquarian who majors in archaic languages may not find that their interests are suitable for their mundane environment or appropriate for fulfilling their dreams of success.

When the education is not geared to a clearly defined goal, it is a delicious luxury but not always marketable. We may certainly pursue our art or music or ballroom dancing, but along the way to perfection, we might as well pick up a class or two on basket-weaving or computers or plumbing. When the ninth house has interpositions with the tenth or sixth houses, it often pertains to on-the-job training: in interaction with the first house, we may be self-taught. In dialogue with the second house, the ninth house implies that trained labor skills command the best livelihood.

In legal matters, the ninth house is the judge and jury, up to and including the Supreme Court. (The suing party is shown by the seventh house; our attorney by the eleventh house and a settlement is represented by the eighth house. Representing our attorney by the eleventh house does not come from traditional astrology but from years of modern observations.) The ninth house parades pomp and circumstances, state formalities or protocol and ceremonies and rituals, notably those of the church with the dogma and doctrine of established religion.

Advertising, marketing, publicity and public representation are symbolized, as well as travel and agencies. (The agent himself performs a third house service.) In business, international import and export are included in the ninth house venue along with the passport and travel arrangements. "Long distance" is a relative term; customary trips (such as a day or two in the city every week) probably fall under third house jurisdiction; if we seldom leave home, a weekend trip where we pack a change of underwear and a toothbrush could qualify for the ninth house.

This area of the chart represents the declared public aim of the business and the image that it presents to the world, its letterhead, stationery and logo and the published Code of Ethics. It is the "happy-face" that we put on before the world and as such may not reflect the actual nature of conditions. What we say in public (ninth house) and what we say or think in private (third house) may or may not be contradictory. What we write and publish in our novels is not necessarily our personal belief system or what we have experienced first-hand. What we publicize by advertising may or may not accurately portray the person or the product that is being promoted. The religion or means of worship that we choose, as indicated by the ninth house, may or may not indicate our inner spiritual quality. This area is pertinent to propaganda, publication, teaching, radio, television and media communication that influences public opinion or reaches the people.

## The Tenth House

*A good reputation is more valuable than money.—*
Publilius Syrus (first century B.C.)

The tenth house, planets posited and the MC and its ruler describes the most appropriate route to success. Though the 1st house and Ascending sign indicate how we define ourselves, the 10th house and MC sign indicate the requisite qualities, conditions and attitudes required to achieve standing and status in the world. It exemplifies our ultimate goals of mundane success and how to go about achieving them and for what we are known, whether that renown is fame or simply personal attributes recognized by others. The MC and the tenth house are covered more fully in Chapter 18, "Success."

## The Eleventh House

*Birds of a feather flock together.*—George Wither, Abuses, 1613

The eleventh house, planets posited, the sign on the cusp and its ruler represent collective agencies, the cabinet, the board of directors, the advisory staff and business consultants. It is the house of counseling, including vocational and astrological counseling, self-help and how-to themes. It is the attorney or legal counsel, a definition that is substantiated by actual examples though contrary to the seventh house named by traditional astrology. When an advisor such as our stockbroker calls on the telephone, we may set up an electional chart for the time of the call to see if the advice is sound (eleventh house).

To build and maintain harmony in our community, we must share and solve problems in a spirit of brotherhood. The eleventh house illustrates our friends, clubs and organizations as well as the degree and nature of our civic involvement in our community. The common denominator of belonging to the Homeowner's Association, the Boy Scouts, the Young Democrats of the Nation, the Ku Klux Klan, the Elks Club, the House of Bridge, the Astrology Club, the Association of Retired Persons, the Black Panthers or the Delta Psi Phi is an unbonded attachment. Our role and personal involvement with the group is shown by the eleventh house planets and rulers which denote our place in our social milieu apart from family, career or work, though it can interface with any of these areas.

As it represented the influence of "who do you know?", it shows how friends can help or hinder our directions and destinations. We are attracted to friendships with people who are role models, as they represent qualities or positions to which we aspire. Our spare time is spent largely with recreation and family, as shown by the third, fifth and seventh houses, or with friends, eleventh house, or with our need to withdraw in private renewal, twelfth house.

Though each of us is all alone in time and space in our own development, that sense of solitude, of being "different", apart rather than one with our own generation is shown more markedly with higher octave planets, Uranus, Neptune and Pluto posited, ruling or in close dialogue with the eleventh house.

Where the tenth house is concerned with ambitions for achievement, status and rewards, the eleventh house is absorbed with aspirations of whatever it is we seek to fulfill our sense of separate self. Both the eleventh and twelfth houses are attracted to and involved with values other than material recompense. This area shows avocational interests, and in charts where there is an interaction between the tenth and eleventh houses, the avocation may ultimately become the vocation.

## The Twelfth House

*Income tax returns are the most imaginative fiction being written today.*—Herman Wouk

Filing our tax return is an eighth house project; however, "skimming" implies covert twelfth house activity. That is the income that is not declared or the money cached in the cookie-jar or in a sock under the mattress (or embezzled from the company). This area shows the ace-in-the-hole of hidden assets or undeclared income, depreciation or underevaluation, tax shelters or clandestine affairs such as espionage and hidden agendas.

In business the twelfth house is hidden costs and unforeseen factors; read the fine print to avoid unpleasant surprises. It is price slashing and cost wars which can be to our advantage or disadvantage depending on circumstances, as well as business negotiations or alliances that are secret. On the plus side, it is the benefit of having medical insurance, unemployment benefits, social security and retirement plans. At optimum, the twelfth house represents power behind the scenes, or support which goes beyond our daily earning patterns.

We who have an active twelfth house are overly sensitive to outside stimuli so seek a tranquil atmosphere for our inner comfort. At periodic times we may feel a call to withdraw into spiritual retreats, ashrams or monasteries. Thomas Merton, with Mercury-Jupiter natally in the twelfth house and Sun-Mars progressed there, Pisces rising and Neptune in a one-degree aspect to three points, wrote in *Seven Storey Mountain* of his first experience with the monastery, "I entered the silence and knew I was home."

Because Merton lived for eight years in the silent cloister, this doesn't mean that he wasn't doing some work around the place for his daily bread. Life goes on during our times away from public view. The twelfth house describes the type of place to retire when work is done and ultimately the nature of retirement from paid labor, as well as unpaid labor or volunteer and charity work.

There may be more than one period of "retirement" in the lifetime, as when a woman is childbearing, or with vacations or episodes of unemployment. When well aspects, this is a safe place in which to retreat from the mundane demands, to dream and replenish our spirit. It is even possible that having a nervous breakdown is the healthiest survival tactic possible under circumstances of unbearable stress.

If there are difficult or no aspects between the twelfth house and the eighth house, such problems can occur of being outside of the system, a lack of hospital, medical or retirement protection. In these cases, watch for an appropriate aspect to move into place to instigate the desired effect.

Chapter 12

# Vocational Indicators

*Every morning I get up and look through the Forbes list
of the richest people in America. If I'm not there, I go to
work.*—Robert Ogden

THE FIRST indication of how and where people can make money
is shown by a planet in the second house in aspect to the MC or to
a planet in the tenth house. The planet ruling the second house cusp
in aspect to the MC/tenth or to the ruler of the MC cusp sign may
serve the purpose but it is not as effective or obvious. The route taken
tends to be circuitous as we must take care of other priorities before
we are even aware, let alone capable of using our financial abilities.

When the planet that rules the second house cusp is placed in another sign and house, its influence is modified and colored by that
sign and house and therefore does not have the clarity of definition
that is suggested by the planet posited. For example, say that we have
Cancer on the second cusp and the Moon is in Virgo in the fourth
house. We may read the delineation of "Moon in the second house,"
but the description will be modified by the actual position of the
Moon (in the fourth house) and by the sign in which it is placed
(Virgo).

When there are several planets in or ruling the second house, all of
which aspect the MC/tenth, consider the one that is in the closest aspect to be the primary indicator. If there is no dialogue between the
second house and the tenth house, the second consideration is the

planet in or ruling the sixth house in aspect to the MC/tenth. The dispositor of either the second or sixth house rulers may also be considered for interaction with the MC/tenth, *the first dispositor only.*

There is an additional vocational indicator of the Ascendant moving into the second house at approximately age 30 (sometime between our teens and late 30's) and moving through this house for the duration of our 30 peak years of earning power. By age 30, we have had our first Saturn return and PR Moon return and should be shaped and molded well enough to live in the mundane world. In Eastern philosophy, for the first third of a lifetime we are considered to be a student, for the second third, a householder, and for the last third, a seeker of wisdom. As the years progress, first house planets also move into the second house, and the planets ruling the second give and receive additional aspects (experience), adding to our vocational repertory and capacity.

Every aspect in the chart represents energy. With the money-work-career houses, discordant aspects show expense, activity and obstacles which require the effort of financial negotiations. *Poverty is not indicated by hard aspects but by the absence of aspects, the absence activity.* Any appreciable change in the income is shown by planetary dialogue involving the second house. Where that gain or loss may occur is shown by the performance demonstrated in different houses and planets.

**Sun in the second house.** With this position, we make money by carrying a position of authority, or by being "the Authority" in our own field. It is therefore important that we have specific education or job training in matters of interest. We tend to official or administrative positions of employment, or self-employment in a field that requires an audience, following or clientele. We are better in partnership or as team players with our Sun in the second house than when it is placed in either the tenth or sixth houses. Free-lance work or middle management is a productive and satisfactory area. Change in the field of expertise is rare; once we find our own niche we tend to stay, often with a long apprenticeship during which we make the modifications necessary to put our own stamp on our vocation.

Not necessarily materialistic, we do take pride in our possessions and value our economic self reliance and ability to be good providers. Mundane considerations strongly influence our goals and major decisions in life, even to the point of putting aside a talent that we love because we can earn a better income doing something else in a sensible field. Whatever the Sun sign, we do have a quality of practical stability; we are aware of fiscal realities as an important part of life and appreciate comfort and gain. Even when work is not necessary due to advantaged backgrounds, we take pride in our capacity as a breadwinner. Not uncommonly we have a golden touch of either shrewd business and financial sense or we marry money.

**Moon in the second house.** We make money by appealing to the public taste or working with the general public, through commodities and food, domestic affairs or the nurturing or care of women, children or others, or in musical fields. We instinctively collect or assimilate personal possessions, which tend to accumulate as a quantity of items. As children, with Moon in the second house we needed to have our rooms cleaned out with a shovel. As we get older, these "items" can be delightful indeed when they turn out to be such trinkets as diamonds or valuable collectibles. Our income tends to be highly variable and the pulse fluctuates from month to month as the Moon waxes and wanes.

We do seem to have a survival instinct of financial skill, but business as an end in itself is seldom the desired primary goal. For the most part, we value comfort and security as the end result of money-making. Consider the sign that the Moon is in, as given in Chapter 10, "Financial Attitude."

**Mercury in the second house.** We make money from verbal, intellectual or artistic skills, from fields of communication or transportation, agencies, scholastic or clerical work. Our best income often comes from contracts, commission, percentages or royalties. We are aware and capable of handling credit statements, costs, prices, expenses and balances.

Though Mercury is considered the god of trade, with this position we do not seem to be drawn into business fields as much as we are attracted to mental expression and mobility, which we value. As a general rule, our timing is good and it is a flexible, comfortable position for Mercury.

**Venus in the second house.** We make money in areas of social interaction, artistic or creative fields, from entertainment or culture, art or decoration, providing beauty or comfort. Despite the association of Venus with the second house as being the natural ruler, this position is remarkably unmaterialistic and our attitude toward income is usually placid. Even when money is tight we are apt to say calmly, "Oh well, easy come, easy go." This may be the result of knowing that something always comes through, a gift or favor. Venus rules gratuities and in the second house demonstrates the generosity of "perks" on the job, a cushy office or an extra bonus.

We do value and appreciate the nice things that money can buy and when affluent, surround ourselves with quality possessions; even on a limited budget, we dress with style and show a gentle flair. (In those cases where Venus is in aspect to Saturn, we tend to lack any fashion sense or we have no interest; we are much more comfortable "dressing down" than putting on finery.)

**Mars in the second house.** We make money in active, competitive fields that require physical labor, skill, training or expertise. We are drawn to production, manufacturer, tools, implements or machines, the construction business, sports or combat. Our income tends to increase in war time or from the stimulus of business competition. We put energy, drive and assertion into our field and often attack red tape or obstacles with impatience. We can be insistent, pushy and combative to drive home the program, production or policy that we value.

We have a vigorous appreciation of the products of success, such as home, property, cars, all the trappings of material possessions, and a pragmatic, realistic sense of the financial necessities. However, money can burn a hole in our pockets, and we are prudent to avoid impulse buying. There can be strife over money at times or financial problems that arise from enmity or jealousy.

**Jupiter in the second house.** We make money from professional fields, business, mass media communication or advertising, teaching, large companies or corporations, law, sales, religion or philosophy. Money is interesting to us; it makes us feel valuable, good, optimistic and cheerful. Whether we have a lot or a little, we appreciate it with a philosophical or even religious wonder *(Praise the Lord for this our bounty),* and when affluent we are generous and philanthropic.

We are protected financially and often fortunate through patronage, support, inheritance or investment. We keep a rose-colored view about money and buy the best quality possible for our income.

**Saturn in the second house.** We make money by slow, shrewd, calculated moves and hard work, often in traditional fields or business administration, management, organization or utilities, trade, real estate or agriculture. We are able to handle a subordinate position for the goal of eventual security, taking a long range point of view. Our education or apprenticeship may be pursued for years to insure the stability of a steady income. We approach financial risk cautiously and during a long period of low income tend to feel insecure, worried and grim, but we will stick to financial discipline for the sake of future goals. We seldom take the gamble of breaking out into a new field unless our economic security is first well established.

If we are born into, or gain financial well being, we then put our work ethic into well structured activities of personal interest. If prestige comes early, there is still labor required to keep that acclaim; when we are content to rest on former laurels we drop out of public sight. For the most part, our sense of self achievement and value are connected to feeling useful.

Mundane responsibilities or financial dependents may deplete our bank account or delay our personal ambitions for a long time. However, the promise of Saturn is a just return, and when our duty is faithfully completed, not only is our valuable security assured but our personal interests may be pursued to a greater depth. With financial duplicity or cheating, loss and is grace follows this position of Saturn as surely as when it is elevated in the tenth house.

**Uranus in the second house.** We make money in fields dealing with the humanities, whether in science or the arts, counseling, human relations, civil or government contracts, electronics or high tech fields. In optimum cases, our income is the result of a unique talent or singular originality. Not uncommonly our income is subject to totally unexpected gains and losses, or from striking an unusual pose that startles the public into sudden recognition. "Overnight success" may be the result of an unanticipated career break.

Vocational changes that give us greater independence in mid-to-later years are common as we value a livelihood in work that is unregimented, though not necessarily unconventional. We put self reliant enterprise ahead of a comfortable, routine income. Often we do well in making a unique or innovative use of our talents or of setting the style or standard in our field.

A contradiction is often seen in our possessions, such as an expensive home and no furniture, or a flashy car and low-income housing, or a shabby residence and a fat bank account. Our best income periods often run counter to those of the general public trend.

**Neptune in the second house.** We make money from providing or giving a service which we consider valuable to the community, whether in the arts or entertainment, public counsel or the ministry, or something as mundane as waiting tables. This position of Neptune inclines us toward poetic, artistic, aesthetic fields that require creative imagination, and if we are drawn to business, our schemes tend to be Utopian and complex. Money may come from music, art or drama, photography, drugs or medications, liquids or the sea.

We may have a financial handicap of someone unable to cope for themselves for whom we must provide. Though we long to retire and be provided for by the efforts of another or benefit from someone else's gifts, when we try to set up a lifestyle that comes without work, the price is too high. It takes a feet-on-the-ground observation of practical reality to keep clear of deception, confusion or muddle in money matters. Nonetheless, at dramatic times of crisis financial salvation often appears that seems miraculous, a boon or a bonus from family, marriage or public support.

It takes years for us to learn to evaluate our own financial worth reasonably. If confusion rears its head about what price to set on our time and effort, it may be recommended that we seek advice and counsel on how to set up a cost-sheet and stay with it. At times we have no sense of money value or the price of things and are seduced by impractical get-rich-quick schemes. "Budget" may be a concept that is foreign to us.

**Pluto in the second house.** We make money from a singular effort within the group, whether that group is the government, a major corporation or a more loosely defined collective which influences the masses in its own way. We may be in mass production, programming, syndication or propaganda. In all cases the income depends to some extent on our cooperation for the general good of the whole, as the team, group or organization is a strong vehicle for our work or the value we espouse. That team may also split into factions at times to jeopardize our position; if we are setting inflexible standards or using underhanded, secretive or dictatorial methods, the group may close ranks to exclude us.

We value fields that allow a certain autonomy, where we can deliver our product or talent at our own pace, or where we have a minority position. Work in the educational system, advertising or television is possible (though Pluto in the ninth house is more favorable for media performers), or we publicly present our views to the masses or to our own clique or following. We may be born with the proverbial silver spoon in our mouths before "Daddy lost it all in the stock market"; we later regain a financial position by our own efforts. Extremes of all or nothing are not uncommon. During one period in our lives our support may be provided by the group (the family, the mate, the congregation, the government).

Our financial values also tend to extremes; we are either highly materialistic or totally indifferent, but in both cases we have a tendency to amass a quantity of certain possessions, such as a collection. The instinct to produce and accumulate is apparent. There may even exist a simultaneous surface and underground quality to our financial life, such as a psychological or religious vocation while we discretely accumulate a stock portfolio or real estate, or hard-hitting business manipulations and negotiations while we privately attend metaphysical or evangelical meetings.

All of us who have Pluto in the second house seem to choose fields or circumstances that pay well, unless Pluto has no dialogue with the MC/tenth, in which case our income is always a step behind expenses.

The phenomena of Uranus, Neptune and Pluto is that they are all three dualistic; they not only run the gamut in various charts but may go to extremes in the same chart, exhibiting their entire spectrum of poverty to wealth.

## Placement of the Planet Ruling the Second Cusp

The house where the ruler of the second cusp sign is posited gives an indication of environments where employment and earning capacity are favored.

**Ruler of the second house in the first house** is one of the two most favorable placements, along with the ruler of the second house in the tenth house, to indicate self employment or a profession vocation. We make money from following our own abilities and interests. We so value working for ourselves that this is the goal toward which all other efforts lead. We also work in leadership roles, such as president of the organization.

**Ruler of the second house in the second house** suggests that our drive to make money is an end in itself, that success is associated with our earning capacity. Even if we are in affluent circumstances where we are not required to work, we want to contribute to our own livelihood and feel a sense of valuable achievement in being paid.

**Ruler of the second house in the third house** depicts an income from communication fields or from work as an agent or go-between, uniting a buyer with the product or service. The job may be in a local office or store or we may sell, represent or display wares. In some exceptional cases we have an intellectual or inventive output that creates a valuable product or service.

**Ruler of the second house in the fourth house.** We value the pursuit of our livelihood at home, or we may be supported in the home when the secluded environment is protected by a private income. We can make money from the land or real estate, gardening or agriculture, famishing or decorating, home goods or fixed holdings of business ownership.

**Ruler of the second house in the fifth house** attracts us into entertainment fields, the care of children, or with the sale and service of toys. Our income may depend on our clientele or following, clients or patients, audience or fans. In exceptional cases there is a personal accomplishment out of our own creative well that is valuable to the children of mankind for future generations.

**Ruler of the second house in the sixth house** generally indicates money from the helping professions or service occupations such as physical or mental medical fields, health foods, clerical work, factory, store or office, providing valuable maintenance and upkeep. If the planet moves into the seventh house it implies that we have pulled ourselves up, that is, we have worked our way up from menial to administrative capacity.

**Ruler of the second house in the seventh house** implies that money is influenced by or comes from marriage or partnership. Our money is better after marriage but not always so in business partnership. For the latter, comfortable aspects between the seventh and eleventh houses are helpful. Our income may be influenced by contests or competition with rivals or exchanges with peers. We value work in a professional capacity where clients are met on an equal level or where there are many one-to-one contacts.

**Ruler of the second house in the eighth house** shows income that is influenced by the buying public or by the present state of the economy. Our support may come from the state, such as grants or subsidy, employment by the government or from a company operating under government contract; there can be welfare benefits (in connection with the twelfth house). The sale of public goods, or working with taxes, insurance, banks and lending institutions is appropriate. The shared resources of our partnership are valuable to our financial position. (An inheritance is more aptly indicated when the eighth house planet is associated with Venus or Neptune plus an active dialogue with the twelfth house.)

**Ruler of the second house in the ninth house** demonstrates that an advanced education is a valuable help to give us expertise in a specific subject or field. When the ninth house ruler is interposited with the 1st house or the sixth house, on-the-job training is indicated. We can make money by influencing public opinion in writing, teaching or public representation, or through travel or work that involves foreign countries, religion or the ministry.

**Ruler of the second house in the tenth house** indicates that we are self-employed, career professionals in our field or have our own business. If not so at present, we keep trying and working toward that valuable goal. When we do hold a job, it is one of such a universal nature that we can always support ourselves.

**Ruler of the second house in the eleventh house** associates the income with a broad choice of fields that range from the humanities to entertainment, from business to the arts. The common denominator is that the income is of less value to us than the achievement of some specific goal or expression of talent, or the fulfillment of a personal quest. We can also work in law, counseling or the helping professions or in an advisory capacity in civic positions.

**Ruler of the second house in the twelfth house** sometimes points to support in retirement, where we are unable or unwilling to contribute to our own livelihood. In other cases we work behind the scenes in industry, institutions or in private or secluded environments. We value the possession of a "nest egg," secret or undeclared funds or money paid "under the table."

# Chapter 13

# Wealth

*I've been rich and I've been poor. Rich is better.*—Sophie
Tucker (1886?-1966)

CONSIDER the horoscope as a blueprint of how things work, a model
of the action as well as the ethic by which we live a successful life on
various levels. For the mundane life, the tenth, second and sixth
houses compose a trine, an indicator of the natural order of position,
money and work. To reach the pinnacle of the chart, the MC, we have
a job, profession or career (tenth) by which we make our livelihood
(second), we do labor (sixth) for hire or recompense (second) to gain
our status (tenth).

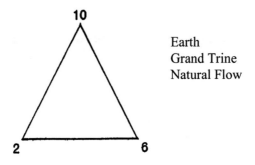

Earth
Grand Trine
Natural Flow

However, incentive is stimulated by external or internal pressure, the demand to do or reach the maximum of our potential as implied by the position of oppositions in the model. With the second

house opposing the eighth house, to accumulate an estate we must generate income. If we want possessions, we must either make money ourselves or be content with the shared resources that come from the partner or other providers. If we are going to buy anything that goes on a charge account or needs financing, the extent of our fiscal power (eighth house) depends on our earning capacity (second house).

The tenth house is opposite the fourth house, pictorially representing the central focus of the dual imperatives, status and territory. With oppositions from the fourth house to the tenth house, once we have found our niche, we are drawn to reach beyond a private life in the home for recognition in a public life.

The sixth house is opposite the twelfth house; to gain a comfortable retirement, we must fulfill the work ethic. To be content in work, we must have times in which we can withdraw for private renewal, to find reason and purpose for our labors.

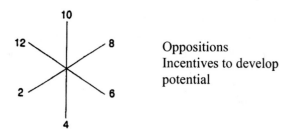

Oppositions
Incentives to develop
potential

Squares in the commercial model stimulate action and purposeful change motivated by strong desire. As a nesting species, we want to have children (second square fifth house) even though they are a major expense for a lifetime. If not children, we have our toys and recreations. As a gregarious species, we want to have friendships and fit into our milieu (second square eleventh house) which can lead to "keeping up with the Joneses" as well as memberships, dues and community involvements.

With the fifth house opposite the eleventh house, our hopes and wishes for our children may be for that which we would wish for ourselves to do or be. If we want to have influence in our social environment (eleventh house) we need to develop the interactive skills of showing interest in others. If we want an audience (fifth house), we have to be in touch with the mores, tastes and appetites of our own culture at our own time in history (eleventh house).

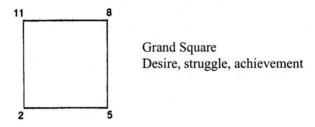

Grand Square
Desire, struggle, achievement

The everyday commercial life is shown by the natural earth houses in the zodiac, the tenth, second and sixth; however the **attainment of wealth, either by one's own means or by the fortunes of the universe, is shown by the water houses.** The interactive grand trines include the sextile points, as earth and water houses sextile each other. This interaction implies that opportunities abound between the natural earth and water houses, such as financial backing from parents (second house sextile fourth house, eighth house sextile tenth house), accumulating money in reserve accounts (twelfth house sextile second house), learning how to manage commercial transactions such as loans and investments (eighth house sextile tenth house), and holding a job in order to buy a home (sixth house sextile fourth house).

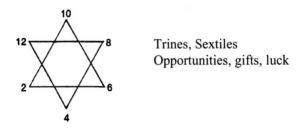

Trines, Sextiles
Opportunities, gifts, luck

Wealth is, of course, a relative term. In 1970 in the United States, 600 people made a million dollars or more. At that time, a few less than 100,000 Americans had a calculated worth of more than a million dollars. By 1976 those numbers had doubled. Ten years later, in 1986, 3,766,706 Americans had a net worth of a million dollars or more. In the most active real estate areas, any of us who turned over property three times in the 1980s could count an inflated million. Pluto in Scorpio took the dollar into the stratosphere to where we could read of a 20-year-old hockey player signing a $21 million contract, rock concerts bringing in $150 million and more, movie releases making $54 million in the first weekend and netting $347 million world-wide with an eight-year-old superstar being courted for his next film with a $6 million contract.

The eighth house is discussed in Chapter 11, "Houses of the Commercial Horoscope," as it pertains to business skills and net worth.

The fourth house denotes fixed wealth, real estate. In the lives of some 90 percent of the world's population, the biggest purchase of our lives, our single greatest possession of value is our home. For many of us, our home represents security for our later years. Fortunes have been made and lost on property development, either for community building or in personal home purchase and sales.

The MC ruler in the fourth house indicates that family help is paramount. There may be a family established business as with Gianni Agnelli who took over Fiat Automobile Corporation, or inheritance such as the $650,000 start given to Howard Hughes by his father, or it can show, for example, that Dad was the bank loan officer and had done business with oil entrepreneurs that helped Junior make the contacts to buy his first rundown oil refinery, as with oil tycoon and cattle baron Robert O. Anderson. However, remember that in career choices the circumstantial directions that pull at a person may synchronize with one of several astrological options. One young man with a Cancer MC and the Moon in the fourth house was the son of a musician; he headed for a career in music until the PR MC squared Uranus in the second house and computers began to absorb all of his time and attention.

Where the fourth house represents **acquisition,** *(Mine!),* the eighth house **symbolizes requisition** *(What's mine is mine and what's yours, I'll take by barter, negotiation, manipulation or conquest).* The twelfth house suggests **abnegation** *(Consider the lilies of* *the field, how they grow; they toil not, neither do they spin. . . . Take therefore no thought/or the morrow: for the morrow shall take thought/or the things of itself.*—Matthew 6:28 and 6:34.)

Sustenance, substance, support that is not accrued from our own labors but that comes to those who toil not, is a product of the twelfth house. This is most remarkably obvious when the ruler of the second house is in the twelfth house (as well as in the eleventh house). We may work as a matter of financial necessity or make money in capacities suggested by either of the two houses but our goal in both cases is not material; it is either to "do our own thing" (eleventh house) or to withdraw into our own private Utopia (twelfth house).

We also see the twelfth house benefits outlined in Chapter 7, "Unemployment," along with conditions which may include a heavy price. An old Spanish proverb says, "Take what you want and pay for it."

As we examine charts of the wealthy, it bears repeating that there is no one formula. Every chart tells a new story; as soon as we find commonalty that is repetitive, the next chart introduces a different pattern that may even have contradictions. For example, Jupiter-Saturn contacts are supposedly "the millionaire aspects." Yes, they are often present in the charts of entrepreneurs but not always. In some cases where Jupiter-Saturn do not contact each other, another significant planet, usually the Moon, is in aspect to one or both. We look first at overall general indicators before considering the specific points that stand out with the greatest frequency.

**In the charts of the wealthy, whatever the source of their riches, we find a connection by both interposition and aspect between earth and water houses. Mutual Reception, in the same way as interposition, unites the symbology of the two planets in a strong union.** (In mutual reception, two planets are each in the sign which is ruled by the other, as we shall see in the following example chart.)

## Example Chart of Wealth

In the chart of Diane von Furstenberg, a powerful complex of Saturn-Pluto contains the MC in Leo, trine the Moon. Jupiter does not

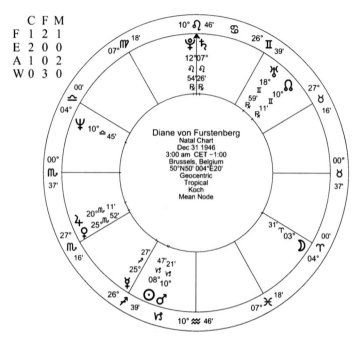

| | C | F | M |
|---|---|---|---|
| F | 1 | 2 | 1 |
| E | 2 | 0 | 0 |
| A | 1 | 0 | 2 |
| W | 0 | 3 | 0 |

Diane von Furstenberg
Natal Chart
Dec 31 1946
3:00 am CET −1:00
Brussels, Belgium
50°N50' 004°E20'
Geocentric
Tropical
Koch
Mean Node

***Diane von Furstenberg: Fashion Designer***

*Declinations: Ψ 2S53; D 3S3; A 11S42; ♀ 15S23; ♃ 16S51; M 17N32;*
*♄ 18N56; ☊ 22N9; ♅ 23N5; ☉ 23S9; ♀ 23N31; ☿ 23S42; ♂ 23S54*

have a trine but it does conjunct Venus, and its dispositor is the elevated Pluto. Mars, ruling the sixth house and co-ruling the second house is conjunct the Sun, ruler of the tenth house, united the three earth houses. It is one degree square Neptune in the twelfth house and one degree semisquare Venus, ruler of the eighth and twelfth houses, to connect the three earth houses to two of the water houses. The dispositor of Mars is Saturn, ruler of the fourth house, the third of the water house under consideration.

By Koch, von Furstenberg's second house ruler is Pluto on the MC, an indicator of being in business for herself; by EQHS the second house ruler is Jupiter in the first house, which gives the same message.

By Koch, von Furstenberg's eighth house ruler, Venus, is in the first house and by EQHS the eighth house ruler is Mercury in the second; the chart is responsive to either house system. The Sun has the requisite dialogue with the fourth house by way of a close quincunx to Saturn on the MC; the Sun and Saturn have, as well, a Mutual Reception (the Sun is in Capricorn, the sign ruled by Saturn, while Saturn is in Leo, the sign ruled by the Sun). The Mutual Reception unites not only the two planets, Sun-Saturn, but in effect, unites the third house and 9th house where they are posited, and the fourth and tenth houses, which they rule. In all, von Furstenberg's chart has a strong message of drive, purpose, efficiency and initiative.

The ruler of the ninth house is Mercury in the second house; as a Capricorn, von Furstenberg chose an appropriate educational major, economics. After marriage, two children and a move to New York City, she opened her own fashion design showroom in 1972 with a loan of $30,000. Her success was beyond all expectations, sweeping her into a position of being one of the outstanding designers; by 1976 her wholesale turnover was estimated at $20 million. In less than five years she built a fashion empire.

## Example Chart of Wealth

Leona Helmsley has Pluto, Sun and Venus conjunct the ASC from the twelfth house; the dispositor is the Moon in the eighth house. The tenth house ruler, Neptune, is in the first house designating a self-directed leadership role in a field in which she is "a natural" by way of its conjunction with Mercury in the first house. Her genius is in promotional planning and execution. The co-ruler of the MC, Jupiter, is in the second house to suggest that her reputation is associated with her livelihood, and success is measured in terms of material expansion.

By Koch, the ruler of the tenth house and that of the fourth house are conjunct in the first house (Mercury-Neptune), and the ruler of the second house is posited in the twelfth house, effectively connecting earth houses with water houses (tenth and fourth, second and twelfth). By EQHS Libra is on the fourth cusp with the ruler, Venus, in the twelfth house while Saturn is in the EQHS second house, ruling the eighth house. In both cases we have several earth and water house interpositions to indicate wealth. The Moon has no trine; however, its

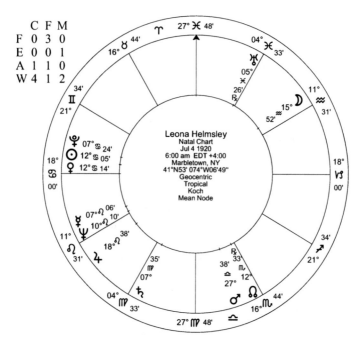

|   | C | F | M |
|---|---|---|---|
| F | 0 | 3 | 0 |
| E | 0 | 0 | 1 |
| A | 1 | 1 | 0 |
| W | 4 | 1 | 2 |

*Leona Helmsley: Real Estate Developer*

**Declinations: M 0S53; ♅ 10S15; & 10N24; ☽ 11S13; ♂ 11S38;
☊ 15S58; ♃ 16N1; ♆ 17N42; ☿ 17N44; ♀ 19N41; A 22N15;
☉ 22N54; ♀ 23N31**

dispositor, Uranus, is in a wide trine to Mars and a trine to Pluto-Sun-Venus.

The MC in Pisces indicates flair, charisma, even brilliance, with the possibility of questionable practices or scandal. Helmsley was gifted in turning over property, and upon her marriage to hotel magnate Harry Helmsley, was able to develop her talent to the fullest. Together they built a net worth of well over a billion dollars in resort hotels. Both rulers of the MC are in Leo and Helmsley exemplified leonine majesty and elegance as well as arrogance in her role as head of the Palace Hotel in New York.

However, Helmsley's private world was steeped in corporate and personal Pisces intrigue; in 1989 she was accused of billing some $4 million in personal expenses to the business and of 47 counts of tax evasion. The PR Neptune was at 12 degrees 37 minutes of Leo, sesquisquare the MC to imply a highly agitating career disruption due to vague, nebulous, confusing scandal and PR MC was square Saturn, presenting a stringent due-bill. Helmsley was found guilty on August 30, 1989; TR Neptune was at 7 Capricorn making a yod to PR MC and natal Mercury, opposite Pluto. She was fined $7 million and served 18 months in prison.

# Chapter 14

# Business Wealth

*Business is a good game—lots of competition and a minimum of rules. You keep score with money.*—Atari founder Nolan Bushnell

AS WE begin our analysis *of Business Wealth,* please review Chapter 6, "Self Employment." The qualifications of self-employment are prerequisite for those of us who become entrepreneurs, who deal with industry and commerce by initiating a variety of business enterprises.

Pluto deals with power issues. Sex, death and money are its broad power bases; business, religion and politics its most potent vehicles for manipulation and control. Close Pluto aspects (one or two degrees) are essential in the charts of most business people and certainly in the charts of industry giants and politicians for the tradeoffs, negotiations and undercover dealings with incorporated groups as well as with individuals; manipulation of public opinion and propaganda to influence the masses; attaining party position and financial backing; jockeying for favors in exchange for monies and position; and receiving and dispensing huge amounts of capital, money that exercises control and money that represents power.

Pluto is particularly productive for business clout when it is in dialogue with the MC, Saturn and the Sun; its potency is more apt to be absorbed by our private life when it is involved with Moon or Venus. Pluto conjunct or in strong relationship to the ASC demonstrates a noticeable display of muscle and influence at the same time that the private agenda is kept a state secret, such as shown in the chart of Donald Trump with Pluto in the twelfth house seven degrees applying to the ASC (as well as in the chart of H. Ross Perot, with Pluto conjunct Moon eight and nine degrees into the first house).

A personal client with Pluto on the ASC from the twelfth house influences the purchasing habits of a nation through her advertising agency, but her private phone is unlisted and few people know that she is, discretely, lesbian. Private individuals with Pluto on the ASC who do not direct that compelling drive into business power nonetheless attempt to rule, control, manipulate or influence their personal environment in positive or negative ways. (Scorpio rising reflects some of this drive but is not as dynamic as the presence of the planet and external results may even be depleted when the focus is limited to a search for identity and satisfaction of personal desires).

For business drive, Mars, Jupiter or Saturn statements stand out, as these planets tend to rule the angles or are posited in angular houses or conjunct the angles, say within 10-15 degrees. (Orbs are flexible and cannot be limited to precise calibration; the MC merits a larger orb for elevated planets.) It is difficult, if not impossible, to have success on any level or in any capacity without the Saturn activity of hard work, long hours, focused ambition and personal discipline; success simply does not "happen" when we are sleep-walking through life.

Both Mars-Saturn and Mars-Pluto aspects often sublimate sexual energy in order to redirect it to pragmatic interests, at times illustrating the goal-propelled workaholic. Mars-Jupiter is an excellent money aspect as it describes the conspicuous consumer: we have to make money to spend it with such zest and optimism. This is where the judgment of Jupiter-Saturn or Moon-Saturn is helpful to add some conservative restraint to a Mars-Jupiter passion of extravagance. In all these examples, we are not as highly motivated with the soft aspects as we are with the hard aspects, with which we may even appear driven.

**The ruler of the MC in the first or second houses, or the ruler of the second house in the tenth or first house are high-score indicators of mundane success. The ruler of the eighth house in the tenth or first houses are potent indicators.**

Lady Luck does not produce fame and fortune by herself, but she is an appreciable player in this game. In the charts of the wealthy, the Moon has a trine in at least eight charts out of 10, Jupiter has a trine in seven charts out of 10, and the second and/or eighth houses also have trines in six to seven charts out of 10. If not trines, we will see a highly favorable position of Moon and Jupiter such as a conjunction or tight sextile to Venus or Neptune, or conjunctions to angles or to the Sun. There are many talented people who never become famous, and capable people who never become rich, while another with less talent or less ability has that magical "luck factor" to be in the right place at the right time knowing all the right people and making all the right moves.

Uranus deals with alternate realities, variant life styles and counter-cultures and is more concerned with social movement and influence than with money. When it makes strong statements in the charts of the wealthy, it is due to an inclination to follow a path less traveled (*I did it my way*). With a successful Uranus, we learn how to make our eccentricities work for us. For us, wealth may be an interesting and enjoyable fringe benefit but is not the purpose in itself. Uranus tends to aspect Sun, MC, or Saturn for our drive of self-determinism and independent enterprise. It is the planet associated with original thought and inventive brilliance, so it plays this role (along with sesquisquares) in the charts of those of us who carve out new directions for ourselves, our careers or even humanity as a whole.

Moon, Venus and Neptune are not conducive to business unless they are in close dialogue with pragmatic planets, usually in conjunction or hard aspect; they deplete the "killer instinct" of a hard core focus of closing in on the deal, therefore are not often found in/or conjunct angles. Home and family are not first priorities for businessmen who work 10-12 hour days; businesswomen who take an hour with cosmetics in the morning and are side-tracked by long lunches and shopping afternoons may lose the cutting edge. When we like to stand around and visit with the reps or customers, we can talk ourselves into and out of a deal in the same hour. If, on the other hand, our business is geared to domestic needs, fashion, public relations, entertainment or some other field that is represented by Moon, Venus or Neptune, it becomes applicable to have those planets in obvious placements. The great designer and fashion entrepreneur Pierre Balmain, for example, has Neptune in a one degree conjunction to the ASC to illustrate imaginative brilliance.

The value of Neptune is that it gives us the ability to conceptualize, to make that quantum leap out of the vision or potential into reality. It may aspect inner planets in the charts of entrepreneurs, but for the most part the placement is succedent, or if cadent, not within 15 degrees of the angle. As a matter of fact, Neptune in a close aspect to angles (a few degrees at most) is suspect as it has such a volatile range. The person all too often has *A Cause,* and a thoroughly righteous man with a divine mission and a gun is rather frightening, as demonstrated in the charts of terrorists and assassins.

The Neptune spectrum can range from an inspiring dedication to relieving world hunger, as shown by Audrey Hepburn, (Neptune in a one-degree opposition to the ASC) to a belief that one has been abducted to a spaceship, as Whitley Strieber wrote of in his book. *Communion* (Neptune in a three-degree trine to the ASC). Astronaut Buzz Aldrin piloted the first earth craft to land on the Moon (Neptune in Virgo closely opposite the MC) while a private client with Neptune in the same sign and position has spent as much time unemployed as she has on the job, as in her heart she longs to be a poet, not working in an office with gray cardboard partitions and electronic terminals.

In any event Neptune is extraordinary. It turns away from the common, ordinary, everyday, mundane beliefs that are considered reality by most people to deal with extended dimensions, which makes it a highly delicate planet to define.

**Insofar as the houses are concerned, the earth houses establish our mundane position:** *in the charts of successful business people, the MC or its ruler makes a strong, usually favorable contact with the second house or its ruler, the sixth house or its ruler, and the eighth house or its ruler.* (Even this rule has alternative possibilities. Say that our second house ruler does not aspect our MC/ruler; the first house planet that moves into the second house may make the requisite aspect to start us on our career.)

There can be excellent income potential shown in a chart in which the twelfth house is not connected with second-fourth-eighth, but stop a minute to consider the extent of what **wealth** represents. If we want to take off work for a month to cruise the Mediterranean on our yacht with twenty of our closest friends, what kind of money are we talking about? This is a twelfth house month of "retirement" that few of us are in a position to consider seriously, and the concept illustrates the difference between a "good income" and great wealth. (The true entrepreneurial type, however, would hardly take a month off work; while away from headquarters, the boardroom, computer, fax and ship-to-shore telephone would all be fully functional on the yacht.)

*In the charts of people who have great financial wealth, the water houses are connected to each other and to the second house in at least one or two interlinking patterns of relationship.* This relationship requires interpositions, such as the eighth house ruler posited in the twelfth conjunct the second house ruler while the twelfth house ruler is in the fourth house. The interpositions are more important than aspects, though they are frequently accompanied by aspects. Various combinations show, for example:

The second house ruler (earth) opposite the fourth house ruler (water) and trine a planet in the twelfth house (water) which rules the eighth house (water); or eighth house ruler (water) in the 4th house (water) with the fourth house ruler (water) at a midpoint sextile to the ruler of the second house (earth) and twelfth house (water) and so on.

To cite actual cases:

Computer industrialist H. Ross Perot has the ruler of the second house, the Sun, in the twelfth, and the ruler of the fourth house. Mercury, in the twelfth. The eighth house ruler, Uranus (in the tenth) is trine Venus in the second.

Travel czar Peter Ueberroth has Pluto in the eighth house, ruling the Scorpio twelfth house, trine Saturn in the fourth house while Saturn rules the second house.

Gianni Agnelli, the head of Fiat automotive industry, has Jupiter in the eighth house, ruling the twelfth house, conjunct Saturn (in the ninth house) which rules the second house, and trine Mars which rules the fourth house. (By EQHS, Mars, co-ruler of the twelfth house, is conjunct the Moon, ruler of the eighth house posited in the fourth house.)

Ted Turner, TV network giant and baseball team owner, has Saturn, the ruler of the second house in the fourth house, and Pluto, ruling the twelfth house, is posited in the eighth house. Pluto easily trines Sun-Venus in the twelfth house by four and five degrees.

Adolphus Busch, founder of the Anheuser-Busch Brewery, has Mars-Jupiter conjunct in the tenth-eleventh houses, ruling and co-ruling the twelfth, fourth and second houses, sextile planets in the eighth house.

## Example Chart of Business Wealth

As an example chart, we shall follow the 12-step program of mundane delineation of the horoscope of industrialist Henry Ford.

1. **Planets east/west, above/below.** The majority of the planets in Henry Ford's chart are on the east (including the ruler of the ASC, Mercury, in the eleventh house), showing less need of involvement or approval from others than self-interest, with an occupied eleventh, twelfth and first houses for absorption in finding his own direction, vision and identity.

2. **Qualities and Elements.** The elements are evenly divided except for lacking water; a drive for emotional outlets is not a strong motivation or distraction. With six fixed signs plus Pluto and Mars both fixed and conjunct angles, he had the perseverance to stay with his goals in a fidelity of effort.

3. **Phenomena.** Neptune is retrograde, suggesting that Ford's early dreams were subordinated as inappropriate for a farm boy, but that they came out in full force through his adult pursuit of a creative vision. Saturn and Uranus are dominant in the chart by way of their greatest number and strength of aspects to display a strong work ethic and independent drive, and Pluto is elevated within 13 degrees of the MC for the potential of exercising power over his environment.

4. **Character.** With the Sun in Leo, Ford portrays the conviction of his own enthusiasms; the Moon in Aquarius denotes his scientific or inventive bent and the ASC in Virgo adds fastidiously accurate craftsmanship.

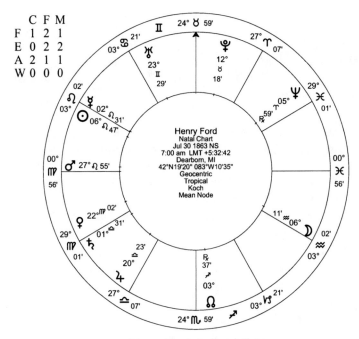

C F M
F 1 2 1
E 0 2 2
A 2 1 1
W 0 0 0

Henry Ford
Natal Chart
Jul 30 1863 NS
7:00 am LMT +5:32:42
Dearborn, MI
42°N19'20" 083°W10'35"
Geocentric
Tropical
Koch
Mean Node

*Henry Ford: Industrialist*

*Declinations: ♀ 0N24; ♆ 1N2; ♄ 1N28; ♀ 2N16; ♃ 6S53; A 11N9;*
*♂ 13N15; ☽ 14S26; ☉ 18N35; M 19N2; ☿ 21N3; ☊ 21S9; ♅ 23N24*

5. **Employment.** With Virgo rising, the modest and industrious natural ruler of the sixth house, and the Sun and Mercury both in aspect to the second house and sixth house. Ford is depicted as a faithful worker, whether employed or self-employed. However, the ruler of the sixth house is Uranus in the tenth house to indicate independent or free lance employment.

6. **Self-employment.** Ford's drive to be self-employed is symbolized by a strong Saturn trine the MC, inventive Uranus in the tenth house in a two-degree semisquare to the Sun, the self-determinism of fixed signs and the personal motivations of houses eleventh-twelfth-first. Further testimony is given by Saturn in a one-degree semisextile to the ASC and trine the Moon. It is unusual to have Venus in the first house for entrepreneurial drive, but in this case the easygoing passiv-

ity of Venus is outweighed by the preceding factors as well as Mars closely conjunct the ASC. As the dispositor of the MC is Venus in the first, it indicates that his career and reputation come from his own personal abilities and interests, a factor that is an outstanding indication of a prestigious life. (By EQHS Venus rules the second house cusp; posited in the first house it is another indicator of leadership vocation.)

7. **Planets in the sixth house.** The Moon in the sixth house shows skill in dealing with people and optimum output through teamwork in a support group. The work fluctuates in time and tempo by mood and "feel." Saturn is co-ruler of the sixth house, its position in the second house implies that a stringent financial necessity is the first work priority. Uranus in the tenth house shows work that gains a reputation for originality (or eccentricity).

8. **Financial Attitude.** With the Moon in Aquarius, economic prudence was outweighed when Ford heard the siren call of change; he left the traditional farm vocation to follow his own path. As his motor company developed into an industrial giant, he devised innovative business methods that introduced brilliant, revolutionary achievements in technology. Venus in Virgo activated his ability of efficient economy with his original operating budget. Ford was unassuming in the position of wealth that he achieved and he took care of his employees, paying the best wages of that era to get and keep quality craftsmen.

9. **Vocational Indicators.** Saturn in the second house represented Ford's practical expediency with his possession of business skills and a valuable ability to work with administration and managerial organization. Jupiter indicates his need to grow and expand in large business or corporations or in professional capacities. Saturn is trine the MC; Jupiter is trine Uranus in the tenth house and Uranus rules the sixth house, which connects the three earth houses in a positive dialogue in air signs.

10. **Wealth.** The possibility of wealth is shown by the second house of income in a relationship with the water houses: Neptune in the eighth house is trine the Sun in the twelfth house as well as Mercury in the eleventh house (ruler of the second house), while Mars (co-ruling the fourth house) is posited in the twelfth house. For the

luck factor, the Moon makes its helpful trine, in this case to Saturn in the second house.

Jupiter posited in the second house is trine Uranus. Both the second and eighth houses have trines. Once Ford had achieved great wealth he set up one of the richest philanthropic foundations of its kind in the world, which we may attribute to the close aspects of Neptune in the eighth house.

The first conjunction in Ford's chart occurred when he was age two, Mercury conjunct Sun in Leo in the twelfth house. As the twelfth house portrays early non-verbal conditioning, we may consider that he learned from his father at that time to set goals of how to gain importance and "be a man" by experiencing his father's expression of authority. The arc between the MC and EQHS tenth cusp is some four degrees; Mars simultaneously reached the ASC at age four. We can picture Ford as a little boy climbing on farm machinery and exploring his physical world, finding out, as he later said, that he was a natural engineer. The first opposition is present at birth, the full Moon within minutes suggesting a demand to do and be the best he could.

11. **Success.** The MC is Taurus, a venue of stubborn determination for Ford to follow in his pursuit of that which he believed to be possible, after a long apprenticeship. The ruler, Venus in Virgo in the first house, depicts a position of personal success and acclaim in detail work to perfect his goal.

12. **The Life Path.** The arc between the MC and the tenth cusp is 6 degrees 10 minutes (no information available); the PR MC reaches the eleventh EQHS cusp at 36 degrees 10 minutes, equivalent in age arc to 36 years, 2 months = September, 1899. In 1899 Ford finished three automobiles, quit his job and went into business. He failed in his first two attempts but (Taurus MC) kept trying.

By progression, the Sun moved into the first house in 1897 when Ford was 34; he had a small farm and married Clara Bryant that year. The following year he moved back to work in Detroit where he built his prototype "horseless carriage" in a shed behind the house. The opposition of Saturn to Neptune (work to turn a vision into concrete reality) dominated much of Ford's life with its one degree aspect from 1891 to 1914, ages 28 to 51. He worked for seven years in a shed behind the house on his first auto, finishing it in the spring of 1896. When he made his first attempt to go into business in 1899, PR Mercury joined Saturn opposite Neptune; he failed twice in the next few years before he began selling his cars. As the aspect continued its approach to partile, Ford Motor Company was born (1903) with twelve shareholders; they sold 5,000 "Fords" in the next two years.

Not only Uranus in the tenth house for the remarkable chapters of his life, sesquisquare the Moon for blazing new trails and creating inventive contributions to give the world, but the conciliation by Neptune on one side and Saturn on the other of an exact full-Moon birth shows remarkable patterns for this unique inventor and manufacturer. Demonstrating the elevated Pluto, Henry Ford did indeed influence his environment; he introduced mass production in the assembly line that changed the methods of manufacturing forever.

Although Henry Ford achieved appreciable money and success relative to his day, wealth today is exemplified by Bill Gates, whose computer software company was assessed as worth $4.4 billion by 1991, when he was 36 years old.

## Example Chart of Business Wealth

Scanning through the 12 steps, we find nine planets below the horizon in the horoscope of Bill Gates, disclosing an essentially private person who keeps a low profile. Earth is lacking; practical expediency is not his driving motivation; with four fire signs and five water signs, he is stimulated by passionate enthusiasm in the matters that interest him. Gates also has five cardinal signs and six fixed signs, indicating extreme initiative and perseverance. The chart signature (five water-six fixed) is Scorpio, adding potency to Gates' Sun in Scorpio.

The Moon in Aries is the most elevated planet, depicting fluctuation of reputation and activity; as the ruler of the first house, it indicates that Gates gains prestige at the peak of his life above that of his birth position. His strong family background and the need for a support team is reinforced by Cancer rising. Gates had an advantaged background as the only son of a lawyer and an educator. He was an underachiever math whiz-kid who caught the computer bug as a kid (Uranus in the first house). He built a homemade computer while at

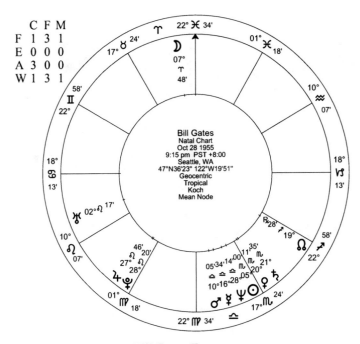

| | C | F | M |
|---|---|---|---|
| F | 1 | 3 | 1 |
| E | 0 | 0 | 0 |
| A | 3 | 0 | 0 |
| W | 1 | 3 | 1 |

Bill Gates
Natal Chart
Oct 28 1955
9:15 pm PST +8:00
Seattle, WA
47°N36'23" 122°W19'51"
Geocentric
Tropical
Koch
Mean Node

*Bill Gates: Entrepreneur*

*Declinations: M 2S57; ♂ 3S6; ☿ 4S37; ☽ 7N33; ♆ 9S17; ♃ 12N58;*
*☉13S12; ♄ 16S16; ♀ 17S40; ♅ 20N12; ♇ 21N48; A 22N12; ☊ 22S55*

Harvard in 1974 with his pal, Paul Allen. They both dropped out of school to form Microsoft Corporation. Five years later he sold the MS-DOS to IBM. His company went public in 1986; by 1991 he was #3 on Forbes' list of "The Richest Americans."

On January 1, 1994, Gates married Microsoft executive Melinda French in a Roman Catholic ceremony on the tiny Hawaiian resort of Lanai. The $35 million house he built on Lake Washington in Seattle has room for their family.

Gates has a Scorpio Sun, Aries Moon and Cancer ASC. Hard planets do not fall on angles in this case but the MC-ASC are in a grand trine to Venus-Saturn in Scorpio. The Moon is trine inventive Uranus, both in angular houses. Jupiter has no trine but it does conjunct Pluto in Leo, square Venus-Saturn for strong dynamics.

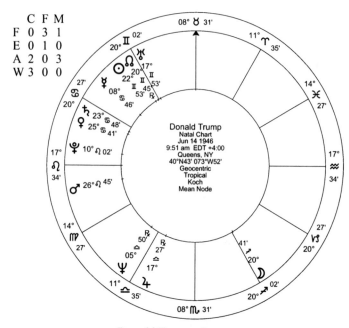

*Donald Trump: Entrepreneur*

*Declinations: Ψ 0S57; ♃ 5S35; ♂ 13N47; M 14N21; A 15N34;*
*♄ 21N30; ♀ 22N50; ♅ 22N57 ☽ 23S6; N 23N8; ☉ 23N15;*
*♀ 23N51; ☿ 25N10*

To connect water houses to the second house we have the rulers of the twelfth house and second house in the fourth house. The ruler of the eighth house in the first house gives Gates another outstanding indicator of being in personal control of his financial position.

## Example Chart of Business Wealth

Donald Trump's chart illustrates a strong position of Pluto and Mars by way of their containment of the ASC: Pluto is square the MC in Taurus, a sign associated with tangible, material returns. While Saturn is not in aspect with Pluto, it is closely conjunct the ruler of the MC and rules the work ethic of the sixth house. Pluto semisquare the Sun portrays the need to learn to carry power through the experience of making decisions and balancing choices (Gemini) by discussing options with a board of directors and an advisory staff (eleventh house).

# Chapter 15

# Performance Wealth

*We are what we pretend to be.*—Kurt Vonnegut, Jr.

THERE ARE movie stars, rock stars, sports champions and authors of best-sellers who make millions, sometimes for one performance alone. For those of us who aspire to their ranks it may be noted that out of all working actors, those who have their Screen Actor's Guild card, only 10 percent make more than what they could make on a minimum wage job and many of them support themselves with mundane occupations in between minor roles. The number of superstars is only a small fraction of entertainers, and the number of millionaire performers is only a small fraction of the number of millionaire business people. Therefore, as a vocational choice, these fields are about as practical as playing the lottery.

As performers, our charts do not have the same patterns as those of business entrepreneurs unless we ourselves are involved in business investments. Turning our funds over to a manager or consultant is putting our money into the hands of our eleventh house advisors which must be taken into consideration. The eleventh house is meaningful in any event as so many openings in competitive fields go to those of us who have contacts, who know someone influential, who have a foot in the door. If we do wish to work in the magical world of show biz (and do not have an "in" connection), our best old entry is to enroll in film production classes (or secretarial areas, or accounting, or computers) and apply for work at the studios. If not then "discovered" while performing at local theater workshops during the evenings, we are at least employed in an environment that we find stimulating.

Whereas success for the businessman is measured in terms of control of a unit of commerce, success for the performer is measured in terms of being heard and having an audience, therefore the third and fifth houses stand out. Of course, the second house has to be outstanding to make staggering amounts of money and the eighth house portrays the type of investments that we make, the fourth house indicates the homes and property purchased and the twelfth house the tax shelters employed, but the water houses simply do not make those connections by way of interpositions that we see in business winner's charts.

Mercury and the Moon are more frequently connected to Pluto in performers charts than with those of business people, to show a contact with the public as well as a gifted feel for the public pulse. Venus, Neptune and Mars are seen posited and conjunct angles more often. In the musicians charts the Moon has strong contacts to angles (mostly the ASC). The Moon has trines in more of the example charts but Jupiter has less; however, Jupiter in or conjunct angular houses is advantageous for successful *exhibition,* a succedent or wide cadent position is not as helpful. An assertive, pushy Mars is also needed to spark our drive to keep coming back after hours or years of rejections at spring tryouts, interviews, auditions and casting calls as well as returned manuscripts.

Whether the performance is a film or concert, a book or play, a sports season or tour, the twelfth house is strongly involved during the periods of creation, rehearsal and preparation that lead up to the exhibition, all the behind-the-scenes activities that are formative (cadent house) prior to their presentation.

Performers' charts markedly demonstrate interpositions connecting the third house and the fifth house with the MC. Consider the following examples:

## Example Chart of Performance Wealth

To illustrate the MC connections with the third and fifth houses, singer Whitney Houston has the Moon (ruling the fifth house) in the

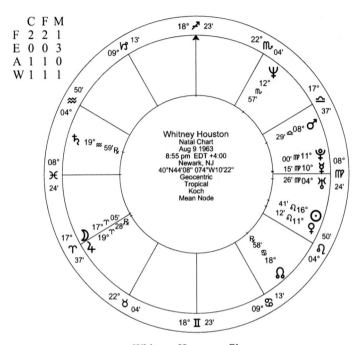

C F M
F 2 2 1
E 0 0 3
A 1 1 0
W 1 1 1

Whitney Houston
Natal Chart
Aug 9 1963
8:55 pm EDT +4:00
Newark, NJ
40°N44'08" 074°W10'22"
Geocentric
Tropical
Koch
Mean Node

***Whitney Houston: Singer***

***Declinations:*** *☽ 1N54; ♂ 3S8; ♃ 6N16; ☿ 7N52; A 8S25; ♅ 10N33;*
*♆ 14S3; ☉ 15N50; ♄ 15S59; ♀ 18N25; ♀ 19N41; ☊ 21N56; M 22S56*

first house conjunct Jupiter in the second house; both grand trine the
MC and Sun-Venus in the sixth house (Venus rules the third and
eighth houses and Jupiter rules the MC). Note that the ruler of the
MC, Jupiter, is trine the MC and the ruler of the ASC, Neptune, is
trine the ASC, a repetitive emphasis on superbly fortunate angles.

Mercury is conjunct Pluto to suggest Houston's range of intensity.
Her twelfth house "down time" contains Saturn retrograde while the
ruler, Uranus, is in the sixth house; this does not imply much leisure
time off from work pressures of rehearsals, commitments and obligations. Saturn closely sextile the second house Jupiter (MC ruler) designates the succession of lucrative opportunities in Houston's steps of
career advancement.

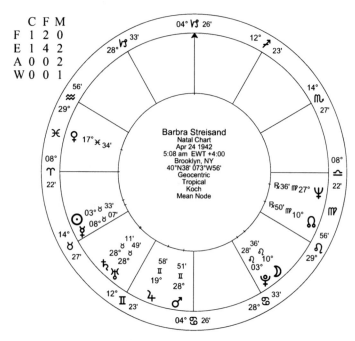

*Barbra Streisand: Singer, Actress*

*Declinations:* Ψ *2N11; A 3N19;* ♀ *5S16;* ☊ *7N3;* ☉ *12N42;* ☿ *14N22;*
☽ *14N60;* ♄ *18N1;* ♅ *19N44;* ♃ *22N50; M 23S22;* ♀ *23N57;* ♂ *24N53*

## Example Chart of Performance Wealth

Barbra Streisand has Moon-Pluto in the fifth house (of her audience) trine the ASC and quincunx the MC. Although the trine portrays her natural sense of showmanship (with Leo), the quincunx indicates that her initial involvement subsequently dissipated: Streisand
described this in an interview when she said she had enjoyed singing
in live performances in the first decade of her career but not since.
The MC connects with her third house (of self-expression) by way of
a trine to the ruler. Mercury, in the first house conjunct the Sun. The
MC ruler, Saturn, is in the second house conjunct Uranus and trine
Neptune, all within one degree; Streisand has had outstanding success, winning every award possible in music, stage and the film industry. Portraying the Capricorn MC and nine planets below the hori-

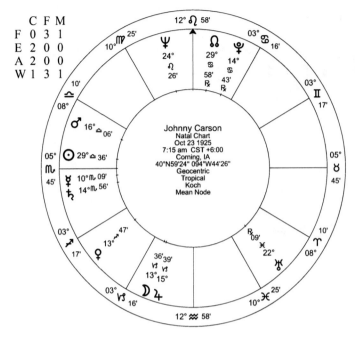

|   | C | F | M |
|---|---|---|---|
| F | 0 | 3 | 1 |
| E | 2 | 0 | 0 |
| A | 2 | 0 | 0 |
| W | 1 | 3 | 1 |

Johnny Carson
Natal Chart
Oct 23 1925
7:15 am CST +6:00
Corning, IA
40°N59'24" 094°W44'26"
Geocentric
Tropical
Koch
Mean Node

*Johnny Carson: Talk Show Host*

*Declinations:* ♅ *3S50;* ♂ *5S38;* ☉ *11S20; A 13S27;* Ψ *13N43;* ♄ *14S20;* ☿ *15S28; M 16N55;* ☊ *20N 9;* ♀ *20N50;* ☽ *21S20;* ♃ *22S54;* ♀ *24S56*

zon along with the second house ruler, Venus, in the twelfth house, Streisand is a perfectionist who is painfully nervous in public performance. Though she occasionally appeared in films, she withdrew from singing for a long period of retirement. Streisand's first concert in 22 years was a Las Vegas smash hit on New Years Eve, December 31, 1993.

## Example Chart of Performance Wealth

We certainly expect TV talk-show host Johnny Carson to have an outstanding Mercury and third house, as well as a ninth house for his media role, and a fifth house for his massive following. Begin with Mercury-Saturn on the ASC in Scorpio, **trine its own dispositor,** Pluto, in the ninth house and square the MC. The third house has Moon-Jupiter in a one degree quincunx with the MC while Jupiter

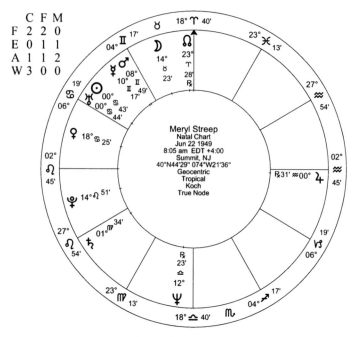

**C F M**
**F 2 2 0**
**E 0 1 1**
**A 1 1 2**
**W 3 0 0**

Meryl Streep
Natal Chart
Jun 22 1949
8:05 am EDT +4:00
Summit, NJ
40°N44'29" 074°W21'36"
Geocentric
Tropical
Koch
True Node

*Meryl Streep: Actress*

*Declinations:* Ψ *3S26;* M *7N19;* ☊ *9N7;* ♄ *12N27;* ☽ *17N52;* ☿ *17N59;*
A *19N33;* ♃ *20S27;* ♂ *21N53;* ♀ *23N27;* ☉ *23N27;* ♅ *23N39;* ♀ *23N41*

rules the second house and co-rules the fifth house. Uranus, posited in
the fifth house is within a two degree quincunx to Neptune in the tenth.

 **Please note how very potent is the reinforcement of connec-
tions that are repeated in various ways, and also, how effective is
the aspect between a planet and its dispositor, or an aspect between a planet that is in the house and the planet that rules the
house.** In Carson's chart, for example, Uranus in the fifth house is
quincunx Neptune (in the tenth house) which rules the fifth house: Jupiter, co-ruler of the fifth house is quincunx the MC.

## Example Chart of Performance Wealth

 To further illustrate the theme of repetitive interaction, we may
note in the chart of award-winning actress Meryl Streep that her fifth

house (audience) Jupiter exhibits a close yod to both of its dispositors, Saturn and Uranus, the rulers of Aquarius. Her third house Neptune (in a powerful Station) is trine, not to its dispositor, but to the ruler of the third house. In the first case, the planet (Jupiter) is given a triple emphasis; in the second case, the house (third) receives a double message of impact.

The indications of outstanding success continue in Streep's chart with the Mars-Mercury conjunction (ruling the MC and the third house) in a grand-trine of Mars to Jupiter (ruler of the fifth house, posited in the sixth house) and Mercury to Neptune in the third house. The second house ruler is exactly conjunct the eighth house ruler in the eleventh house; a business manager would be invaluable for her financial affairs.

## Example Chart of Performance Wealth

**Sports figures** do not have this same pattern since third house personal expression is not an essential factor. Having an audience is important and if they are part of a team, Pluto plays a role; the seventh house indicates the competitor. Sports figures show evidence of more energizing squares than soft aspects and we find Saturn-Mars either in aspect or strongly placed for the discipline of practice and sense of timing as well as physical stamina. In the chart of hockey superstar Wayne Gretzky, who accumulated 62 National Hockey League records by 1994, Mercury is in the first house, ruling the fifth house (and the eighth) and opposite Uranus in the seventh, T-square the MC. Scorpio is on the MC, Pluto is in the seventh house and Mars in the fifth house. Though his chart has a number of squares, Venus in the second house is trine the MC. Gretzky signed a contract with the Los Angeles Kings in 1993 for $8.5 million a year.

## Example Chart of Performance Wealth

Writers are included in this section; they are performers in the sense that they too are driven by the need to express and must have an audience.

Stephen King, whose horror genre writing earned him a four-book contract for $38 million in 1989, has Neptune-Mercury containing the IC, a fourth house Jupiter trine the ASC and Mars in the twelfth

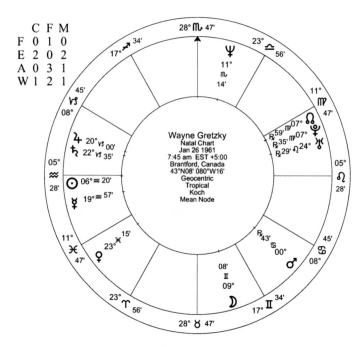

|   | C | F | M |
|---|---|---|---|
| F | 0 | 1 | 0 |
| E | 2 | 0 | 2 |
| A | 0 | 3 | 1 |
| W | 1 | 2 | 1 |

Wayne Gretzky
Natal Chart
Jan 26 1961
7:45 am EST +5:00
Brantford, Canada
43°N08' 080°W16'
Geocentric
Tropical
Koch
Mean Node

*Wayne Gretzky: Hockey Player*
*Declinations: ♀ 2S28; ☊ 9N4; ♆ 13S31; ♅ 14N5; ☿ 16S14; ☽ 16N40;*
*☉ 18S41; A 18S54; M 19S54; ♀ 20N46; ♄ 21S28; ♃ 22S5; ♂ 27N9*

house. The Moon in the fifth house is grand trine to the MC and Pluto in the first house for his mass audience appeal, and the third house Sun-Venus in sextile to Mars-ASC motivate King, along with Mercury, for his drive of expression.

Science fiction master Ray Bradbury once said in a lecture, "If you want to be a writer, write 500 short stories. I guarantee that nobody can write 500 **bad** short stories." His point is well taken; three of the great secrets of reaching success are practice, practice and more practice. Of all *published* writers, five percent make enough money to live on their writing alone. If writing is our goal, we'd best not give up our day job as we write our first 500 short stories or articles.

Stephen King, for example, was down to his last penny in 1973 with the phone service cut off due to nonpayment of the phone bill

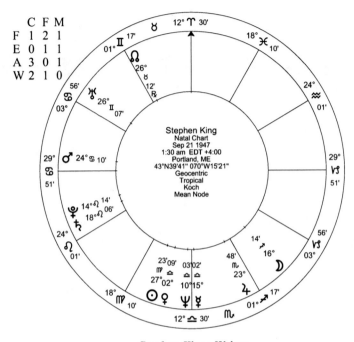

**Stephen King: Writer**

*Declinations: ♀ 0N21; ☉ 1N2; ♆ 2S37; M 4N57; ☿ 6S17; ♄ 16N11;*
*♃ 18S2; ☊ 19N4; A 20N11; ♂ 22N6; ♀ 23N9; ♅ 23N31; ☽ 24S35*

when he received his first book advance of $2,500, for *Carrie*. King's
PR ASC was leaving the conjunction to natal Saturn and applying to
progressed Saturn in the first house. The most remarkable success
stories synchronize with Saturn aspects so often that we can only
draw the conclusion that hard work and personal discipline are highly
productive. King later sold the paperback of *Carrie* for $400,000 as
well as selling the movie rights.

**Note that the more successful the person, the more obviously
the astrological patterns are displayed, graphically repeating indications which are reinforced in a variety of different ways.**

# Chapter 16

# Inherited Wealth

*Work is the curse of the drinking class.*—W.C. Fields
(1879-1946)

IN THE charts of those who inherit wealth there is a remarkable inference: When our parents make their fortune after the time of our birth
there is a different pattern than if they are already wealthy at the time
we were born. *This implies that the natal horoscope portrays conditions at the time of our birth and is subject to change according to the
circumstances of our external environment as well as the way that we
deal with the days of our lives.*

For example, the two sons that Jennifer Jones had with her first
husband, Robert Walker, were born in Queens, New York, before
Jennifer and Robert moved to Hollywood to achieve film success.
Both boys have Sagittarius on the cusp of the eighth house and Jupiter
in the twelfth house, one with a sesquisquare to Neptune and the other
with a quincunx to Neptune. Robert Jr. has the eighth house ruler in
the twelfth conjunct the EQHS fourth ruler: *the water houses did not
connect with the second house until he was 12.* Michael has the eighth
house ruler in the twelfth house with *no connection to the second
house until he was 15.*

Another point must be acknowledged with these charts, as well as
those of people born to royal families and that is, the indications listed
will not be as obvious with Placidus or Koch house systems as those
calculated in Equal House charts. In the prior horoscopes, those of

business wealth and performance wealth, there was less difference between the various house systems than found here, especially in the charts of royalty, as the European locations are further north than the United States and have a greater incident of intercepted signs. They vary so much in EQHS that for many of the examples the difference merits the comment that is included.

The example charts are of people who inherit great wealth. For those of us who are not wealthy but nonetheless have some inheritance there are lesser aspects of the same nature. For example, a woman who inherited money that was equivalent to a third of the price of a modest home put the money immediately into a house purchase. She had a natal sextile of the eighth house ruler to Neptune and at the time of the inheritance had, in the fourth house, the Sun conjunct Mercury, the ruler of the Virgo eighth house. The ruler of the natal Pisces second house is Neptune, which received a trine from the PR MC that year.

**The most commonly seen indications of inherited wealth are:**

1. The second or the eighth house are ruled by Taurus or the dispositor is in Taurus or, Venus or Neptune are posited in the house.

2. To a much lesser degree, the second or eighth houses are ruled by Libra or Sagittarius, or have Jupiter or the Moon placed there. The Moon in the eighth house often refers to family money, but this indicator is not consistently reliable.

3. Neptune is in contact with the eighth house. All nature of aspects are represented between Neptune and the eighth house planet or ruler, but the hard aspects show difficulties with the inheritance, either in obtaining it or how it is handled, or the estate becomes an issue of ensuing distress.

4. The water houses are connected with the second house. This is not customarily by interpositions (as with the entrepreneurs) but with aspects.

## Example Chart of Inherited Wealth

In Christina Onassis' horoscope, Venus is in the eighth house. The chart is in Koch; EQHS gives a ninth house cusp of 25 Capricorn,

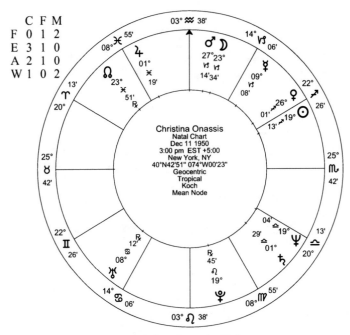

*Christina Onassis: Heiress*

*Declinations:* ♄ *1N24;* ☊ *2S22;* ♆ *5S60;* ♃ *12S2; A 19N13; M 19S20;*
♂ *21S57;* ♀ *22N60;* ☉ *23S0;* ♅ *23N31;* ♀ *23S52;* ☿ *25S18;* ☽ *25S40*

adding the Moon to the eighth house, square Neptune. Onassis' great
wealth, inherited from her father, Aristotle Onassis, put her in a position where she had to be cloistered, or protected, (Moon square Neptune) due to the threat of kidnaping and the invasion of her privacy by
the press. She was known for her sensitivity to the possibility of fortune hunters. *(Does he love me for myself or my money?)*

For the connection of earth and water houses, the second house
ruler (Mercury by either house system) is in the eighth house. Venus,
in the eighth, rules the sixth and is conjunct the Sun, ruler of the
fourth. (By EQHS, the Moon is in the eighth house conjunct Mars,
which rules the twelfth.) Incidentally, note that the MC is Aquarius
and Uranus is in the second house; her reputation was associated with
her money.

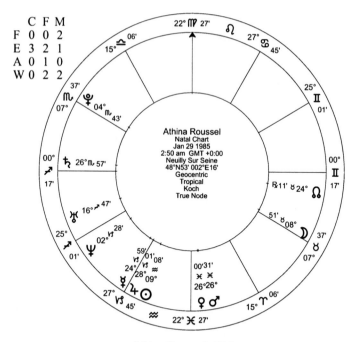

**C F M**
F 0 0 2
E 3 2 1
A 0 1 0
W 0 2 2

Athina Roussel
Natal Chart
Jan 29 1985
2:50 am GMT +0:00
Neuilly Sur Seine
48°N53' 002°E16'
Geocentric
Tropical
Koch
True Node

***Athina Roussel: Heiress***

*Declinations:* ♀ 0S50; ♂ 1S52; ☿ 2N46; M 2N60; ☽ 13N10; ♄ 17S24;
☉ 17S58; ☊ 18N49; A 20S13; ♃ 20S51; ♆ 22S18; ☿ 22S31; ♅ 22S47

## Example Chart of Inherited Wealth

Athina Roussel, daughter of Christina Onassis and her husband,
Thierry Roussel, inherits fortunes from both her mother and father,
making her possibly the richest little girl ever born. (Note that EQHS
adds Jupiter to the second house along with Neptune and Mercury,
with the eighth house ruler (Moon in Taurus), opposite the twelfth
house planet (Pluto) and trine the fourth house ruler (Neptune in the
second house), coordinating all the water houses effectively with the
second house.) The requisites are met equally well with Koch, with
eighth house ruler, Mercury, in the second house sextile the twelfth
house co-ruler, Mars in the fourth house. The MC is Virgo: Mercury
is in the second with either system. Her reputation, just as that of her
mother, is connected with her money and how she handles it.

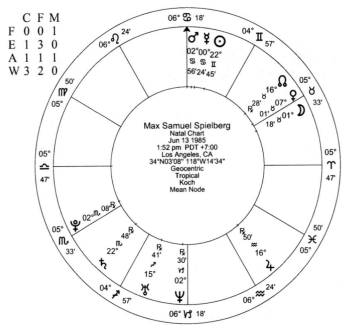

|   | C | F | M |
|---|---|---|---|
| F | 0 | 0 | 1 |
| E | 1 | 3 | 0 |
| A | 1 | 1 | 1 |
| W | 3 | 2 | 0 |

Max Samuel Spielberg
Natal Chart
Jun 13 1985
1:52 pm PDT +7:00
Los Angeles, CA
34°N03'08" 118°W14'34"
Geocentric
Tropical
Koch
Mean Node

*Max Samuel Spielberg: Heir*

*Declinations: A 2S18; ♀ 3N50; ☽ 10N31; ♀ 11N19; ♄ 16S14; ♃ 16S27;*
*☊ 17N9; ♆ 22S15; ♅ 22S42; ☉ 23N15; M 23N17; ♂ 24N17; ☿ 25N2*

## Example Chart of Inherited Wealth

Max Samuel Spielberg is the son of movie tycoon Steven Spielberg and actress Amy Irving. His parents married November 27, 1985, and separated in 1989, with a settlement of $100 million for Irving. Max has Taurus on the eighth cusp with Venus posited in Taurus making a trine to Neptune. The fourth house ruler is Saturn in the second house. The ruler of the second house is Pluto trine Mercury (ruler of the twelfth house) and opposite Venus in the eighth house. Note the MC in Cancer and the Moon in Taurus conjunct the eighth house Venus, representing family money.

The charts of those born to royalty present more variables. There are people born to the noble houses who have quiet and conservative lives, comfortably living in the genteel circumstances which reflect "old money." These people have mild indicators of wealth such as the placements listed above for inheritance, but without all the factors included. They may, for example, have Moon trine Jupiter and Venus ruling the second or eighth houses, but with no Neptune aspect to the eighth house, or there is no connection between the second house and the water houses.

Historically, some royal figures have lives embroiled in wars and disputes, others are known for profligate extravagance, and there are those who attempt to live normal lives in spite of being born to an inflexible situation. This is not a job from which one can very easily resign, and in this sense, royal figures have less freedom and certainly less privacy than the average citizen. The ninth house often makes strong statements, such as interposition with the first house, fourth house or MC for those who are involved in public affairs that require rituals with pomp-and-circumstance.

Oppositions between the ruler of the MC and the ruler of the ASC occur when we are doing that which we must, fulfilling a duty that comes with the territory and which cannot be avoided. Other planets in opposition to the MC may imply that we find it necessary to make a difficult choice. For example, the Duke of Windsor shocked the world when, after ruling as Edward VIII for less than a year, he abdicated "to marry the woman I love." His Venus at 23 Taurus opposes the MC at 2 Sagittarius.

The twelfth house tends to stand out when there is no necessity to go into paid-hire, and it is common in these situations to see trines from the twelfth house planet or ruler to the second, fourth or eighth houses. In the charts of the wealthy, the sixth house is kept very busy with planning and executing the maintenance of an estate with administrative skill, as well as keeping up social obligations and correspondence. Shopping and decorating is time consuming, as is the care and maintenance of the body with manicures, hair styling, health workouts, massage, getting the perfect tan and shopping for a wardrobe that is appropriate for public functions as well as for the country club.

However, there are people born to the purple who rule their country with great power and influence, interacting with their ministers in much the same way that an industrialist manages the manipulation of

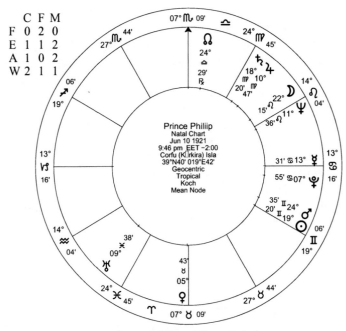

| | C | F | M |
|---|---|---|---|
| F | 0 | 2 | 0 |
| E | 1 | 1 | 2 |
| A | 1 | 0 | 2 |
| W | 2 | 1 | 1 |

Prince Phiilp
Natal Chart
Jun 10 1921
9:46 pm EET −2:00
Corfu (Klirkira) Isla
39°N40' 019°E42'
Geocentric
Tropical
Koch
Mean Node

***Prince Philip of Great Britain***

***Declinations:*** *♄ 6N38; ♃ 8N40; ♅ 8S41; ☽ 9N46; ☊ 9S56; ♀ 11N1;*
*M 13S55; ♆ 17N22; ☿ 19N57; A 22S47; ☉ 23N1; ☿ 24N2; ♂ 24N3*

great wealth. In these charts the patterns will be similar to those of
Business Wealth. In the chart of Queen Elizabeth II (Koch houses) the
connections of the second house to the water houses are illustrated by
Saturn (second house ruler) square Jupiter (twelfth house ruler), Venus (ruler of the fourth house) posited in the second house and the Sun
(ruler of the eighth house) semisextile Mercury in the second house.
By EQHS, Jupiter (the ruler of the twelfth house) is posited in the second house conjunct Mars (ruler of the fourth house) opposite Neptune
(in the eighth house), a rather more graphic portrayal. The eighth
house rule is the Sun, posited in the fourth house.

## Example Chart of Royalty

The chart of Prince Philip shows appropriate patterns for an example of royalty. The MC is Scorpio with both rulers in the sixth house,

suggesting that his public role, though powerful, is nonetheless a subordinate position as consort to Queen Elizabeth II. The EQHS tenth cusp is Libra with Venus in Taurus, indicating a life path of peacemaker and balancing factor to stabilize his home and family, easy-going and affectionate. Venus rules the fourth house by Koch; by EQHS it is posited in the fourth house trine Jupiter in the eighth house. Jupiter rules the twelfth house and is conjunct Saturn, co-ruler of the second house, coordinating the second house with all the water houses. As Prince Philip made an influential and wealthy marriage, we see the ruler of the seventh house (Moon) in the eighth with either house system. By EQHS, Saturn in Virgo is in the ninth, indicating the duty (and boredom) of long detailed public functions of state. The ninth house ruler. Mercury, is in the seventh house; these functions are due to the position that resulted from his marriage.

In the charts of those who "marry money" there is an obvious connection between the seventh house to the second and/or eighth houses. For example, Joan Kennedy, the former wife of Senator Edward Kennedy, has Pisces on the seventh cusp and Aries on the eighth cusp; Mars is conjunct Jupiter in the third house; Jupiter is one degree sextile to Venus, ruling the second house. Ethel Kennedy has Virgo on the seventh cusp and Libra on the eighth cusp; Venus is conjunct Mercury in the first house and both planets had moved into the second house when she married Robert Kennedy.

## Example Chart of a Wealthy Marriage

Kathy Ford became an heiress on September 29, 1987 upon the date of death of her husband, Henry Ford II. As a young woman, she was married and pregnant at 15. Her first husband was killed in a car crash December 12, 1959, leaving her with two babies. With Mars-Saturn on the IC she was down but not defeated; she became a top model, glamorous and fashionable. She met Henry Ford in 1970, and they became lovers for a 10-year affair before they married October 14, 1980. Natally the ruler of the eighth house is the Sun, posited in the second house. The PR Sun had just completed the trine to Pluto in the seventh house at the time of the marriage.

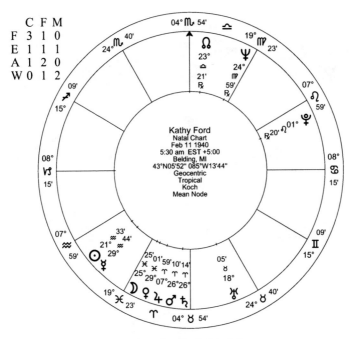

**Kathy Ford: Model**

*Declinations:* ☽ *0N14;* ♀ *1S4;* ♃ *2N7;* ♆ *3N8;* ♄ *7N56;* ☊ *8S25;*
♂ *10N29;* ☿ *13S3; M 13S10;* ☉ *14S19;* ♅ *16N56; A 23S11;* ♀ *23N38*

# Chapter 17

# Lottery Winners

*How little you know about the age you live in if you think that honey is sweeter than cash in hand.*—Ovid (43? B.C.-A.D. 18)

ONE WEEKEND Carol and Ron and two other couples pooled their cash and bought 300 one-dollar lottery tickets. On Sunday afternoon they lit the barbecue fire, opened the first bottle of wine and began to scratch the surface of the 300 tickets to look for cash prizes. It was one of those wonderful balmy days with friends and laughter, good company, good food and cheer . . . but no big bucks in spite of the fact that Scratchers offer the best overall odds of any of California's five lottery games. There were enough small bill winners to recoup about a third of their money.

The lottery is big business. Since the California lottery began in 1985, sales have totaled $16.1 billion (as of October, 1993) with a total number of 925 people winning a million dollars or more. Out of every lottery dollar, 50 cents goes to the winners, 34 cents to public education, 6½ cents to retailer commissions, 3½ cents to game costs and 6 cents to operating expenses.

The earliest government-sponsored lotteries were organized in France in 1520. In 1680, England held an historic lottery to raise funds for improving London's water supply equipment. Spain developed the "el gordo" game and Ireland, the sweepstakes. Though private lotteries were popular in the United States, it was not until 1963 that the government began to sponsor lotteries. It was then that New Hampshire authorized a sweepstakes lottery and designated a portion of the profits to its educational system. The games proved so popular that by the end of the 1980s more than half of the states had approved lotteries.

Odds of winning vary for the different games. In California, for example, the "Daily 3" pays up to as much as $500 for three winning numbers; the odds are 1 in 1,000. "Deco" pays off on winning cards that are drawn six days a week; the odds are 1 in 28,561. "Fantasy Five" requires the selection of five winning numbers for drawings that are held three days a week, with various winning amounts that can go over $100,000; the odds of choosing all five of five winning numbers is 1 in 575,757.

The California lottery game which builds up gigantic jackpots is "Super Lotto" as it is held over for the next bi-weekly drawing when no one has picked all six winning numbers. This is the game that pays off in the millions. The odds of winning all six of the six winning numbers are 1 in 18,009,460. Why bother to play in a contest against odds of 18 million? Because of the 925 people who have already won. *(Why not me? I might be the one to hear those magical words, "You will receive a check for $125,000 a year for the next 20 years!")*

In a study of the charts of Lucky Winners, the patterns are similar whether the gamble is in a state lottery, keno, poker, a slot machine, a sports pool or a game show. It is the **amount** that makes the difference: does it change our life, from one day to the next, suddenly and forever to win an obscene amount of money? In theory, winning a million dollars would not show an appreciable difference, astrologically, in the chart of a multi-millionaire, as it would not make a marked change in their lives as they were at the time.

The *Big Win* is the amount of money, *in comparison* to what is customary for us that is sufficient to make a sweeping change in our life style. For the sake of number crunching in this study, we may call a half-million dollars the minimum consideration. The following patterns are those which are observed to be most obvious and consistent:

1. The Moon in a trine or grand trine (which in half of the examples involved Venus or Jupiter). In those few cases where the Moon

does not have a trine in the natal chart, it is necessary by progression at the time of the Big Win.

2. Natal Jupiter in at least one trine.

3. Natal Jupiter in aspect to Neptune. This does not have to be one of "the big four"; it is often one of the lesser aspects, such as a semisextile or semisquare.

4. Natal Mars in aspect to Jupiter or Neptune.

5. Natal or progressed Venus or Jupiter in aspect to Uranus (one degree for progressed aspects)

6. Natal or progressed Venus or Jupiter retrograde.

7. Natal Pluto conjunct or opposite the ruler of the second house within four to five degrees, or in some other aspect to the ruler of the second house within one or two degrees, or in progressed aspect within one degree.

8. A close natal sesquisquare between two planets within one degree to show the potential for a sudden change of direction in the life, or a progressed sesquisquare between two planets, one degree. (This sesquisquare most frequently involves the MC, Moon, Venus, Jupiter or Pluto.)

9. Natal or progressed interpositions or close aspects between the twelfth house to the second and/or eighth houses.

10. Transit Uranus in an aspect up to two or three degrees to the natal or progressed MC or the natal or progressed ASC. (The reason that we find a valid Uranus transit within several degrees is because Uranus will go back and forth over an aspect three times during its change of station: the aspect is valid from the first one-degree application until the last one-degree separation.)

To be a big-time winner, we do not have to have all 10 of the indicators but we do need at least six or seven. **The greater quantity of lucky indicators and the more obvious they are in the chart, the greater the chances are of winning a fortune.**

A lesser winner, for example, is Hugh Jeffcoat. He was interested in astrology as a tool to aid gambling. On July 29, 1981, in Reno, Nevada, he won $10,322 for an investment of $39 in Keno. The win was at 9:54 p.m. PDT; he was paid the money at 10:30 p.m. PDT. He has natal Moon trine Mercury, natal Jupiter trine the Sun, a semisextile between Jupiter-Neptune and Mars sesquisquare Jupiter, PR Uranus is conjunct Venus and transit Uranus is trine the PR MC within three degrees.

Mimi Levine won an all-expense-paid trip to England to the British Astrological Conference in York. She bought her ticket on June 26, 1983, 1:53 p.m. EDT, New York, New York and was notified the following Saturday afternoon. She has no trine with her natal or progressed Moon, natal Jupiter is trine Pluto, there is no Neptune-Jupiter contacts but natal Mars is square Jupiter and PR Venus is square Uranus. TR Uranus was two degrees from the PR ASC when she was informed that she was a winner.

## Example Chart of a Lottery Winner

Fred Drago was a law enforcement officer for 28 years. On April 30, 1982, he went into McDonald's fast-food restaurant for lunch where he was handed a game ticket with his hamburger at 3:30 p.m. CDT, 88W07, 30N41. The ticket was a winner of $500,000.

Drago has the Moon trine Venus and yod Jupiter-Uranus. Jupiter does not have a trine, nor is PR Jupiter in aspect; we may assume that Drago did not go on a big-time spending spree. There is no contact between Jupiter and Neptune or between Mars to Jupiter or Neptune. Venus is square Uranus, PR Venus is quincunx Uranus. There are no Venus or Jupiter retrogrades. Pluto is in a wide sextile to the second house Mars while the second house ruler, Mercury, is in a one degree square to PR Pluto. The natal sesquisquare of Mercury to Uranus is greater than our one degree orb limit. The Sun had progressed from the twelfth house into the second house. TR Uranus was two degrees applying by retrograde motion to quincunx the PR MC and sextile PR ASC. In all, Drago had six of the requisite indicators of lucky money.

## Example Chart of a Lottery Winner

Compare the prior chart with that of Kenneth Greene, who won $13 million. Greene was a disabled truck driver who had not worked in three years. His wife, Joanne, was holding two jobs to support the family, and they were at rock bottom in their financial struggle. Jo-

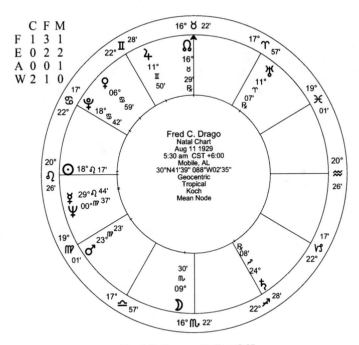

|   | C | F | M |
|---|---|---|---|
| F | 1 | 3 | 1 |
| E | 0 | 2 | 2 |
| A | 0 | 0 | 1 |
| W | 2 | 1 | 0 |

*Fred C. Drago: Police Officer*

*Declinations: ♂ 3N18; ♅ 3N44; ♆ 11N48; ☿ 12N58; ☽ 14S6; A 14N41;*
*☉ 15N21; M 16N44; ☊ 16N48; ♃ 21N27; ♀ 21N33; ♇ 21N45; ♄ 22S14*

anne's parents were not able to help as they were about to lose their home of the past 30 years for non-payment of the mortgage.

When Greene bought a lottery ticket on November 25, 1992, the clerk (in error!) sold him a ticket for Megabucks instead of the lesser-winning Massachusetts Mass Cash ticket. Megabucks had not had a winner for seven weeks and the prize money had accumulated up to $13 million. On December 21, Greene was cleaning out his wallet of old tickets when he checked the numbers on the one he had bought a month before. It had all the winning numbers.

When Greene and his wife went to the lottery headquarters the next day, they were given a first payment of $6.5 million. Joanne was laughing and crying; she nearly passed out twice. The family, including Misty, 15, and Ken Jr., 3, could anticipate a Christmas to surpass

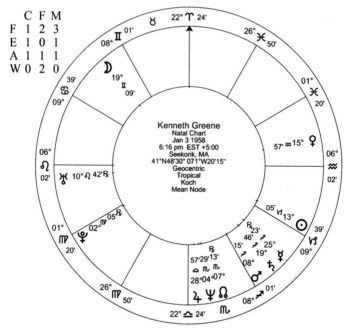

*Kenneth Greene: Truck Driver*

*Declinations: M 8N44; ♃ 9S56; ♆ 11S23; ☊ 14S20; ♀ 14S40; ♅ 18N12;
A 18N46; ☽ 19N44; ☿ 20S16; ♀ 21N36; ♂ 21S39; ♄ 21S43; ☉ 22S48*

their wildest dreams.

1&2. Greene has the Moon trine Venus four degrees, trine Jupiter nine degrees.

3. Jupiter is conjunct Neptune.

4. Mars is semisextile Neptune.

5. Venus is opposite Uranus.

6. PR Venus is retrograde.

7. PR ASC is conjunct Pluto (second house by Koch; first by EQHS).

8. Mars is sesquisquare the MC by one degree, and PR MC is sesquisquare the Sun.

9. There is no interposition between the twelfth house and the sec-

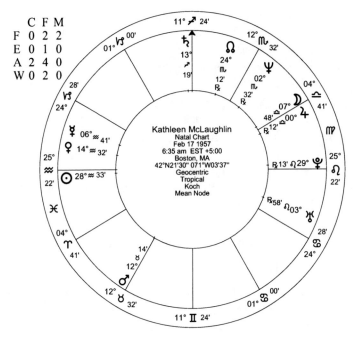

**Kathleen McLaughlin: Bank Employee**

*Declinations:* ♃ 1N17; ☽ 6S24; ♆ 10S42; ☉ 11S59; A 13S4; ♂ 16N27; ♀ 17S23; ☋ 18S42; ☿ 19S47; ♅ 19N53; ♄ 20S41; M 22S9; ♇ 22N24

ond or eighth houses (However, the ruler of the twelfth house, the Moon, is opposite the ruler of the second house, Mercury, by six degrees).

10. Transit Uranus at 15 Capricorn is sesquisquare PR ASC-Pluto. Nine of the 10 indicators are present by EQHS, 10 by Koch.

## Example Chart of a Lottery Winner

Kathleen McLaughlin was a Customer Service Representative for a Shawmut, MA, Bank. She had never played the lottery before, and she picked numbers that were a combination of her birthday and age and her husband's birthday and age. She won the $27 million Massive Million Jackpot December 13, 1991.

1&2. McLaughlin has Moon-Jupiter trine Mercury.

3. Jupiter is semisextile Neptune.

4. Mars is in a wide opposition to Neptune, within nine degrees, and sesquisquare Jupiter by three degrees.

5. Jupiter is sextile Uranus.

6. Jupiter is retrograde.

7. Pluto is semisextile Jupiter, ruler of the second house by EQHS (with no aspect to the second house with the Koch house system)

8. The Moon is sesquisquare the ASC, PR MC is sesquisquare Pluto.

9. Mercury in the twelfth house is trine the Moon in the eighth house by two degrees and the PR Mercury in the second house is opposite the Moon, one degree.

10. Transit Uranus is conjunct the PR MC.

Ten of the ten indicators are present by EQHS, nine by Koch.

## Example Chart of the Mate of a Lottery Winner

What of the families of the Lucky Winner? James McLaughlin is Kathleen's husband, a self-employed carpenter who planned to continue his business after his wife won $27 million December 13, 1991. Their first goals were to buy a new car and set up educational accounts for their children, Jennifer and Tom.

1&2. McLaughlin has Moon-Mars in a grand trine to Saturn-Venus and MC-Uranus-Jupiter.

3. Jupiter is square Neptune.

4. Mars is trine Jupiter.

5. Venus is trine Uranus.

6. Jupiter is retrograde.

7. PR Pluto is in a one-degree square to the second house Venus.

8. The Sun-Mercury is sesquisquare Pluto and the PR MC is sesquisquare PR Mars.

9. The eighth house ruler, Venus, is in the second house semisquare Mercury, ruler of the twelfth house, and the two planets are separating from a PR square.

10. Transit Uranus at 12 Capricorn is three degrees from sesquisquare the PR MC. McLaughlin not only has all 10 indicators,

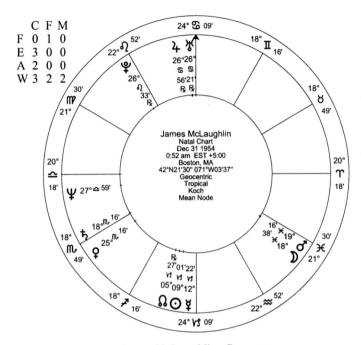

*James McLaughlin: Carpenter*

*Declinations: ☽ 0N10; ♂ 4S50; A 7S56; ♆ 9S11; ♄ 15S10; ♀ 15S18;*
*♃ 21N9; M 21N17; ♅ 21N25; ♀ 22N24; ☉ 23S8; ☊ 23S20; ☿ 24S48*

but Mars, ruling his seventh house, has five trines, one of which is to
Venus, ruler of his eighth house, posited in the second house.

# Section 4

## Success

# Chapter 18

# The Midheaven

*The two hardest things to handle in life are failure and success.*—Anon.

SUCCESS IS **the attainment of a designated goal or purpose. The first requisite is definition.** When we say, "I want to go to Hawaii," that is a wish. When we say "I want to go to Hawaii," and put the first dollar into a piggy-bank for that purpose, we have taken the initial step to a successful goal. When we say "I want to go to Hawaii on my next birthday, I shall stay at the Honolulu Hilton, it will take this amount of money which I shall make by doing this nature and amount of work and put aside at this rate," we are on our way to white beaches and flower leis.

A vague definition such as "I want to be a movie star," or "I want to be rich," are wishes. A clearly defined goal *which is realistically accessible* within a specific time window is the most appropriate method to attain a desired outcome. If, for example, championship chess is our goal, we must learn the rules, be able to concentrate, and spend the time and energy necessary to perfect our game. In the same way, success means learning the rules of the game and putting in the time and effort necessary to reach the winner's circle. Natural ability is a great help but not the prime requisite. **Perseverance, self-motivation, self-discipline and focus are the secrets of winning.**

Astrologically, success is symbolized by the MC, the top point of the angle that bisects a horoscope vertically, the southernmost point.

Public figures tend to have the ruler of the MC above the horizon somewhat more than below the horizon, with the eleventh house well represented. The fourth house also stands out in close dialogue with the MC/tenth house, indicating that we are "at home" with our reputation, that we have found our own niche.

The term *Midheaven* comes from the Latin, Medium Coeli, meaning middle of the sky, and in time is designated by 12:00 noon. This point signifies the ultimate elevation, the epitome of personal ambitions, our public persona rather than our character or private temperament. It illustrates our reputation, status or public standing.

The horoscopes of public figures are easier to delineate than those of average citizens, for three reasons. One, their charts repeat a theme in a number of ways. Two, their charts as a whole coordinate with the MC, and three, they are using fully all the tools at their command. The more contradictions in the chart, the more that the overview is in conflict with the MC, the more that we are reluctant to work with the MC, the less apt we are to achieve success in mundane terms.

An analysis of Chapter 2, "Overview", is an essential preliminary to the question of success. Then, building upon the foundation shown by the overview, consider how we are going to work with the tools designated by the MC. Does our chart elements and qualities, our Sun, Moon and ASC synchronize with our MC requisites? Consider all aspects to the MC as messages that reach a public broadcasting station; are these messages coordinate or contradictory to ourselves as we are portrayed in the overview, and do they compliment the MC?

**Success is shown in a chart by the extent to which we assume the role symbolized by the MC voluntarily and constructively.** *The extent of the contradiction between the MC and our basic nature shows the extent of distress or inability to function in a successful societal role.*

For example, consider a situation where we might have a fixed Sun and Moon and an abundance of fixed signs, with the MC in a cardinal sign. This shows a contradiction between our nature and the *conduct necessary to achieve status and recognition*. Consider, for example, that we have a gentle character (soft planets and easy aspects) along with a pragmatic MC and planets in the tenth house making stressful aspects. The requisites of the hard MC/tenth house would be overwhelmingly difficult for our aesthetic nature. Conversely, when we have a strong, pragmatic character, we would have difficulty achieving success through adequately expressing a gentle, passive MC/tenth house (soft planets and easy aspects). Success requires a first priority of coordination between the tenth house and the rest of the chart.

**As we analyze the qualities requisite to mundane success, another dimension is implicit and that is, being a winner or a loser in this game of life involves more than being rich and famous. The greatest success of which we are capable is that which demonstrates a quality of spirit. Though we may indeed achieve all our mundane goals, we fail in the deepest sense of our humanity when we demonstrate the MC symbology in negative discord or antisocietal actions.**

To evaluate the MC, first delineate the MC sign, then the planet that rules the MC sign, then the sign in which the ruler is posited. If planets in the tenth house are in another sign than that of the MC, consider the symbology of that sign as well, and its dispositor (first dispositor only). In signs that have dual rulership, look at the sign position of both rulers. For Scorpio, the sign that Pluto is in describes our generational identification and cultural patterns and the sign that Mars is in implies our personal energy level of self-assertion, construction or destruction. For Aquarius, Uranus signifies our peer identification or isolation, and Saturn testifies to our personal level of maturity. For Pisces, Neptune suggests the social and ethical ideals of our era, and Jupiter our personal growth patterns.

Evaluate planets in the tenth house and elevated planets which conjunct the tenth house from the ninth house. Any planet within 15-20 degrees on either side of the MC is strongly influential. The farther the planets are from the MC, the more the influence drops off insofar as judging career and success; there is no hard line of demarcation but a gradual decrease of intensity. The most elevated planet, even in the eighth or eleventh house, is more obvious by dint of being "in the light" as compared to planets below the horizon.

All vocational fields are represented by each of the 12 signs on the

MC; however, career selection through astrology begins with the requisites of the MC sign and planets and is then defined to more specific vocational areas by the second house of livelihood (Chapter 12, "Vocational Indicators.") We are noted as well for other qualities and matters as shown by other planets and houses that aspect the MC.

The more tenanted and more complicated the MC, the more visible we are, being seen *as our public image.* In these cases, that which is in view on the surface is not always what we get in private. People still have full and detailed personal lives, which we often find surprising when scandal explodes around our public idols. Several planets in the tenth house illustrate the point that a reputation is established on a variety of levels for different reasons.

Those of us with many planets in the tenth house are not at all ostentatious; however, we are not generally people who are approachable on a level of familiarity. Our self-contained poise does not encourage intimacy; there is a certain dignity, an assurance that respect is our natural due. We are attracted to positions of authority through our own abilities that are supplemented by assistance from influential family, alliances and friends. We often work in public fields with large concerns and civic issues, such as government and industry, and all fields that are marked by pragmatic areas of expertise rather than aesthetic or artistic areas. Even when less-well-known (private rather than public figures), in subordinate rather than leadership careers, we show an awareness of our dignity and stature.

A cardinal stellium in the tenth implies that we keep moving up, improving with age and experience. The fixed stellium indicates that a longer apprenticeship is needed in order to attain and hold our position, and the mutable stellium testifies to our flexibility, with career changes when progress is blocked.

With the inclusion of EQHS, the tenth house cusp and its ruler is a description of our life path that is more personal than the public image exhibited by the MC. (Aspects to the tenth cusp are not noted, as all the cusps are the same degree as the ASC in EQHS).

# Signs on the MC and Planets
# Posited or Conjunct the MC

## Aries on the MC

With Aries on the MC, we have enthusiastic zeal for a career in which we can initiate self-assertive action to win or accomplish a goal. To achieve our maximum success, we compete with open challenge and daring. We act to gain constructive results and take shrewd commercial initiative. We fail to succeed when we avoid constructive action but complain that we are being acted upon. With rash or violent anti-societal acts we antagonize or hurt others. We make impulsive commercial moves without listening to advice. When we recklessly sail into the fray without proper precautions, we are subject to danger.

The career fields we choose are highly competitive either in mundane terms of fiscal achievement or in competitions such as sports, games or politics. There may be physical activity and dexterity shown in our vocation, avocation or lifestyle, such as dance, physical culture, sexual conquest, playing a musical instrument or manual labor. Dangerous employment choices may include such activities as driving a taxi cab, working in a liquor store or as a hotel night clerk. We often conquer obstacles through pitting our skills against odds.

We manage to score a high incident of crime or danger, trouble with the law, government or authority with an Aries MC. The examples include drug-crazed killer Tex Watson, a member of the Manson gang, as well as one of his victims, Sharon Tate, and politician George Wallace who was paralyzed by an assassin's bullet. Actress and burlesque dancer Liz Renay spent a year in jail due to her connection with gangster Bugsy Siegal, and priest-activist Philip Berrigan went to jail as a political demonstrator. Joan of Arc headed an army and was captured and burned at the stake, where General Norman Schwarzkop led the Desert Storm offensive January 17, 1991. Hollywood director Sam Peckinpah was a great success making films that focused on violence.

To evaluate the capacity of success of an Aires MC, consider all planets in the tenth house, the sign where Mars is posited and the aspects of both the MC and its ruler, Mars. Life is not one dimensional and no one factor in the chart tells a complete story. In the prior mentioned charts, Tex Watson has Mars in Leo on the Ascendant with Pluto; he went to prison. Sharon Tate had Mars in Sagittarius in the 6th house square Neptune. She was an actress. (At the time of her murder progressed Ascendant was sesquisquare Mars and progressed Mars was opposite Jupiter in the twelfth house.) The other examples continue to exemplify the theme.

The position is certainly not always traumatic. Other people with an Aries MC are personable and popular. Maurice Chevalier had Mars in the fourth house conjunct Jupiter in Sagittarius; he was a dancer before gaining recognition as an effervescent and charming actor and, to mirror Mars opposite Pluto, became internationally known. He was also a shrewd investor in real estate (fourth house).

Prince Andrew of England, with Mars in the sixth house conjunct Venus, gained the nickname in the tabloids of "Randy Andy." He further satisfies the Mars directive with his career in the Air Force. His elder brother, Prince Charles, on the other hand, has Mars in the fifth house conjunct Jupiter and opposite Uranus (ruling his Aquarius seventh house); his public image has been subject to bad press focused on his marriage. (In this example, Charles' chart illustrates that the first priority of delineation is the planet posited: his Moon in the tenth house portrays a reputation that waxes and wanes.) Actor Eddie Albert has Mars in Gemini in the eleventh house conjunct Venus; he is a vocal and impassioned environmentalist. (He also has Sun in the tenth house in unassuming Taurus, and has had great career longevity and popularity).

When we have an Aries MC with Mars posited or conjunct the MC, we tend to direct our action toward achieving competitive results such as Olympic gymnast Mitch Gaylord. We display rash daring, as Jean Genet related in his autobiography, *A Thief's Journal*, or we are known for trauma such as astrologer Marcia Moore who disappeared; her skull was found several years later. An Aries MC shows the need for combat, challenge or accomplishment which adds excitement to our lives.

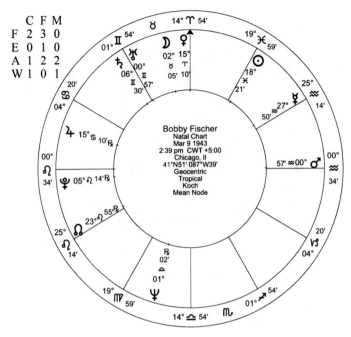

***Bobby Fischer: Chessmaster***

*Declinations:* ♆ *0N52;* ☉ *4S36;* ♀ *5N23; M 5N52;* ☽ *7N40;* ☊ *13N16;*
*☿ 14S7;* ♄ *19N50; A 20N2;* ♅ *20N14;* ♂ *20S51;* ♃ *22N57;* ♀ *23N59*

## Example Chart of an Aries MC

Bobby Fischer won his first chess championship at age 14; by his Saturn return he became the World Chess Champion when he defeated Russia's Boris Spassky in a contest that concluded August 13, 1972. Fischer exemplifies both the positive and negative connotations of an Aries MC. He initiated self-assertive action in his challenge to win: Mars is in Aquarius in a grand air trine to Neptune and to both of its dispositors, elevated Saturn and Uranus. The MC ruler, Mars, exactly on the seventh house cusp, also signifies the opponent, the adversary. It is opposite the ASC and Pluto, T-square the Moon; Fischer is convinced that he is being singled out as a minority (Pluto in the first house) in danger; he once had his dental fillings removed to prevent the KGB from transmitting messages through them. (Paranoia itself may be more adequately described by his third house Neptune yod to Mercury-Moon.)

Venus in the tenth house exemplified a non-competitive position; for many years the chess world regarded Fischer as no longer a challenger in the game. Whenever he surfaced, the elevated Moon once more stirred up the gossip that he was boorish and offensive with legendary temperament and eccentricity (Moon T-square Mars and Pluto). Neptune sextile to the ASC and grand-trine to Mars and Uranus (all within one degree for many years) contributed to his long retirement as well as to his growing isolation from reality.

After a 20-year self-imposed exile from chess, Fischer played his old opponent again on September 2, 1992 on the island of Svetistefan, Yugoslavia. When he accepted the challenge, the PR ASC was opposite PR Mars, second to eighth houses; he needed the money. When the match began TR Mars-Jupiter were on the IC; they progressed to T-square Mars-ASC as Fischer took an adversarial position to most of the world, railing against Jews, the U.S. government and the news media. TR Mars opposed the Moon in November when he won $3.35 million for the 10-game match.

## Mars in the Tenth House

With this position, we are noted for being go-getters who put energy into a personal goal or creation, with a drive for accomplishment and to gain and produce pragmatic results. We often have an impact on our environment as we keep pushing forward for constructive aims.

Our path is not smooth as there are rough periods of frustration or even trauma; we may reach the top championship but very few of us keep it beyond a certain time span or specific period of award. The intense competitive stress of Mars pressure at the career peak is difficult to maintain in a smooth and constructive application of energy. Most of us have periods of greater or lesser lengths of time when we maintain our winner's status, but we can't keep up the high pressure focus indefinitely. When we are sports figures, we are outstanding during our season of acclaim, as shown by Olympic figure skater Nancy Kerrigan. In our jobs, with Mars in the tenth house, we dominate when we are in command or we may work in a field that requires a de-

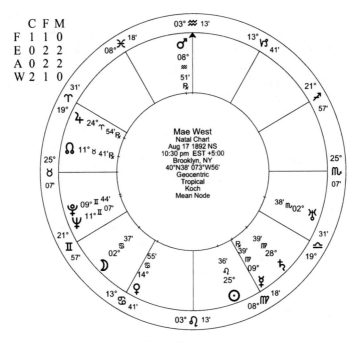

|   | C | F | M |
|---|---|---|---|
| F | 1 | 1 | 0 |
| E | 0 | 2 | 2 |
| A | 0 | 2 | 2 |
| W | 2 | 1 | 0 |

Mae West
Natal Chart
Aug 17 1892 NS
10:30 pm EST +5:00
Brooklyn, NY
40°N38' 073°W56'
Geocentric
Tropical
Koch
Mean Node

*Mae West: Actress*

*Declinations: ♄ 2N30; ☿ 3N41; ♃ 8N16; ♀ 10N49; ♅ 11S57; ☉ 12N60; ☋ 15N15; ♀ 17N22; A 19N3; M 19S27; ♆ 20N35; ♂ 24S27; ☽ 27N22*

gree of manual labor or physical activity. Entertainers such as Elvis Presley and Jimi Hendrix exemplified the raw sexuality, passion and devil-may-care recklessness that can lead to a traumatic downfall.

## Example Chart of Mars in the Tenth House

Mae West is legendary for her insouciant wit and insinuation, drawling such lines as "Are ya glad to see me or is that a gun in your pocket?" Much of her success came from playing on her reputation (tenth house) of liberated and unconventional (Aquarius) sexuality (Mars). She never actually disrobed or used profanity in her fifteen plays and eleven movies from the 1930s to the 1970s; if she were in today's films we might speculate a different scenario. Her reputation extended into her private life as she was known for having muscular young men as companion (Mars co-rules the seventh house).

With the MC square its ruler, Uranus, in the sixth house, West was confined by type-casting. She could only play the certain type of role that was uniquely hers. The MC is quincunx the Moon in the second house; her income fluctuated widely with inconsistent bursts of activity and Mars in the tenth house repeats the theme with a quincunx to Mercury (ruler of the second house) in the fifth house of her fans. The eighth house ruler, Jupiter, in the twelfth house suggests that she handled her income with enough profitable investments in real estate (trine Sun) to protect her during the times she did not work, but its opposition to Uranus (ruling the sixth and tenth houses) implies that she was disappointed many times with projects which fell through.

## Taurus on the MC

Those of us with Taurus on the MC display practical stability with a career in which we feel comfortable and worthwhile. To achieve out maximum success, we take a long apprenticeship, practicing and learning by experience and repetition. This type of assimilation prepares a firm foundation for our accomplishments, and we stick to our goal or game plan. We fail to succeed when we place personal indulgence and indiscriminate sensuality ahead of common sense. With obdurate intolerance, we lack focus and show an over-sensitivity of personal ego. We may have financial problems or be drawn into questions of fraud or theft.

Even when our career fields do not deal directly with business or finance, we are generally aware of fiscal realities. Practical and mundane considerations require our attention. Many of us marry well or choose alliances that are materially beneficial.

We are remarkable for standing up for our personal beliefs or value system, either through our ethics or our work. The examples include religious innovators Martin Luther and Paramhansa Yogananda, as well as evangelist Edna Ballard whose religious movement brought in quantities of lucrative "love offerings" before she was indicted for fraud. People whose lives and reputations were distinguished by their beliefs include the boxer Muhammad Ali, a conscientious objector in war time, and singers Judy Collins, a peace activist and Anita Bryant, a homophobic activist. Michel Gauquelin spent a lifetime establishing a research methodology for his subject, astrology. The crime cases involve money, such as the jewel thief known as the Mayfair Boy, James Earl Ray, who had a long record of robbery before he assassinated Dr. Martin Luther King, and John Mitchell, Wall Street lawyer convicted ofWatergate charges.

Some of us are noted for our good looks or graciousness; those who are entertainers are able to command great popularity. Actress Marilyn Monroe had the ruler of her Taurus MC, Venus, in Aries in the ninth house trine Neptune in the first house and sextile Jupiter in the seeventh house adding to her charisma and appeal. Singer Eiton John has Venus in Aquarius in the sixth house opposite the Ascendant; he is bisexual and bizarre, with outstanding talent and appeal. It is also easy for those of us with a Taurus MC to take the path of least resistance, and we may withdraw from active assertion to follow a role that is comfortable. None of us are loners; a loving alliance is important to our well-being.

A Taurus MC shows the need for love and/or money, with a dedicated value system to add stability and direction to life. If these areas are lacking or break down, we feel that life is meaningless. To evaluate our capacity for success, consider all planets in the tenth house, the sign where Venus is posited and the aspects of both the MC and its ruler, Venus. With a Taurus MC and Venus posited or conjunct the MC, we appeal to the public taste and values, as advertising tycoon Mary Wells Lawrence demonstrated successfully, or we are noted for popular appeal, as shown by contemporary and country singer Anne Murray (who has Venus in the ninth house conjunct her Taurus MC).

## Example Chart of a Taurus MC

Grizzled and bearded guitarist, singer and composer, with long hair tied in a pony-tail, Willie Nelson has long been one of the top country-western performers. He paid his apprenticeship dues by traveling for more than 200 days a year playing clubs, bars and concert halls. His Taurus MC is exhibited by his easy-going, down-home comfortable charm that has worn well for the past 40 years. As hard-working as his Saturn opposite the ASC implies. Nelson's tenth house Venus takes priority in describing his reputation; he is known as a lover as well as an entertainer, with three marriages that lasted 10 years, 10 years and 18 years, and a total of five children.

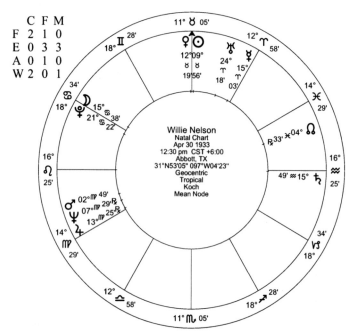

| | C | F | M |
|---|---|---|---|
| F | 2 | 1 | 0 |
| E | 0 | 3 | 3 |
| A | 0 | 1 | 0 |
| W | 2 | 0 | 1 |

Willie Nelson
Natal Chart
Apr 30 1933
12:30 pm CST +6:00
Abbott, TX
31°N53'05" 097°W04'23"
Geocentric
Tropical
Koch
Mean Node

*Willie Nelson: Country Western Singer*

**Declinations:** ☿ 3N18; ♃ 7N49; ♅ 8N54; ♆ 9N33; ☊ 9S35; ♂ 12N26; ☉ 14N48; ♀ 14N51; M 15N10; A 15N55; ♄ 16S47; ♀ 22N45; ☽ 26N23

In a further demonstration of his Taurus MC, Nelson was acclaimed for his work with a cause in which he believed, Farm Aid, raising millions with his concerts to help farmers struggling against foreclosure. The Sun-MC-Venus are trine Neptune-Jupiter in the first house to mirror Nelson's phenomenal success with his fans (Jupiter rules the fifth house) and the extent of his wealth (Jupiter and Neptune co-rule the eighth house).

However, Jupiter sextile the Moon makes a yod to Saturn, suggesting a personal crisis involving the eighth and eleventh houses; his business affairs were in shambles when his manager (eleventh house) failed to pay income taxes (eighth house) for seven years. In November 1990, the IRS seized 22 of Nelson's properties to pay his bill of $16 million. Nelson's eighth house rulers in the first house, as well as a Taurus Sun and MC, suggested that he would have been wise to maintain a tighter personal audit of his financial affairs. The ruler of the second house is Mercury in a semisextile to MC-Venus. As a semisextile is an uneven aspect, Mercury took precedence while he was traveling (ninth house) and Venus took over when he was on stage (tenth house).

## Venus in the Tenth House

Even when highly capable, we who have Venus in the tenth are not taken too seriously and we are more apt to be considered "light-weights." We are most successful when cultivating that reputation, such as entertainers Goldie Hawn, Brooke Shields and Sally Struthers. A hard-working actress with Venus in the tenth house who made literally hundreds of films, Loretta Young, was known as "Hollywood's gorgeous hack." We can also have a reputation for games or play, such as chess champion Bobby Fischer, playboy Prince Aly Khan and daredevil Evel Knievel. When we are in business, a tenth house Venus more appropriately represents entertainment or pleasure fields, decoration or show than technologies or standard necessities.

We who have deeper reputations are those who have additional planets posited in the tenth house, such as mathematician Albert Einstein, artist Paul Gauguin and writers Johann von Goethe and Upton Sinclair, and the presence of Venus adds a reputation of being likable, gentle and easy-going, or of being sybaritic, or non-competitive, non-assertive. Many of us receive "lucky" breaks from helpful friends or family or affluent marriages and alliances. Content and comfort in love relationships is one of our major priorities; even if we live alone, we have deeply bonded friendships and associations. Venus and the Moon are both interior planets and are not usually directed toward public attainment until after our first priority of private needs are adequately met.

## Example Chart of Venus in the Tenth House

Son of former U.S. President Ronald Reagan, young Reagan studied ballet from 1976, first in Los Angeles and then with the Jeffrey School; he spent the 1981-82 seasons touring small American cities with the troupe. A Pisces MC contained by Mars in Pisces and Venus in Aries is appropriate for dance but the chart shows so many career

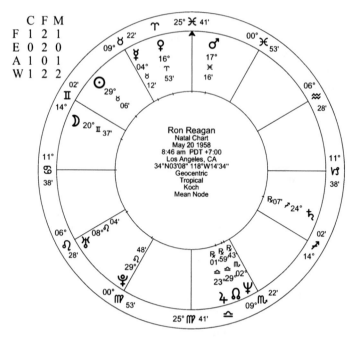

**C F M**
**F 1 2 1**
**E 0 2 0**
**A 1 0 1**
**W 1 2 2**

*Ron Reagan: Noted Family*

Declinations: M 1S43; ♀ 4N52; ♂ 6S45; ♃ 7S36; ☿ 9N57; ♆ 10S43;
☊ 11S51; ♅ 18N52; ☽ 19N9; ☉ 19N58; ♄ 21S53; ♀ 22N23; A 22N56

possibilities that it is difficult to focus on one.

The second house ruler, the Sun, is in a semisquare to Venus in the tenth house and quincunx to Neptune which rules the MC, not the strongest career directives to follow. Uranus in the second house is trine Venus in the tenth house and sesquisquare the MC, while Pluto in the second house is trine Mercury in the tenth house, pointing to all four of these planets as possible vocational indicators; the entertainment business (Venus), communications fields (Mercury), the humanities (Uranus) or the mass media (Pluto).

Reagan left ballet in January 1983, to begin work as a radio correspondent (Pluto-Mercury). He was on the staff of ABC's *Good Morning America* as a contributing reporter for four years and has dabbled in entertainment appearances on TV. Unfortunately his work is not taken seriously (Venus); in what role does a producer cast the son of a president? He was more noted for his family connections than for his talent (MC rulers in the fourth house). Mars in a T-square to Moon-opposite-Saturn could give a concentrated drive were they not distracted by so many operative signals. The Moon rules the ASC and is placed in the twelfth house in a trine to Jupiter in the fourth house, making it easy and comfortable to take a retiring position.

## Gemini on the MC

We who have Gemini on the MC express versatility in a career in which we have mobility. To achieve our maximum success, we use our mind, skills and wits. We write, sing or play, talk to others, counsel and listen. We go to school to study and keep learning our craft, and when troubled, talk it out. Versatile in our career, we are willing to make thoughtful changes and we often travel. We fail to succeed when we gossip, lie, exaggerate, conceal and commit perjury. We are prone to confidence games or instigating arguments and law suits. Instead of thinking it through, we chatter heedlessly; we yield to persuasion and change course in midstream. We can be highly nervous, erratic, scattered, and amoral.

Our careers lean toward a high incident of intellectual, communication and transportation fields. These include politics, flying, teaching, psychology, law, science, art, computers, almost any area that shows the common denominator of our dexterity and active mind. Entertainers and writers stand out, as well as musicians and dancers. Some of us are calm and low key but most have a high degree of nervous vivacity, and some of us go over the edge of the rationale.

Our multi-talented ability is demonstrated by writer-composer-actor Oscar Levant, as well as the avant-garde composer-teacher John Cage. Our erratic nature is shown by Charles Baudelaire, who moved monthly and dyed his hair green, as well as writing great poetry, and by flamboyant writer Oscar Wilde. Two singers with a Gemini MC who are talked about and get a great deal of press coverage are Madonna and k.d. lang. Many of us with this position are prodigies with a brilliant youth; others among us have notoriety in youth, as the kidnapped Patty Hearst or Gregory Godzig, whose peak reputation was that of being a 17-year-old murder victim of John Wayne Gacy. Novelist Francoise Sagan wrote and published her first book at 18, and Louisa May Alcott wrote stories about young people.

A Gemini MC shows our need to pursue intellectual interests and express a variety of abilities. To evaluate our success, consider all planets in the tenth house, the sign where Mercury is posited and the aspects of both the MC and Mercury. With a Gemini MC and Mercury posited or conjunct, we have a natural drive to express mental skills, such as writer Francoise Sagan, or we are noted for restless changes and versatility, as film director Vittorio De Sica.

### Example Chart of a Gemini MC

"It's no wonder you have trouble with men, Jane," her sister said. "It's because you talk too much." True, Jane Austen never married. As a young girl she was as romantic and high spirited as a young colt, but she turned away suitors. The ruler of the seventh house is Neptune on the ASC, and none could measure up to her high ideals. Expressing her Gemini MC and Mercury in the third house in Sagittarius, Austen became the first historically renowned woman novelist of England.

Austen was the seventh of eight children born to a scholarly village rector. The family read aloud and made up stories in the evenings. Her Sun (on the IC) gave her a buoyant and expressive home base (Sagittarius) from which she was able to reach out for her own recognition (opposite the MC). Austen wrote from age 12, finishing her first novel at 15 and publishing six novels between 1811 and 1817.

Though the MC is strongly aspected, the second house contains its own ruler, Venus, which does not contact the MC and is not an appropriate vocational indicator. The sixth house of work is co-ruled by Saturn which is conjunct the Moon in the first house; both trine the MC to indicate their role in her career and reputation. Her instinct (Moon) was to work (Saturn) in a cultural expression (Libra) to communicate (Gemini). The Moon rules the eleventh house (personal motivation). Neither money nor fame were the goals; Austen simply had something to say and meant to say it. As a spinster she lived at home; that her support came from her family may be indicated by the ruler of the eighth house in the fourth house. Her health was not strong and Austin died at age 41, June 18, 1817.

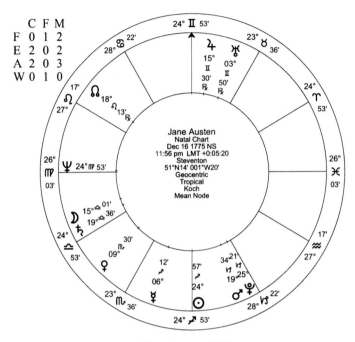

| C | F | M |
|---|---|---|
| F | 0 | 1 | 2 |
| E | 2 | 0 | 2 |
| A | 2 | 0 | 3 |
| W | 0 | 1 | 0 |

Jane Austen
Natal Chart
Dec 16 1775 NS
11:56 pm LMT +0:05:20
Steventon
51°N14' 001°W20'
Geocentric
Tropical
Koch
Mean Node

*Jane Austen: Writer*

*Declinations: A 1N34; ☽ 2 1S55; ♆ 3N10; ♄ 5S28; ♀ 11S46; ☊ 15N45; ☿ 20S13; ♅ 20N50; ♃ 22N6; ♂ 23S10; M 23N22; ☉ 23S22; ♀ 23S43*

## Mercury in the Tenth House

Our life experiences would make a story—and they often do. At times our names are even recorded in history. We communicate our knowledge, as did the brilliant examples Albert Einstein, Guglielmo Marconi, Friedrich Nietzsche, and Jules Veme, or we often are writers or spokespeople who represent communication fields, such as TV host David Frost, writer-editor Gloria Steinem and comedian-commentator Lenny Bruce. If not public figures discussed in the tabloids, we are at the very least talked about in our own circle.

The fields we choose lean toward the intellectual, verbal and clerical, but we also enter sports fields and business, as well as showing some evidence of music and dance. Mobility does have a measure of priority in our lives, as many of us travel or make residential moves,

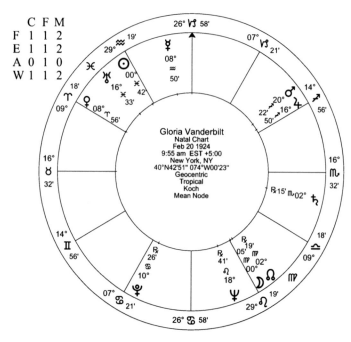

**C F M**
F 1 1 2
E 1 1 2
A 0 1 0
W 1 1 2

Gloria Vanderbilt
Natal Chart
Feb 20 1924
9:55 am EST +5:00
New York, NY
40°N42'51" 074°W00'23"
Geocentric
Tropical
Koch
Mean Node

***Gloria Vanderbilt: Designer***

***Declinations:** ♀ 3N14; ♅ 5S59; ♄ 9S48; ☊ 10N42; ☉ 11S13; ☽ 11N16;*
*♆ 15N29; A 16N49; ☿ 19S20; ♀ 20N36; M 20S46; ♃ 22S7; ♂ 22S56*

often for career reasons or as part of the job.

It is not common to find Mercury alone in the tenth house as Mercury and Venus are close to the Sun and often two if not all three are in the same area. We must also note that Mercury is extremely flexible and responsive to sign and aspect so ranges through a variety of influence. The reputations that we gain may be historically brilliant or simply denote that we are a person who chatters along with our own stories.

## Example Chart of Mercury in the Tenth House

Gloria Vanderbilt's name was newsworthy from the time of her childhood when her aunt, Gertrude Vanderbilt Whitney, sued for and won custody of her at age nine. She was called "poor little rich girl," as her father's death left her an orphan with a multi-million dollar fortune. Her inheritance is indicated by the twelfth house ruler, Mars, in the eighth house conjunct Jupiter and trine Neptune in the fourth house.

Mercury retrograde in the tenth house rules the second house (of livelihood) and is square Saturn (the ruler of the Capricorn MC) in the sixth house (of labor) to imply a drive toward a career that Vanderbilt herself achieved through the work ethic. Saturn in Scorpio certainly added perseverance that endured through times of being unseen (or underground, so to speak) alternating with times of exposure to the press. The placement of Mercury in Aquarius (ruling the second house) suggests that Vanderbilt put a measure of value on her independent career accomplishments.

True to the versatile nature of Mercury, Vanderbilt made periodic sorties into various fields, dabbling in the theater for a few years before stepping into the fashion field. She had four marriages, the most prestigious of which was to conductor Leopold Stokowski, 40 years her senior, with whom she had two sons. She testified again to the message of Mercury in 1985 with the publication of her autobiography.

## Cancer on the MC

Those of us with Cancer on the MC feel deeply about a career in which we can nurture to the needs of others with a service or product, or to the needs of our home or national homeland. The domestic bond plays an important role. To achieve our maximum success, we care for God, flag and country, apple pie and Mom, with strong associations of loyalty and support. We are curious and responsive to our environment and have adequate emotional outlets. We fail to succeed when we are sexually immoral, moving from partner to partner and lover to lover with no lasting bonds or permanent home base. We cut off family ties and tradition. We have no empathy for others but are ourselves touchy, thin-skinned, weepy and long suffering.

Our career fields show a response to human needs in politics, humanities, medicine, teaching, and counseling, the manufacture of goods, music, entertainment or play. Musicians and dancers do well with this position, and the entertainers represented are markedly versatile.

The most obvious trait is the family bond, as in the examples of musician Dweezil Zappa, son of musician Frank Zappa, and actress Tatum O'Neal, daughter of actor Ryan O'Neal. Artist Rosa Bonheur's father and four siblings were also artists. Donald Kinman was living with his mother when he committed his second murder. Actress Sally Struthers gained fame in a TV series called *All In The Family,* and she is, as well, an activist for the relief of hunger among children.

There is a suggestion of mysticism and certainly a link to the family of mankind, as shown by humanitarian Dr. Albert Schweitzer, writer Anais Nin and Saint Therese de Lisieux. Others among us find that necessary supportive link with our partner, such as Marge Champion and Ruth St. Denis who both danced with their husbands. Twin brothers August and Jean Piccard were both scientists, and Jacques Cousteau worked with a team that included his son Philippe in underwater explorations. Bill Clinton speaks of his concern for the effect that his position as U.S. President has upon his family as well as his care for the welfare of his nation.

In the negative examples we see a large amount of indiscriminate sexual activity and either difficulties with children or a loss or lack of issue. There are a number of examples of alcohol or substance abuse that we deal with in ourselves or in our family environment. The anti-societal cases include serial killers Dennis Nilsen and Jeffrey Dahmer, both of whom killed to keep their victims from leaving them, and who kept the bodies at home "for company." Dahmer lived with his mother until he was eighteen when she took his younger brother and moved away; he then lived with his grandmother for five years. A distorted hunger for closeness may have been a factor in both of these cases.

Emotional and creative satisfaction in our careers or private lives takes a high priority. To evaluate the capacity of success of a Cancer MC, consider all planets in the tenth house, the sign where the Moon is posited and the aspects of both the MC and its ruler, the Moon. With a Cancer MC and the Moon posited or conjunct, we must have emotional outlets, as pianist Van Cliburn does with his music, or we may be noted for marriage or domestic associations, or family connections, as Harpo Marx, one of the famous Marx Brothers.

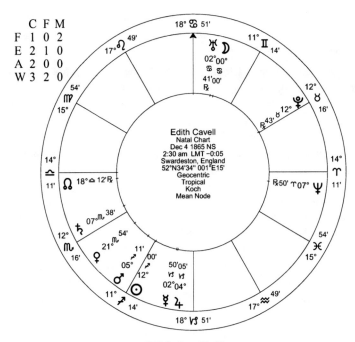

*Edith Cavell: Nurse*

*Declinations: ♀ 0N28; Ψ 1N41; A 5S36; ☊ 7S44; ♄ 11S56; ♀ 17S4;*
*☽ 18N40; ♂ 21S25; M 22N8; ☉ 22S15; ♃ 23S23; ♅ 23N41; ☿ 25S40*

## Example Chart of a Cancer MC

Before age 30, Edith Cavell was a colorless governess who taught and cared for the children of an affluent family, suggested by the Moon (children) ruling the MC (career) in the ninth house (teaching). In 1885, her father (tenth house, a parent) took ill, and she responded to his need (Cancer MC) by returning home to nurse him through his declining years and death. The experience of nursing was so fulfilling for her that she continued in this career and (Moon conjunct Uranus in Cancer in the ninth house) instigated and organized a school of nursing in Brussels in 1907.

Cavell's second house Venus in Scorpio is trine the MC to suggest social work and it is in a wide opposition to its dispositor, Pluto in the eighth house to equip her with the emotional depth to handle life-and-death situations. Her sixth house contains Neptune, trine to Mars in the second house to imply sacrifice and drama in her work, perhaps even remarkable adventures.

When World War I broke out, PR Uranus had moved into a one-degree conjunction of the Moon to portray further changes; Cavell made her hospital a way-station for Allied soldiers to escape from German captors. In 1915, the escape route was broken and Cavell was arrested; she was executed by firing squad October 12, 1915, in Brussels. The PR ASC in Scorpio trine MC at the time of Cavell's death indicates the fame that endured for her heroism.

### Moon in the Tenth House

We who have the Moon in the tenth house are team players and we do our best with the "nest" of a support group, the family, organization or partner. Our reputation may be linked with family, such as both Amy and Billy Carter, as well as Great Britain's Prince Charles. Our reputation fluctuates, or pulses; periodically we attract gossip around or about us. We seldom stay consistently before the public; our exposure waxes and wanes. The sports figures and entertainers among us gain more publicity for the roles portrayed than for our private lives. Even Doris Day, one of the most widely known actresses in history, is more recognized for her image as the world's favorite virgin than for her private life and succession of four husbands. (In her later years, she became known for her interest in animal rights and for the care of her own dogs.) The limelight does not seem comfortable on a full-time basis; withdrawal into domestic privacy is customary.

Our career tends to shift in a two-to-three year cycle. Even when we are strongly fixed and stay in one job or situation for a lifetime, the mood, time, tune or tempo changes at roughly the same interval that it takes the progressed Moon to go through one sign. Some of us make frequent changes of our residence rather than our job.

We are financially aware and lean toward fiscal and business interests even when this is not our primary area of activity. Fields are shown in which we respond to the public weal, from service and commodities to music and entertainment, to working with women or children, even to military careers where our need for a support team is sat-

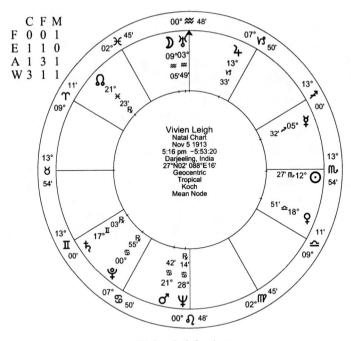

**Vivien Leigh: Actress**

*Declinations: ☊ 2S49; ♀ 5S54; ☉ 15S35; A 16N3; ☿ 17N35; ♅ 19S54;*
*M 19S58; ♆ 20N5; ♄ 21N5; ☽ 21S25; ♃ 23S3; ♂ 23N5; ☿ 24S1*

isfied. The nature of the Moon is to seek nourishment, and in maturity, to nurture others. A financial start often comes from our family or our marriage partner.

We demonstrate a few cases of multiple marriages, as emotional involvements have a high priority. Our emotional health requires a comforting and mutually caring domestic situation. If this is not present, we who have Moon in the tenth house may turn to inward brooding and solitary habits.

## Example Chart of the Moon in the Tenth House

Vivien Leigh attained great publicity and popularity, winning an Oscar as Best Actress for her role in *Gone With the Wind*. On Christmas Day, 1938, she was informed that she had won the coveted role of

Scarlett O'Hara; the three stars of the film Signed their contracts January 13, 1939. During the filming of GWTW, Leigh's PR Venus in Scorpio was trine its dispositor, PR Mars in Cancer; her portrayal of Scarlett as saucy, impertinent, sexual, flirtatious, courageous, intense and persevering magnificently reflected the planetary positions.

The Moon and Uranus in the tenth house conjunct the MC, all in Aquarius. The three points sextile Mercury, the ruler of the second house of livelihood, to indicate that Leigh could work before the public in a fluctuating career (Moon) with verbal expression (Mercury) and further, that her reputation would vary widely from "brilliant" to "unstable" (Uranus). Leigh was known for her 23-year marriage to Sir Laurence Olivier, continually explosive and turbulent. She withdrew periodically from her public life in search of a more secluded and nourishing environment. Emotionally erratic, Leigh suffered from manic-depression and was nearly catatonic in her later years from shock treatments (Uranus posited and ruling the MC, conjunct Moon). She died of tuberculosis in London on July 8, 1967.

## Leo on the MC

We who have Leo on the MC take pride in a career that allows us to express authority. For our maximum success, we present our public position with dignity and some reserve. We set goals and maintain a focus on our chosen direction without compromising our values. Though we appreciate praise, that is not the yardstick of our measurement; we maintain integrity in our belief of personal worth and the value of our work. We fail to succeed when we show righteous superiority and unreasonable, narrow views. Arrogantly we presume that we are a law unto ourselves and act on self-aggrandizing passions without any goal greater than, "Look, look at me!"

Our career fields show positions of authority or command, often with an audience or a following, and we habitually accumulate honors and awards. Some of us have difficulty in handling conflict or rivalry and are troubled by subordinates who threaten to surpass us, though generally we stick to our guns, even under fire, to spend a lifetime developing the excellence of our work, as shown by Sigmund Freud, Upton Sinclair and Louis Pasteur. In the examples, entertainers are not as numerous as we might expect, but those who are represented have great popularity and a large following, such as veteran TV host Johnny Carson and the promising, short-lived young actor River Phoenix. We who enter the business fields stand out with an air of command. Though a few of us are representative of our group, most of us work alone or in leadership roles. Uri Geller, with his psychokinetic exhibitions has the most singular distinction, but many of us are "one of a kind" to some extent.

A Leo MC is representative of our need to be distinct, one of the elite rather than part of the common herd. We do not care to take orders, and being part of the team is not a high priority. To evaluate the capacity of success of a Leo MC, consider all planets in the 10th house, the sign where the Sun is posited and the aspects of both the MC and its ruler, the Sun. When we have a Leo MC and the Sun posited or conjunct we have a natural ability to carry authority, as shown by evangelist Jerry Falwell, or we may be noted for our family position, as Princess Anne of England.

## Example Chart of Leo on the MC

Tom Dooley came from a prosperous family and an advantaged background, as may be suggested by a Leo MC; he had a good education and completed medical training to become a physician. Dooley joined the United States Navy to serve as an M.D. and impressed by his experiences in the far east, turned his entire focus on the relief of suffering. Neptune closely conjunct the MC inspired his belief system to a cause based on the highest ideals, and with a Capricorn Sun ruling the MC, he put that vision into concrete, responsible practice.

Dooley's first hospital was a 30-mat hut in Laos that he established in September 1956, which developed into a fully staffed clinic within a few years, aided by Medico. In northern Vietnam he was known among the people with whom he worked as "the splendid American." When a reporter asked him, "What do you get out of this deal, Dooley?" he replied, "Plenty. My life is more worthwhile." The ruler of Dooley's second house of livelihood is Jupiter, which portrays the advantage of his education directed to the professions; it is opposite the MC and Neptune to indicate the management, organization and hard work that Dooley assumed in order to achieve the maximum of his capacity of growth and dedication. His Sun (ruling the

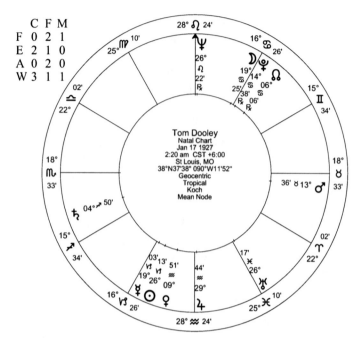

**Dr. Tom Dooley: Humanitarian**

*Declinations:* ♅ 2S9; M 12N2; ♃ 12S27; ♆ 13N10; A 17S21; ♂ 17N28; ♀ 19S10; ♄ 19S16; ☉ 20S55; ☿ 21N16; ☽ 23N9; ☊ 23N15; ☿ 23S43

MC) is conjunct Mercury in the third house; he is the author of *The Night They Burned the Mountain.* In 1959, at age 32 Dooley had surgery for cancer; he died two years later, January 18, 1961.

## Sun in the Tenth House

With the Sun in the tenth house, we "show" well. We have a dignity that carries us through blunders that could bring disgrace to anyone less poised. We generally present a self-assured mien and hold public positions with confidence. Marilyn Monroe's legendary insecurities were put aside when she stepped into the limelight; Angela Davis refused to be relegated to stereotypical minor posts as a woman and a black American; even with 20 years in prison Albert Speer was never given the denigration of other Nazi officials but was always acknowledged as an aristocrat.

Acclaim is the natural habitat for those of us who have the Sun in the tenth house, and we step up to external expectations naturally. Many of us are leaders in our field, such as explorer Admiral Richard Byrd and tennis champion Billie Jean King. We win awards, as did producer David O. Selznick, actor Jack Nicholson and pianist Van Cliburn. We are not "retiring" people; even with setbacks or obscure periods we come back to the fore, and all of us (with very few exceptions) show career longevity and popularity. Though good earning power is shown, recognition and status stand out as our first priority.

## Example Chart of Sun in the Tenth House

Demonstrating a tenth house Sun, musician Jim Morrison became a legend in his own time. Recreational drugs that led up to heroin, years of alcohol abuse, addictions, decadence and outrageous behavior were all overlooked by his adoring fans as only part of his mystique. He was the founding member of *The Doors,* one of the top rock groups of the 1960s, exemplar of that brief magical period when the world's youth wore colorful clothes and long hair and the sweet smell of marijuana drifted across the parks and "love-ins." Morrison played his Scorpio MC to the hilt, dressing in skin tight black leather and projecting blatant sexuality; his music beat with the pulse of the rock generation. *Light My Fire* and *Riders on the Storm.* At the same time his 2nd house co-ruler Jupiter screamed "excess!" with its close square to the MC; its trine to Mercury allowed him liberty without an apparent price during his peak superstar prestige. In March 1971, weary and disillusioned, beset by legal problems and years of substance abuse, he moved to Paris to regroup. He died there of a heart attack July 3, 1971, after snorting heroin.

## Virgo on the MC

When we have Virgo on the MC, we are adaptable to career variations that allow us to develop a useful expertise. To achieve our maximum success, we are helpful and humane with a witty down-to-earth approach. Unpretentious, we perfect our talents with practice and experience. We fail to succeed when we are critical complainers and use others unfairly. We are mental or physical hypochondriacs with eating disorders and multiple health problems. We vacillate, moving from job to job as none seems to meet our standards.

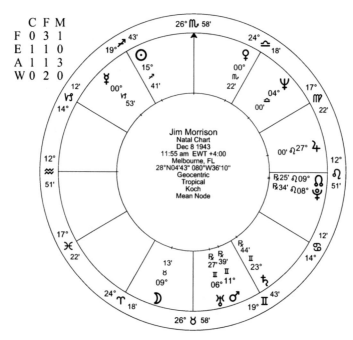

|   | C | F | M |
|---|---|---|---|
| F | 0 | 3 | 1 |
| E | 1 | 1 | 0 |
| A | 1 | 1 | 3 |
| W | 0 | 2 | 0 |

Jim Morrison
Natal Chart
Dec 8 1943
11:55 am EWT +4:00
Melbourne, FL
28°N04'43" 080°W36'10"
Geocentric
Tropical
Koch
Mean Node

*Jim Morrison: Rock Musician*

*Declinations: Ψ 0S20; ♀ 9S22; ☽ 9N43; ♃ 13N19; A 16S58; ☊ 18N13;*
*M 19S29; ♅ 21N18; ♄ 21N54; ☉ 22S41; ♀ 23N25; ♂ 24N22; ☿ 25S43*

Our career fields are often in intellectual and communication fields, sometimes in transportation areas. We may work in healing or dietary careers. All fields are represented with the common denominator of skills that are perfected through work to a fine degree of excellence. Highly flexible, we seek variety in life's experience and most of us change jobs or careers several times. Even if there is one career, there is an avocational interest or second career in the wings, such as pursued by Hildegard Neff, an actress and a writer. Ken Uston, a stockbroker and a gambler and Shirley Temple Black, an actress and a diplomat.

Others among us have multiple abilities; some of the most brilliant minds and talents in history are shown with the Virgo MC. Leonardo da Vinci, Benjamin Disraeli, Friedrich Nietzsche and Raphael show the epitome of human development in craftsmanship. Sports champions also exemplify the presence of a second career as the average sports figure has a limited peak period.

Some health and physical abnormalities are evident, such as Henri Toulouse-Latrec with stunted legs, and the phenomenal George Lippert who was born with three legs. Chanteusse Edith Piaf had a stunning history of alcohol, drugs, hepatic comas, jaundice, ulcers and seven operations, and martial arts expert Bruce Lee died of a massive brain hemorrhage. Heavy drug and alcohol abusers include Elvis Presley. Internally or externally, problem solving takes priority in our lives.

A Virgo MC shows an impetus to do something useful and worthwhile in life, to make some viable contribution through service to others that makes a difference, either in the world as a whole or simply in our private reality. There are periods when work dries up or is dull, perhaps for years at a stretch. A physically and emotionally healthy lifestyle helps us to avoid (or resolve) problems. To evaluate the capacity of success of a Virgo MC, consider all planets in the 10th house, the sign where Mercury is posited and the aspects of both the MC and its ruler, Mercury. With a Virgo MC and Mercury posited or conjunct, we strive for career variety and mobility, such as shown by the multiple talents of Mickey Rooney, or we are noted for perfecting our field, as did composer George Gershwin.

## Example Chart of Virgo on the MC
Dr. Timothy Leary began his academic vocation doing graduate work at Berkeley in psychology where he helped devise early group therapy techniques, illustrating the Virgo intellectual qualities as well as those of the MC ruler, Mercury in Scorpio. The ruler of the second house of livelihood is Saturn in the ninth house of higher education, conjunct the MC. He became a professor at Harvard University, a prestigious and honorable position, until he was fired for experimenting with hallucinogenic drugs, which may be illustrated by Mercury sesquisquare (trail-blazing) its dispositor, Pluto.

Though Neptune, ruling drugs, has a trine to the ASC, Pluto is more indicative of the psychedelic experience, that of being the microcosm within the macrocosm, of being one cell within the body of

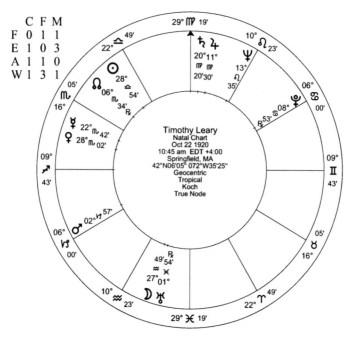

**Dr. Timothy Leary: Psychedelicist**

*Declinations: M 0N16; ♄ 5N32; ☽ 7S36; ♃ 8N8; ☉ 11S5; ♅ 11S32;*
*☊ 13S43; ♆ 16N47; ♀ 19N35; ♀ 20S25; ☿ 21S6; A 21S55; ♂ 25S7*

the whole, and Pluto not only has the close aspect to Mercury, (ruler of the MC) but it is in a one-degree quincunx to Leary's ASC.

Uranus stands out (in Pisces) conjunct the Moon (in rebellious Aquarius) square Venus and Mercury and trine the Sun to exemplify the slogan that Leary coined, "Turn on, tune in and drop out." Verbalizing Mercury (twelfth house in Scorpio), he touched the core of the underground subculture of his day to become the archetypal spokesman of the flower-children. The twelfth house also pointed to his 29 arrests for drug possession and to his exile in Europe when he escaped from a federal work camp in 1970. He was later paroled. Leary's books and lectures further explore the heights and depths of a Scorpio twelfth house with the philosophical voice of a Sagittarius ASC.

**Mercury in the tenth house follows Gemini on the MC.**

## Libra on the MC

Those of us with Libra on the MC express social and intellectual initiative in a career that allows us to have comfortable interaction with others. To achieve our maximum success, we are pleasant, agreeable and helpful. Interested and caring, we treat others as equals. We deal with the public to improve social conditions in a manner that is just and fair. As we appeal to the public tastes, we are highly popular. We fail to succeed when we are lazy with our only effort being that of avoiding work. We seduce others with our charm but, lacking true ethics, are superficial and two-faced. We are pleasure-seeking dilettantes who take the path of least resistance.

Our career fields are those that appeal to the public tastes and social mores of our time. We are not loners; even those of us who tend to be shy or reclusive mingle socially and in public places, and our job or career puts us into people-oriented situations. Those of us who are socially noteworthy have a high level of visibility with a Libra MC, such as presidential brother Billy Carter, who was more noted for being a beer-drinking good-ole-boy than for running a peanut plantation, and Marion Davies, publicized as the mistress of William Randolph Hearst rather than for her capable business acumen and philanthropy.

The partner, family, or social position plays a large role in our lives, as portrayed by evangelist Tammy Faye Bakker, world known for her marriage to Jim Bakker as well as for her trowel of cosmetics. Those of us who are noted for more substance often express a social consciousness, as demonstrated by the feminist works of Betty Friedan, the fables of Hans Christian Anderson and the philosophical works of Herman Hesse and Alan Watts. Cosmopolitan editor Helen Gurley Brown appropriately wrote *Sex and the Single Girl.* Sociopathic cult leader Jim Jones, with Libra on the MC had sufficient charisma to lead a thousand people to their death.

Generally, we are delightful companions personally or in the workplace, more noted for popularity in our profession than for depth unless other factors add additional dynamics. Always remember to evaluate the total MC/tenth house, as illustrated by actor Charles Bronson with his Libra MC and two planets in Scorpio in the tenth house. He gained great popularity in roles where he dealt out justice

(Libra) with a vengeance (Scorpio). Actor Alan Alda and dancer Fred Astaire are two examples of the extent of devotion that a Libra MC inspires in fans.

We demonstrate a strong requirement to respond and mix with others. We are noteworthy in social positions or in social causes. To evaluate the capacity of success of a Libra MC, consider all planets in the tenth house, the sign where Venus is posited and the aspects made by both the MC and its ruler, Venus. With a Libra MC and Venus posited or conjunct, we are noted for our social position or our artistry, both of which are illustrated by Viscount Linley Armstrong-Jones, or we may be known for a light and delightful popularity, as actress Goldie Hawn.

### Example Chart of Libra on the MC

For his livelihood, Adams followed traditional roles (Saturn in the second house); he taught, lectured and worked in advertising (Jupiter) while establishing his position with important art shows (Venus in the second house, ruling both the MC and the sixth house). His work is now shown in many galleries and his prints are available to lift the spirit of all who see them. Adams lived in one of California's most beautiful locations, Carmel; he died in nearby Monterey April 22, 1984, survived by his wife of 56 years and two children.

**Venus in the tenth house follows Taurus on the MC.**

### Scorpio on the MC

We who have Scorpio on the MC apply intense application to a career in which our constructive action makes an impact on the environment or values of others. To achieve our maximum success, we handle power with discretion and tact, persistently cooperating in teamwork for the general good. We handle groups with concern for individual rights. We fail to succeed when we resort to manipulation and scheming. We live off other's money and power. Inflexibly, we stay in a job or position we hate and set ourselves apart from the group by passive resistance.

Our career fields are strongly represented in business, government and military areas, employment in national concerns and large power-structures. Many of us find that our rise and fall depends on the

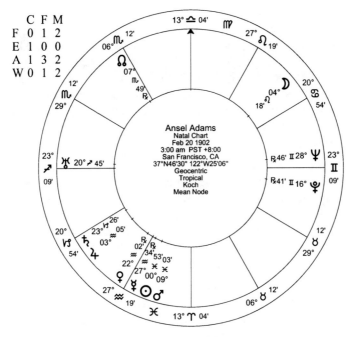

C F M
F 0 1 2
E 1 0 0
A 1 3 2
W 0 1 2

Ansel Adams
Natal Chart
Feb 20 1902
3:00 am PST +8:00
San Francisco, CA
37°N46'30" 122°W25'06"
Geocentric
Tropical
Koch
Mean Node

***Ansel Adams: Photographic artist***

*Declinations: M 5S10; ♀ 6S2; ☿ 8S50; ♂ 9S5; ☉ 11S10; ♀ 13N43;*
*☊ 13S47; ☽ 14N17; ♃ 19S49; ♄ 21S18; ♆ 22N17; ♅ 23S11; A 23S17*

political or cultural tone of our time in history, such as Field Marshal
Erwin Rommell, or Nicolo Machiavelli and Prince Zoorosh Ali Reza
Pahlavi (whose charts, 491 years apart have remarkable similarities).

Others among us speak for our sex or our generation, such as writers F. Scott Fitzgerald and Germaine Greer. Extremes are shown in
our lives, vivid peaks and valleys and great transformations. The directions that we take may be influenced or changed forever by the
death of another or by a personal trauma in our environment or to our
associates. Sex may well play a leading role, or conversely, be sublimated to more compelling priorities. Entertainers are not highly represented by this position; however, we do well as musicians, both as
single artists and in group performances.

A Scorpio MC shows a requisite for us to deal with issues of power and control (or the lack) in ourselves and with others, which not infrequently leads to counseling vocations aimed at the goal of renovation. Sylvia Kars worked for 14 years as a medical assistant before she became a surrogate sensuality partner and sexual therapist, reflecting her Scorpio MC and Venus-Mars in Scorpio in the ninth house. In most cases of a Scorpio MC, more is known about our public life than about our private life. For example, as well as Ray Bradbury's name is known to sci-fi devotees, information about his private life seems nonexistent.

To evaluate the capacity of success of a Scorpio MC, consider all planets in the tenth house, the signs in which both Pluto and Mars are posited and the aspects made by both the MC and its dual rulers. With a Scorpio MC and Mars posited or conjunct, we are drawn to roles where we exercise a degree of power or influence, as feminist Germaine Greer exhibited, or we are noted for the absorbing intensity of our performance, such as actresses Susan Sarandon and Sean Young.

A Scorpio MC with Pluto posited in Scorpio occurs in the charts of people born between 1983 and 1995 (the last time was circa 1740). These people will make their mark on the cultural and economic civilization of the 21st century and may well be influential regarding issues that deal with life and death, such as medical or insurance fields or exploring new depths of psychology and research.

### Example Chart of Scorpio on the MC

Anna Mary Robertson is one of America's great primitive artists who never had an art lesson in her life. Where Ansel Adams' chart displays Venus in the second house and Neptune in the seventh house (both natural Venus-ruled houses). Grandma Moses, as she is known, has Neptune in the second house and Venus in the seventh house. Her life demonstrates the Scorpio MC in that she spent decades that were "secret" in both the sense that she was unknown to the world, and that her talent lay underground; unseen, unrecognized and untapped for the bulk of her lifetime.

The two MC rulers are both cadent in the twelfth and third houses not highly visible positions, but both apply to an angle, suggesting their dormant impact. Neptune in the second house showed a life of service and sacrifice before flowering (retrograde) into an expression

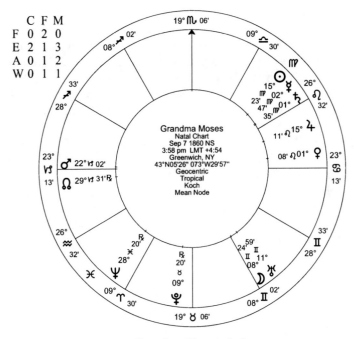

| | C | F | M |
|---|---|---|---|
| F | 0 | 2 | 0 |
| E | 2 | 1 | 3 |
| A | 0 | 1 | 2 |
| W | 0 | 1 | 1 |

Grandma Moses
Natal Chart
Sep 7 1860 NS
3:58 pm  LMT +4:54
Greenwich, NY
43°N05'26" 073°W29'57"
Geocentric
Tropical
Koch
Mean Node

*Grandma Moses: Artist*

*Declinations: ♀ 0S57; ♆ 1S55; ☉ 5N46; ☿ 11N60; ♄ 12N12; ♀ 16N11; ♃ 16N51; M 17S31; ☊ 19S57; A 21S27; ♅ 22N11; ☽ 25N46; ♂ 26S26*

of the arts. Neither of the second house co-rulers, Saturn and Uranus aspect the MC to apply for the position of vocational indicator; Uranus is semisextile the MC ruler Pluto to depict a long interior development prior to a sudden change of direction.

A farm wife and mother, it was not until the children were grown and she was widowed that Grandma Moses began to pursue her hobby of painting. The Scorpio MC indicates her profound sense of duty and commitment to her course of action; it was the death of her husband that freed Robertson for her transformation of emergence. She also survived the death of five of her ten children. Grandma Moses wrote her autobiography, *My Life's History,* when she was 92. She died December 13, 1961, at Hoosier Falls, NY, age 101.

**Mars in the tenth house follows Aries on the MC.**

## Pluto in the Tenth House

This is a position of power and prestige for those of us who respond to the law of supply and demand. We act at the appropriate time to represent a need in the mass unconscious of a specific societal group. That need may be for a hero to emulate, such as Marilyn Bell, the swimmer for whom a nation cheered or an educational leader such as Maria Montessori, but more often is for cult figures who challenge the existing taboos and set new societal standards, anti-heroes such as beatnik writer Jack Kerouac, or musician Alice Cooper. The counter culture movements against established mores may fester underground until released by a spokesman or archetypal image embodied by those of us with Pluto in the tenth house. Our performance and display is carried off with intensity and range, and our quality of sincerity is captivating. Many of us have dual careers, one that is publicly known and a second that is minor or avocational.

Few of us seem to be aiming for power overtly: those for whom this was the end goal did not fare well. Kate Chase, who tried to manipulate the First Lady role for herself through her father and then her lover, concluded her life in ignominious obscurity; evangelist Edna Ballard, and government official H.R. Haldeman both had their downfall from the misuse of their potency. They did exemplify some of the most potent vehicles of manipulation, Chase through family bonds and then, through sex, Ballard through religious fervor, and Haldeman through politics. The title that he chose for his book. *The Ends of Power,* 1978, accurately mirrored his tenth house Pluto.

Others among us are thrust into a public position where we feel that external expectations are a coercive imposition on our private lives, such as Princess Anne of England or presidential daughter Susan Ford. Though a taste of clout can be insidious, all of us seem to experience the loss of potency at some time in our lives (kidnaped and held incognito for ransom, so to speak), either in personal experience or in our career positions. We may withdraw, going underground when overwhelmed with our powerlessness. Even the most visible among us, the public figures and champions have periods of "invisibility", of having to reassess priorities and regenerate directions and capacities.

The most remarkable factor of Pluto in the tenth house is that we are operative on several levels. In some cases this denotes a private life that is inversely different from our public image. The "All-American Sweetheart" on the stage may be a sex-kitten at home or vice versa; the public sophisticate may, in private, cook pasta and raise geraniums; the religious leader may visit prostitutes while the tough executive privately writes poetry. Though not all of the examples are as extreme, there is in all of us an inviolate sense of privacy.

All social and economic strata are represented as well as all vocational fields, but the most outstanding common feature we have is that of appearing before or influencing the masses. Though we work in group environments, represent a group or are part of a group we ourselves have a singular role or distinction. We are the minority figure within the group. Even though we have periods of acclaim alternating with periods of invisibility, career longevity does stand out. If defeated, we rise again from the ashes, stronger in our rebirth than we were before. We are purposeful; only those of us who are ineffectual move from one field to another at random.

## Example Chart of Pluto in the Tenth House

Omar Sharif is an Egyptian in a Western world, a rare figure in Hollywood's upper echelon of talent, a minority role that is markedly singular. In films he usually portrays an Orinetal or Balkan leading man and is often cast as the great screen lover. Privately he is divorced with one son and does not have the reputation (that many actors attract) of being a womanizer.

Pluto in the tenth house may very well give a public image that stands apart from the way the person sees himself, as well as showing that the person "wears two hats." Sharif is not only a famous actor but he is a champion bridge player. With the MC in Cancer he fits into a game that emphasizes teamwork. Those who are active in the world of bridge know each other, a family in a sense who meet at tournaments and contests. Sharifs active seventh house suggests his involvement, initiative and zest (Aries) in meeting competitors and his Moon conjunct Venus (Gemini) suggests his pleasure in a game in which he may use his skill and wits, often playing with mentally agile women. For Sharif, the game involves travel and teaching; he is also the author of best-selling bridge books.

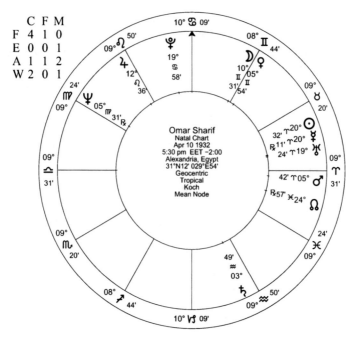

|   | C | F | M |
|---|---|---|---|
| F | 4 | 1 | 0 |
| E | 0 | 0 | 1 |
| A | 1 | 1 | 2 |
| W | 2 | 0 | 1 |

Omar Sharif
Natal Chart
Apr 10 1932
5:30 pm EET −2:00
Alexandria, Egypt
31°N12' 029°E54'
Geocentric
Tropical
Koch
Mean Node

***Omar Sharif: Actor***

***Declinations:*** *♂ 1N27; ☊ 1S37; A 3S47; ♅ 7N3; ☉ 8N2; ☿ 9N59;*
*♆ 10N13; ♃ 17N58; ♄ 19S31; ♀ 22N34; M 23N4; ♀ 24N14; ☽ 27N3*

## Sagittarius on the MC

With Sagittarius on the MC, we apply enthusiasm and eager application to a career that allows us growth and freedom of choice. To achieve our maximum success, we learn from education and experience to keep reaching for more and better. We have faith in deity and in our own philosophy and set our sights on high goals. We fail to succeed when we act upon impulse toward undisciplined indulgence and extravagance, and are wild, restless and scattered, pretentious and lawless.

Our career fields are largely represented by business concerns and the government. Art, literature, publishing and educational fields are also illustrated. We are not people who are happy with a status quo but who seek always to keep movement and growth in our careers.

Even when established in a successful position, we continually send out feelers for the next area to explore, the next class to take, the next project to start. A few of us switch jobs and careers but most move ahead in a series of surges to improve our lot, similar to the way that a galloping horse lunges forward. We easily gain prominence as we want to be noticed.

Our performance is quite visible, or what we have to broadcast is heard loudly and clearly, as in the lives of drummer Ringo Starr and conductor Leopold Stokowski, or politicians Abraham Lincoln and Conrad Adenauer. Even those of us with a modest temperament manage to gain publicity for some distinction and recognition appropriate to our social class or time in history. The examples include Empress Catherine the Great, historic scientists Tycho Brahe and Alexander Graham Bell, and astrologer Evangaline Adams.

The publicity that we attract so easily may include a rowdy or devil-may-care scandal, such as that gained by Edward, Duke of Windsor for his affair with Wallis Simpson, singer Janis Joplin for exemplifying the flower children's explosion out of conventional boundaries, and David Carradine for taking naked acid-trips around his neighborhood. Comedian Benny Hill gained fame for his tongue-in-cheek "naughty" skits.

We demonstrate a sense of adventure with which to explore and experience areas that go beyond former boundaries. To evaluate the capacity for success of a Sagittarius MC, consider all planets in the tenth house, the sign where Jupiter is posited and the aspects made by both the MC and its ruler, Jupiter. With a Sagittarius MC and Jupiter posited or conjunct we spread our wings in freedom to soar, as international conductor Zubin Mehta, or we may be noted for exhibition or display, as artist Pierre August Renoir.

## Example Chart of Sagittarius on the MC

Illustrating a Sagittarius MC as well as the ruler, Jupiter, in Sagittarius, William Butler Yeats was drawn toward travel, literature and discussion from the time of his youth. He published his first book at age 21 and became one of the great Irish authors and poets. His early poems were elaborately crafted with what he later termed "embroidery." The Sagittarius MC as well as the ruler, Jupiter, retrograde may

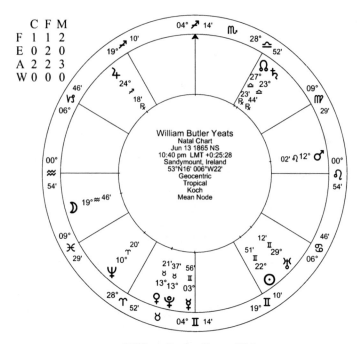

|   | C | F | M |
|---|---|---|---|
| F | 1 | 1 | 2 |
| E | 0 | 2 | 0 |
| A | 2 | 2 | 3 |
| W | 0 | 0 | 0 |

William Butler Yeats
Natal Chart
Jun 13 1865 NS
10:40 pm LMT +0:25:28
Sandymount, Ireland
53°N16' 006°W22'
Geocentric
Tropical
Koch
Mean Node

***William Butler Yeats: Writer***

*Declinations: ♀ 1N9; Ψ 2N43; ♄ 6S47; ☽ 10S21; ☊ 10S57; ♀ 13N12; ♂ 18N29; ☿ 19N13; A 19S58; M 21S1; ♃ 22S55; ☉ 23N16; ♅ 23N40*

suggest that Yeats' initial development surged forward, followed by a period of assimilation of his intellectual growth and an inner re-examination of his philosophy; he later honed his work into finely crafted simplicity, and in 1923, at age 58, won the Nobel prize for literature.

His own philosophy developed in complexity with an active interest in mysticism and astrology; his horoscope, drawn in his own hand was found among his papers. Yeats' plays and essays were pictorial of his era (MC ruler in the eleventh house), and he was active in the formation of the Irish theater. The second house ruler, Neptune, is posited in the second house trine the MC to portray a natural growth of vision and sensitivity. Yeats died near Nice, France, January 29, 1939.

## Jupiter in the Tenth House

Publicity, attention and approval flow easily into our lives when we have Jupiter in the spotlight. We either have an advantaged birth to noted or affluent parents, as shown by Patty Hearst, Susan Ford and Zubin Mehta or we make advantageous marriages or other alliances. If not born to the purple, we ourselves assume or gain a public position that takes us into the mainstream or the limelight, appropriately for entertainers, politicians and lecturers. In other cases our work makes us highly visible in recognition of our capacity. An example of success in the publishing field is Helen Gurley Brown, author of the best-seller *Sex and the Single Girl* and editor of *Cosmopolitan* magazine.

As with the Sun, Jupiter "shows" so well in the tenth house that we can get away with activities that could blacken the reputation of those less fortunate, such as publicly known drug abuse or casual morality in sexual or business conduct. This does not mean that we lack ethics or morals, but it does imply that many of us lean toward excess or occasionally court reckless adventures. Not uncommonly, we are extravagant in our life style, and approach our projects or pleasures with panache. Menial positions or modest goals are not on our agenda. We all tend to bite off big chunks of whatever we do; as a result we reap large wins and accrue large losses.

Some of us with a tenth house Jupiter are publicly or privately religious, such as Saint Bernadette, Maimonides, Daniel Berrigan and Marge Champion, who is active in her local church work.

## Example Chart of Jupiter in the Tenth House

John Charles Fremont showed ability as a gifted minor, entering the College of Charleston at 15. Five years later he took a post as a mathematics teacher aboard a sailing vessel which cruised along the South American coast for over two years. He was offered an appointment as professor of mathematics but after having a taste of travel and adventure he chose not to follow the early opportunities into academia suggested by a retrograde Jupiter. Instead, he became a topographical engineer and surveyor and in 1841 began the adventure that made him famous: mapping the Oregon Trail. Charting unknown territory is further suggested by Jupiter's sesquisquare to Pluto plus the MC sesquisquare Mars conjunct Uranus in the second house.

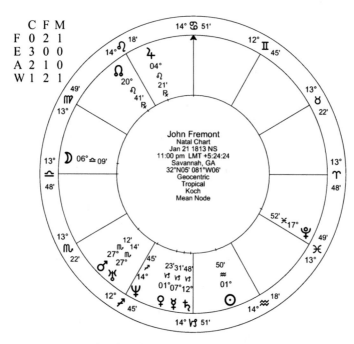

```
        C F M
    F   0 2 1
    E   3 0 0
    A   2 1 0
    W   1 2 1
```

*John Charles Fremont: Engineer, Explorer*

*Declinations: ☽ 1N4; A 5S27; ☊ 14N53; ♀ 18S27; ♂ 18S52; ♅ 19S20;*
*☉ 19S46; ♃ 19N52; ♆ 21S9; ☿ 22S18; ♄ 22S24; M 22N38; ♀ 22S38*

The Cancer MC illustrates Fremont's involvement with his team in a number of expeditions through unexplored Americana, taking precedence over staying in an established home with his wife and family (Moon in the twelfth). It was said that "from the ashes of his campfires have sprung cities." In December 1849, Fremont was elected one of the first two California senators, and he was a presidential contender in 1856. After leaving political life he began to build a railroad, but overextended and lost his fortune in the attempt (Mars-Uranus in the second house sesquisquare the MC). He settled in the Arizona territory as governor. Fremont died in New York City, July 13, 1890.

## Capricorn on the MC

Those of us who have Capricorn on the MC display practical initiative with a career in which progressive ambitions can be pursued.

To achieve our maximum success, we perfect our skills with a patient application of effort to work our way up, step by step. Recognizing that delay and failure may be part of the journey but not the destination, we keep going. We take responsibility for our own actions and direct our most ambitious goals toward civic welfare. We fail to succeed when we are fearful and craven, contesting authority while harboring ambitions beyond our ability or willingness to work, wanting the gain without the required effort. We use others ruthlessly, hiding our envy in an ingratiating, false servility.

Our career fields customarily exhibit keen awareness of material realities and fiscal considerations. Even those of us with an artistic temperament put a price tag on our services and know that we pay our dues for status earned. Government posts are appropriate but upper echelon positions rare with Capricorn on the MC; the career requires more business sense and organizational skills than public self-promotion. Many of us find contentment in a stable minor position in our field; the "superstar" is rare. However, our hard work and long hours gain respect.

Many of us show our gifts in youth and move toward more serious career goals as we mature. After the experience of recognition early in life, it comes as a shock of ice water to hit a stone wall, a holding pattern. Former freedoms are restricted by the responsibilities that come with maturity. Marriage and children or aged dependents, poverty and loneliness, hard work, poor health, or various problems severely test our patience. Even the most famous among us have some period that may extend for years of tedious work and delays that are grim along our way upward.

The greatest areas of success are in fields where we pay our dues by application of effort in preparation for our advancement. Some of us resign ourselves to the secure boundaries of mediocre posts as steady pay and fringe benefits are appreciable when we have done without.

The most exceptional people among those of us who have Capricorn on the MC take responsibilities that are greater than themselves, such as nurse Clara Barton who founded the American Red Cross, and scientific geniuses Nicola Tesia and Enrico Fermi. Reverend

Robert Burton descriptively wrote *Anatomy of Melancholy.* Others gained a poor public image such as heiress Barbara Hutton who flaunted her wealth during the depression, professor Angela Davis who was once on the "Ten Most Wanted" list of the FBI, and author Henry Miller, whose work was banned for years due to censorship.

A Capricorn MC shows the need to place responsibility and duty above our personal ambitions. To evaluate the capacity of success of a Capricorn MC, consider all planets in the tenth house, the sign where Saturn is posited and the aspects of both the MC and its ruler, Saturn. With a Capricorn MC and Saturn posited or conjunct, we must assume the responsibilities of our position, as does both Queen Elizabeth and Princess Margaret of England, or we may be noted for downfall and restriction when we do not observe the law, as Nathan Leopold, imprisoned for 35 years for murder.

### Example Chart of a Capricorn MC

One of the greatest French novelists of the 1900s, Marcel Proust was noted for a complex literary style. A Capricorn MC, emphasized by a retrograde Saturn in Capricorn may certainly show that early abilities are put in a long holding pattern due to external limitations before its full measure of development is realized, but that persevering and disciplined work can endure well past a lifetime.

The ruler of Proust's second house is Venus in the fifth house, trine MC to indicate that he was able to successfully gain a following for his society love stories, full of minute detail (Virgo). The sixth house Mars square the MC and Saturn show his difficulties in publication as well as his health problems.

Well educated, Proust's reputation first began when he was 21 in the cafes and salons where Parisian intelligentsia gathered. By age 31 he was reluctantly forced by failing health to retire to a quiet and disciplined life style. With much time on his hands he read extensively and began a long and leisurely work that grew to fifteen volumes in his lifetime.

After years of work and long delays, he published the first volume himself and in spite of excellent reviews, had difficulty finding a publisher for the second. The Capricorn MC seemed to imply that the

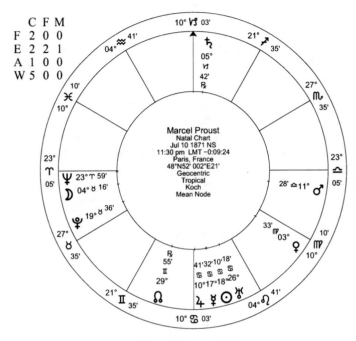

```
C  F  M
F  2  0  0
E  2  2  1
A  1  0  0
W  5  0  0
```

**Marcel Proust: Writer**

*Declinations:* ♀ *3N22;* ♂ *4S41;* ♇ *7N45;* ☽ *8N48;* A *8N59;* ♀ *11N1;*
♅ *21N24;* ☉ *22N13;* ♄ *22S35;* ♃ *23N2;* M *23S5;* ☊ *23N27;* ☿ *23N43*

world was reluctant to give him credit even after years of work; his writing was called immoral and decadent for several decades before his brilliance was acknowledged. When Proust died November 18, 1922, in Paris, three volumes of his work were still in manuscript form.

## Saturn in the Tenth House

Business, science and the professions are appropriate fields; however, music and the arts are also evident. Social and literary figures are seen less often. The astrological tradition that Saturn in the 10th house portrays a career peak followed by a downfall has some evidence but is not uniformly valid. A few examples of people who demonstrated the rise and fall were John Mitchell of Watergate fame, Nazi commander Hermann Goering, Queen Catherine de Medici, and the assassinated John F. Kennedy. Oscar Wilde was disgraced due to the social mores of his time. Saturn does not indicate downfall in a moral life but does point to a stringent demand for duty and propriety. Those of us who observe the ethic of responsibility gain respect and stability.

All of us with Saturn in the tenth house seem to want some measure of privacy, if not solitude, in our personal lives, though conscientious about our public position. We walk the straight and narrow path as we are aware of external expectations; if not, we can easily get public disfavor and a cold shoulder. We are highly subject to criticism if we step out of line. We are often perfectionists, and yes, ambitious. We work hard to gain and hold a position and want to be recognized for our skills and abilities. Success does not come easily; even those of us who are born to affluence or have ease indicated by other factors in the chart choose a stable amount of discipline in our life style and feel the greatest sense of accomplishment when we are working to perfect our abilities.

Saturn in the tenth house demonstrates all career fields as well as all social and economic strata; the common denominator is our sense of duty and responsibility as a prime ethic. Any downfall that we may experience comes from not living up to this code.

### Example Chart of Saturn in the Tenth House

An American poet of unparalleled brilliance, Emily Dickinson was born to a founding family that could trace its background to nine generations in America and thirteen in England. Her father was a lawyer who served two terms in Congress and her mother a housewife who "did not care for thought." She completed her education in South Hadley seminary where she was "cramped, curbed and repressed in every natural desire or impulse," a grim description of a tenth house Saturn that went retrograde two days after her birth.

Dickinson's MC ruler, Mercury, is in the second house conjunct the Sun; they do not aspect the MC. Her reputation was not based on her form of livelihood (which was being steward to her father's household), but for her valuable mental gifts. Mercury is semisextile its own dispositor, Jupiter, in the third house. Had she been born a century later in ordinary circumstances where she might have needed

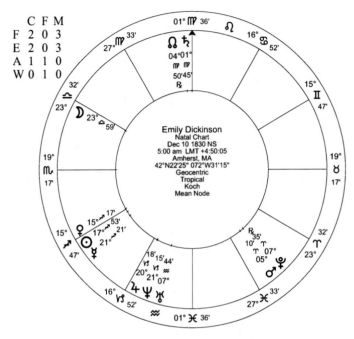

*Emily Dickinson: Poet*

*Declinations: ♂ 1N53; ☽ 5S45; ☊ 9N50; M 10N55; ♄ 12N12; ♀ 12S38;
A 17S34; ♅ 18S57; ♆ 21S16; ♃ 22S16; ♀ 22S34; ☉ 22S55; ☿ 24S42*

to seek employment, she would probably have worked in a clerical vocation, perhaps literature or teaching.

In the spring of 1854 Dickinson had an unhappy love affair with a married man whom she renounced and in the following decade withdrew from the world, only going outside at dusk to water her garden. Out of this strange, shy, solitary genius came the most lilting, insightful and exquisite poetry, with all the joy and soaring spirit that Venus, Sun and Mercury in Sagittarius could express. Her drive to create is also implied by Mars-Pluto, both ruling the ASC and posited in the fifth house; Mars also rules the sixth house of work. It was not until some years after her May 16, 1886 death that her complete poems were published.

## Aquarius on the MC

We who have Aquarius on the MC have stable ambitions with a career in which our innovative originality is unstructured. To achieve our maximum success, we make original contributions and independent decisions and are inventive in our field. We contribute to civic or humane interests and dare to take the road less traveled. We fail to succeed when we become isolationists; nervous, erratic and eccentric, we rudely treat others like objects and take stands that are perversely opposed to public standards. We precipitously cut off ties and antagonize others with dictatorial methods. Though democratic in concept we are autocratic in method.

Our career fields lean strongly toward free-lance employment. Entertainers, literary figures, and athletes stand out as we are independent agents in these fields. This is not generally a job-changing position, we may go along for years in a conventional mode but gradually (if not suddenly), we add an innovation to our field that gives us a unique recognition. In some dramatic cases we break out of the mold from one day to the next. We do not follow a typical stance.

The writers among us are graphic examples as they include Jules Verne with his prophetic science fiction, Vance Packard whose diagnosis of trends led the field, and Mary Shelley, author of the timeless classic, *Frankenstein.* Johannes Kepler combined astrology and astronomy in his work, Ellen Yoakum used her hands to heal and astrologer Zipporah Dobyns focused her work on tracking and defining thousands of asteroids. There are some obvious rebels in the examples but most of us assume an average appearance and keep our eccentricities confined to private interests. Our lives do tend to have abrupt transitions, such as that of novelist Jack London.

An Aquarius MC shows the need to be different, unusual, unconventional. To evaluate our success, consider all planets in the tenth house, the sign were Uranus and Saturn are posited and the aspects of both the MC and its co-rulers, Uranus and Saturn. With an Aquarian MC and Saturn posited or conjunct we tend to develop a precise, cool control, as shown by actress Glenda Jackson. With Uranus posited or conjunct the MC we may well break with established mores, such as activist Madalyn Murray O'Hair, or we are noted for novel eccentricities, as comedienne Phyllis Diller.

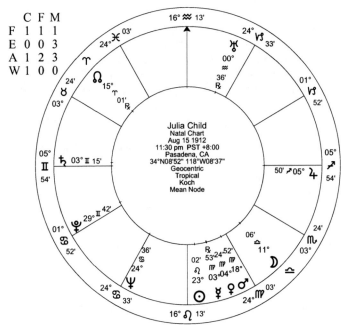

*Julia Child: Chef*

**Declinations:** ☽ 4S11; ♂ 5N11; ☊ 5N21; ☿ 5N40; ♀ 11N15; ☉ 13N51; M 15S59; ♀ 17N23; ♄ 18N49; ♅ 20S37; Ψ 20N43; ♃ 20S45; A 21N18

## Example Chart of Aquarius on the MC

Cookbooks cover miles of shelves in the bookstore and the role of a master chef is not unique in history; however, Aquarius on the MC is never the standard representative of their field. Julia Child learned French and haute cuisine at the Cordon Bleu school and published her first cookbook in 1961. She not only brought French cooking to everyday American housewives with her books but began a weekly TV show in Boston in 1962 which was highly popular; her MC ruler, Aquarius, suggests electronic media communication in the ninth house.

Cancer on the second cusp is appropriate to Child's vocation, and the Moon in Libra, fifth house, is trine the MC for her audience appeal and poise.

Child's turning point began in 1948 when she and her husband Paul moved to Paris for his work. She was restless with extra time on her hands and began going to the famed cooking school Her PR Uranus was three minutes from partile quincunx Pluto and TR Uranus was conjunct Pluto. Child not only found her own world of distinction but has since opened new doors for many other cooks who are willing and eager to experiment with original methods. At age 80 she continues to lecture, write articles and demonstrate her craft on TV.

**Saturn in the tenth house follows Capricorn on the MC.**

## Uranus in the Tenth House

Those of us with this planetary position switch jobs or even change fields from one day to the next, more obviously and often in charts that are primarily cardinal, but even in fixed charts we will break conventional patterns or instigate new methods in our established vocation. We are seldom revolutionaries in a political or military sense but consistently so in a societal, cultural and intellectual mode. We are seldom inventors in scientific fields, but always so in our approach to our work and our lives, and in our particular area of expertise.

As vivid individualists, we who have Uranus in the tenth house stand out distinctly. Many of us have career contradictions, where we are considered brilliant or outstanding by some while others think that we are crazy or too far out; some of us have career reversals in publicity and popularity. Examples include educator Richard Alpert who moved from the educational field, to psychedelic drug use, to seeking spirituality as Ram Das; Cassius Clay who embraced the Moslem faith as Muhammad Ali, Italian dictator Benito Mussolini, and Madalyn Murray O'Hair, who took her battle all the way to the Supreme Court against prayer in public schools. All have contradictions implicit in their public position.

Others among us have a more or less consistent reputation but are known as being exceptional or different in some way in our field. Benjamin Disraeli was the first Jew to become Prime Minister of England, Maharaj Ji was a religious leader from age 14 and both Michelangelo and William Blake were light years beyond the normal range of humanity in their genius.

Even the least known private figures among us have abrupt changes in our lives of one chapter closing as the next one opens. None are obscure or retiring; all of us are positive and active, event-oriented and progressive, and we frequently make innovative contributions. Though all social and economic strata are shown, we seem to have the ability to turn adverse conditions to advantage, financially as well as in an upward career progression.

## Example Chart of Uranus in the Tenth House

In this instance we see the rebel incarnate, a compelling and overwhelming iconoclast ready to break any convention in order to change society. David Duke has Uranus contained by the Sun and Mercury in the tenth house, reinforced by the Moon in Aquarius. He gained infamy by parading in a Nazi uniform as well as the white robes of a Klu Klux Klansman, founding the National Association for the Advancement of White People and being linked to a failed plan to set up a white supremacist government on the island of Dominica in the Caribbean. As a fanatic segregationist he has achieved his goal of getting the attention he wants by attempting to single handedly set America back 200 years.

Duke's second house ruler is Venus, placed in the ninth house in a close semisextile to Uranus. He displays a natural instinct for novel publicity and has also demonstrated a ninth house ability to handle public representation as well as politics.

In 1988 Duke won the political nomination to the radical Populist Party, whose members include neo-Nazis, Klansmen and skinheads. From his early 'teens PR Jupiter had made a trine to Uranus to give Duke acclaim among his followers, but that trine began to move out in the 1990s. At the same time PR Uranus moved slowly into a square to 1st house Mars, suggesting that Duke could be a "loaded cannon," an explosive force to incite social controversy.

## Pisces on the MC

With Pisces on the MC, we are emotionally adaptable with a career in which we explore extended dimensions. To achieve our maximum success, we demonstrate a dedication to our work and exercise creative imagination, even brilliance. We often have a sense of flair

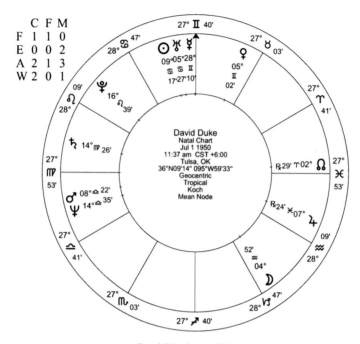

| | C | F | M |
|---|---|---|---|
| F | 1 | 1 | 0 |
| E | 0 | 0 | 2 |
| A | 2 | 1 | 3 |
| W | 2 | 0 | 1 |

David Duke
Natal Chart
Jul 1 1950
11:37 am CST +6:00
Tulsa, OK
36°N09'14" 095°W59'33"
Geocentric
Tropical
Koch
Mean Node

***David Duke: Politician***

*Declinations: A 0N49; ☊ 0N49; ♂ 3S20; ♆ 4S15; ♄ 7N59; ♃ 9S49;*
*♀ 19N28; ☉ 23N7; ☽ 23S8; M 23N26; ☿ 23N29; ♀ 23N31; ♅ 23N36*

and charisma. Our faith in deity, infinity, and our inner realities sustains us. We fail to succeed when we are unstable and yield to the sensational. Deceitfully we say one thing and do another, or try to play both sides against the middle. Subject to scandal or gossip, we are parasites to society. We may well get a reputation of being weird or unrealistic as we withdraw into our private reality.

The career fields shown by the examples are surprisingly high in government figures, religious devotees and musicians. Many skirt the edge of a nebulous position or a questionable relationship to the law, such as Larry Flynt, publisher of pornography who was "born again," and Bhagwan Rajneesh, who established an ashram in Oregon only to finally flee his strife-torn Utopia amid cries of greed and graft.

When we are politicians, we often have scandal touch our lives such as Edouard Daladier who negotiated with Hitler and was later imprisoned, or Umberto Nobile who commanded a dirigible that crashed in the Arctic; when the survivors were rescued, cannibalism was suspected. Others among us are touched by drinking or drug problems. Our archetypal appeal to the public attracts great popularity and the gossip which surrounds us at times is quite delicious, such as that gained by entertainers Cher and Jane Russell. Colorful people all; our lives hold great drama and sometimes mystery. Producer Steven Spielberg captured the magical romance of his Pisces MC in his films.

Many of us exhibit a metaphysical side, a longing for the infinite experience, and we demonstrate the nameless discontent of searching for oneness with the divine or that magical-something-more. We hear the call of both the world of the senses and the music of the spheres. We are drawn to simultaneously follow the path of the mundane and the path of the spirit.

To evaluate the capacity of success of a Pisces MC, consider all planets in the tenth house and the sign where both Neptune and Jupiter are posited and the aspects of both the MC and its rulers, Neptune and Jupiter. With a Pisces MC and Jupiter posited or conjunct, our universal appeal is captivating, as shown by singer Dinah Shore, or we may be noted for whimsy, as comedienne Lily Tomlin. With Neptune posited or conjunct the MC, we strive toward infinite dimension, as did composer Richard Strauss or occult writer H. Rider Haggard.

## Example Chart of Pisces on the MC

Dr. Robert Gale obtained his medical degree in 1970 and his Ph.D. in 1978. Mars-Saturn (or Mars-Pluto) are commonly seen in the charts of physicians and surgeons. He was raised by a supportive, cultured and affectionate family and married Tamar, an Israeli archeologist whom he met in Jerusalem in 1974. They have three children and the family converses in both Hebrew and English.

On April 25, 1986, the Chernobyl atomic reactor failed dramatically; Gale applied immediately to Russian and American sources to offer his help. Disregarding his own safety, he took a team of three to work with the Soviet team over a span of three trips, racing against

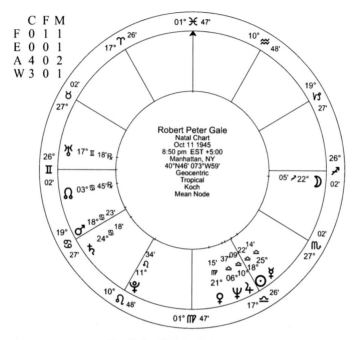

|   | C | F | M |
|---|---|---|---|
| F | 0 | 1 | 1 |
| E | 0 | 0 | 1 |
| A | 4 | 0 | 2 |
| W | 3 | 0 | 1 |

Robert Peter Gale
Natal Chart
Oct 11 1945
8:50 pm EST +5:00
Manhattan, NY
40°N46' 073°W59'
Geocentric
Tropical
Koch
Mean Node

*Dr. Robert Peter Gale: Physician*

*Declinations: ♆ 1S20; ♃ 3S0; ♀ 4N45; ☉ 7S12; ☿ 9S31; M 10S51;*
*♄ 21N3; ☽ 22S16; ♅ 22N51; ♂ 22N56; ♀ 23N12; A 23N23; ☊ 23N25*

time to save radiation victims with bone-marrow transplants. With his passionate concern for human life Gale is awed by the example of Chernobyl as one possibility for the future of mankind.

Nine planets are below the horizon; Gale is not generally known in the same way as people who have elevated planets or many planetary contacts to the MC. The public image that we see of a selfless humanitarian who stepped up to the height of greatness in the face of a universal drama is an appropriate representation of his Pisces MC. Also note the two co-rulers of Pisces, Jupiter and Neptune closely conjunct in Libra, the sign of balance and justice.

Vocational indicators are obscure in Gale's chart. Saturn in the second house does not aspect the MC or MC rulers; it illustrates his value of a mature sense of responsibility but is not the implied vocational indicator. The dispositor (and ruler of the second cusp) is Moon in the sixth house to indicate his daily work fluctuation with people but is not in aspect to the MC/rulers so does not qualify as the vocational indicator. The Moon's dispositor is Jupiter which co-rules the MC, giving us our first vocational clue, that of an educated professional man. The sixth house co-rulers are Mars in the 1st house and Pluto in the third house. Mars in a wide square and Pluto in a close semi-sextile to Jupiter. All the clues which we may follow point to Jupiter. This not only implies the professions, but is the ruler of the MC, and Gale was famed for a brief period in the public limelight.

*When it is difficult to find clear cut indicators of the vocation, look to the first conjunction and opposition which occur in the chart for influential circumstances.* The Moon opposed the ASC when Gale was four months old; there are no further oppositions until later in his life. The Sun made its first conjunction to Mercury at age seven, Venus was conjunct Neptune at 13, Mars conjunct Saturn at 13-15 and Venus conjunct Jupiter at 15-16. Even without information about Gale's childhood and youth, we can draw an inference of progressive development from these conjunctions; that he formed early goals based on a love of culture and justice (Sun-Mercury in Libra), his teen-age romanticism and idealism were stimulated (Venus-Neptune), he grasped his own gut feeling of satisfaction in hard work directed toward a specific goal (Mars-Saturn in Cancer) and he found pleasure in his achievement of academic honors (Venus-Jupiter in Libra).

**Jupiter in the tenth house follows Sagittarius on the MC.**

## Neptune in the Tenth House

Those of us who have Neptune in the tenth house may dream the impossible dreams of Don Quixote to create a better world, as did Red Cross founder Clara Barton or social reformers Carl Marx and John Ruskin; or follow a religious or mystical ideal as did Saint Bernadette, Paramhansa Yogananda and Edna Ballard. On the other hand we may be a sophisticate, a cynic or a sensationalist, as actresses Jean Harlow and Beverly Aadland or pornographer-occultist Conrad Moricand, or even dissolute and perverted as cattle-rustler-killer Harry Tracy or deviate John Wayne Gacy, who buried 33 young men in his cellar.

Outside of such vivid extremes, we average people with Neptune

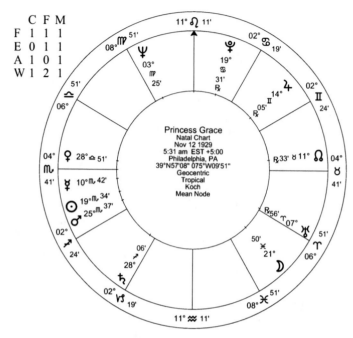

| | C | F | M |
|---|---|---|---|
| F | 1 | 1 | 1 |
| E | 0 | 1 | 1 |
| A | 1 | 0 | 1 |
| W | 1 | 2 | 1 |

*Princess Grace of Monaco*

Declinations: ♅ 2N29; ☽ 6S59; ♀ 9S39; ♆ 10N50; A 13S5; ☿ 14S5; ☊ 15N30; M 17N25; ☉ 17S38; ♂ 19S23; ♃ 21N42; ♀ 21N43; ♄ 22S35

in the tenth house give an impression that's not clearly definitive. If gossip and speculation surround us and our sincerity is questioned, it may very well be that it is due to the illusion of our public image; this is not really whom we see ourselves to be. It is very easy for us to gain a superimposed image, overestimated or underestimated, idealized or fantasized that may not be in keeping with the facts. We might go along with that public image when we feel that it is to our advantage in order to avoid confrontations or exposure.

For the most part we are gentle people who try to avoid stress, sometimes charismatic and gifted, often with a hunger for a better life, for magic, for the infinite, that we don't know how to assuage. Though all fields are represented, our leaning is toward the arts, religion, and service occupations. The emphasis is seldom on business or management. Though all strata are shown the strongest leaning is toward genteel culture. We are often retiring in nature, and may well achieve our goal of actual withdrawal into a cloistered existence.

### Example Chart of Neptune in the Tenth House

What better example of Neptune in the tenth house can we find but that of the young woman who left American to become a real-life princess as the wife of Prince Rainier of Monaco: Grace Kelly. Her whole life seemed enchanted and perfect. She was born to a well-to-do family, her delicate and cultured cool beauty made her a natural photographic model for magazines and television, and then she became a movie star. Even her films were glamorous and dramatic; the closest she came to gritty drama was *Country Girl,* 1954.

Kelly met Prince Rainier in the spring of 1954, they met again Christmas of 1955 and married on April 18, 1956, the fairy-tale ending of a perfect story, to live happily ever after. Or did she? Does Venus in the twelfth house show that a price was paid for the realization of her dream? Is the Neptune portrait the real person, or will we always wonder if the charismatic image concealed other dimensions? Princess Grace died of injuries suffered in a car accident on September 13, 1982; the cause of the accident was never entirely clear.

## The House Position of the MC Ruler

(For the life path, consider the house position of the EQHS tenth house cusp.)

**With the MC ruler in the first house,** we choose fields that express our personal interests, abilities and convictions; however, if the planet is unfocused we may change jobs restlessly or carelessly. We tend to measure success in terms of personal satisfaction or achievement, and often work alone or as boss. Self directed, we strive toward our own career or free-lance work.

**With the MC ruler in the second house,** we choose fields that are practical, tangible and lucrative. We tend to measure success in terms of material reward and comfort. Frequently we get "lucky" breaks and material benefits. Our reputation may be associated with our income.

**With the MC ruler in the third house,** we choose fields that allow self-expression of our intellect or talent. This is often an indication of original thought. We tend to measure success in "being heard," and strive for continual growth in our studies and ideas. Many thinkers, writers and entertainers have this position.

**With the MC ruler in the fourth house,** we choose fields in which we are the center; we are team players with supportive ties but we want to stand out as a focal point. We tend to measure success in appreciation, acceptance, strokes. Many of us have property or own businesses; family is important; perhaps we have noted family members.

**With the MC ruler in the fifth house,** we choose fields in which we gain an audience, clientele or following. We have strong belief systems, in ourselves or our field and tend to measure success by the extent of authority we carry; it's not that we want to be the boss but that we want others to recognize our worth. Often there is protection in family or marital support.

**With the MC ruler in the sixth house,** we choose fields in worthwhile areas of service to feel useful. We tend to measure success with being productive, skilled or accomplished in whatever we do. Modest and discreet, we seldom show off and are uncomfortable with notoriety, but we do want our finished product to be recognized.

**With the MC ruler in the seventh house,** we choose fields in which our interaction with others is acknowledged. We want peer recognition and approbation and tend to measure success in competitive terms, winning over an opponent or proving a point. As teamwork or partnership is essential, we make important alliances.

**With the MC ruler in the eighth house,** we choose fields that hold emotional impact and may even court crises. We tend to measure success by breaking records or pushing the edge of the envelope to the outer limits. Many of us exert power, financially, psychologically, or by our influence on the lives of others or on society itself, even to the practice of crime or violence. We seldom have sedate lives, there is a restless search for some peak or ultimate experience.

**With the MC ruler in the ninth house,** we choose fields where we can display or exhibit our skills and beliefs. We tend to measure success in terms of recognition, of being heard, visible and known, outspoken and on-stage. We often write, publish, teach, perform, entertain and may be seen in religious, political or psychological pulpits.

**With the MC ruler in the tenth house,** we choose fields where the finished product, rather than our personal self, gains recognition. We tend to measure success by achievement peaks but recognize that long time spans are requisite in a successful game plan. We are known usually for a specific accomplishment, or for certain times before the public rather than for our life as a whole.

**With the MC ruler in the eleventh house,** we choose fields that meet societal needs in civic involvement. We are part of our culture, of our time in history, and want to know where and how we fit into our world today. We often have a strong social consciousness, an awareness of our nation and planet but with an openness toward alternate lifestyles. We tend to measure success by our contribution and involvement.

**With the MC ruler in the twelfth house,** we choose fields where we blend in as part of the mainstream, such as social institutions or industries, at the same time as we branch off to swim upstream with interests that are counter-culture. Frequently, we follow pursuits that are off the beaten path. We markedly are involved in several fields simultaneously, exploring extended dimensions.

## The Progressed MC

The main theme of the life is designated by the natal chart, and our development of that theme is shown by progressions. The MC sign and the sign in which the ruler is posited remains the prime directive; however, the signs through which the MC moves by progression symbolize the public environments and experiences that shape and develop us. The same principal is true with the ASC sign, the Sun sign and every other point in the chart that changes signs. We retain the original model (birth chart) but frequently modify the size and shape, dress it differently according to our time and place and put emphasis on the activities that fit into our age and sex (progressed aspects).

We achieve success
when we live the good life,
laugh freely
and love well.

# Appendix

**Data and Sources**
All data is classified according to the Rodden rating system:
AA = Birth certificate, state, church or family records
A = Accurate data from person, family or associate
B = Biography or autobiography
C = Caution, no source of origin
DD = Dirty Data, more than one time/date/place/source
(B.C. is Birth Certificate; B.R. is Birth Records)

**Aadland, Beverly**  September 16, 1942  Los Angeles, CA
Entertainer  11:45 AM PWT  118W15 34N04
A: Laura Breska quotes her mother
**Adams, Ansel**  February 20, 1902  San Francisco, CA
Photographic Artist  3:00 a.m. PST  122W25 37N47
B: Autobiography, 1985, p.5, "about three in the morning."
**Adams, Evangeline**  February 8, 1868  Jersey City, NJ
Astrologer  8:30 a.m. LMT  74W05 40N44
B: Autobiography, *Bowl of Heaven*, p.27
**Adenauer, Konrad**  January 5, 1876  Cologne, Germany
Politician  10:30 a.m. LMT  6E59 50N56
AA: Gauquelin Vol 5 #1846
**Agnelli, Giovanni**  March 12, 1921  Turin, Italy
Industrialist  2:30 a.m. MET  7E40 45N03
AA: Ciro Discepolo quotes B.C.
**Albert, Eddie**  April 22, 1908  Rock Island, IL
Actor  11:30 a.m. CST  89W06 42N16
A: LMR quotes him, 1971 (Edward Albert Heimberger)
**Alcott, Louisa May**  November 29, 1832  Germantown, PA
Writer  00:30 a.m. LMT  75W11 40N03
AA: Data recorded by her father in biography
**Alda, Alan**  January 28, 1936  Manhattan, NY
Actor  5:07 a.m. EST  74W01 40N48
A: Philip Sedgwick quotes him to mutual friend (Alphonso D'Abruzzo)
**Aldrin, "Buzz"**  January 20, 1930  Montclair, NJ
Astronaut  2:17 p.m. EST  74W13 40N50
AA: GBAC (Edwin Eugene Aldrin, Jr.)
**Ali, Muhammad**  January 17, 1942  Louisville, KY
Boxer  6:35 p.m. CST  85W46 38N15
AA: B.C. in hand, ECS (Cassius Marcellus Clay, Jr.)

**Aly Khan, Prince**     June 13, 1911     Turin, Italy
Royalty     2:00 p.m. MET     7E40 45N03
AA: Dana Holliday quotes Leonard Slater, *Aly,* copy of B.C. (Aly
Suleiman Khan)

**Andersen, Hans C.**     April 2, 1805     Odense, Denmark
Writer     1:00 a.m. LMT     10E23 55N24
AA: Luc De Marre quotes parish records

**Anderson, Robert O.**     April 13, 1917     Chicago, IL
Entrepreneur     5:00 a.m. CST     87W38 41N53
AA: B.C. in hand, Wilson

**Andrew, Prince**     February 19, 1960     London, England
British Royalty     3:30 p.m. GMT     0W10 51N30
AA: Newspaper announcement in hand from Gwen Stoney (Andrew Albert
Christian Edward Windsor)

**Anne, Princess**     August 15, 1950     London, England
British Royalty     11:50 a.m. GDT     0W10 51N30
AA: AFA February 1966 quotes official data (Anne Elizabeth Alice Louise
Windsor)

**Armstrong-Jones, Linley**     November 3, 1961     London, England
British Royalty     10:45 a.m. GMT     0W10 51N30
AA: Dana Holliday quotes official records

**Astaire, Fred**     May 10, 1899     Omaha, NE
Dancer, Actor     9:16 p.m. CST     95W56 41N15
AA: Ed Helin quotes B.C. (Frederick Austerlitz)

**Austen, Jane**     December 16,1775     Steventon, England
Writer     11:45 p.m. LMT     1W20 51N14
A: *Pioneer to Poet* quotes a letter from her father, "before midnight."

**Bakker, Tammy Faye**     March 7, 1942     Intl. Falls, MN
Evangelist     3:27 a.m. CWT     93W25 48N36
AA: B.R. in hand, ECS (Tamara Fae LaValley)

**Ballard, Edna**     June 25, 1886     Chicago, IL
Religious Founder     8:30 a.m. CST     87W38 41N53
A: Phyllis Stanick quotes her to Lucy Thompson

**Balmain, Pierre**     May 18,1914     St Jean de Maurienne,
France
Designer     8:15 a.m. GMT     6E21 45N17
AA: B.C. in hand, ECS (Pierre Alexandre Claudius Balmain)

**Barton, Clara**     December 25, 1821     Oxford, MA
Nurse     11:40 a.m. EST     71W52 42N08
B: T. Pat Davis quotes *Story of My Childhood,* 1907, "just pre-noon."
(Clarissa Harlowe Barton)

**Baudelaire, Charles**    April 9,1821    Paris, France
Poet    3:00 p.m. LMT    2E20 48N52
AA: Gauquelin Vol 6 #63 (Pierre Charles Baudelaire)
**Bell, Alexander Graham**    March 3,1847    Edinburgh, Scotland
Inventor    7:00 a.m. LMT    3W13 55N57
AA: Chrys Craswell quotes B.C.
**Bell, Marilyn**    October 19,1937    Toronto, Canada
Swimmer    6:00 a.m. EST    79W23 43N39
A: AA June 1959 quotes her mother
**Bernadette, Saint**    January 7,1844    Lourdes, France
of Lourdes    2:00 p.m. LMT    0W03 43N06
AA: Luc De Marre quotes Choisnard for B.R. (Marie-Bernarde Soubirous)
**Berrigan, Daniel**    May 9, 1921    Virginia, MN
Pacifist    6:30 p.m. CST    92W32 47N31
AA: ECS quotes Bob Garner for B.R.
**Berrigan, Philip Francis**    October 5,1923    Two Harbors, MN
Pacifist    00:45 a.m. CST    91W40 47N01
AA: CSH quotes B.C.
**Black, Shirley Temple**    April 23, 1928    Santa Monica, CA
Actress, Diplomat    9:00 p.m. PST    118W29 34N01
AA: B.C. in hand
**Blake, William**    November 28, 1757    London, England
Artist, Writer    7:45 p.m. LMT    0W10 51N30
A: Given by his friend Varley
**Bradbury, Ray**    August 22, 1920    Waukegan, IL
Writer    4:50 p.m. CST    87W50 42N22
AA: B.C. in hand, ECS. (CST confirmed by Waukegan Library)
**Brahe, Tycho**    December 24, 1546 NS    Skane, Denmark
Astronomer    10:47 a.m. LMT    13E08 55N59
A: Sloane mms #1638 quotes his own chart. (Dec 13 OS, 22:47 after noon)
**Bronson, Charles**    November 3, 1921    Croyle, PA
Actor    11:00 a.m. EST    78W48 40 N24
AA: CSH quotes B.C. (Charles Buchinsky)
**Brown, Helen Gurley**    February 18, 1922    Green Forest, AR
Writer, Editor    3:00 a.m. CST    93W26 36N20
AA: B.C. in hand, ECS from Bob Garner (Helen Marie Gurley)
**Bruce, Lenny**    October 13, 1925    Mineola, NY
Satirist    11:24 a.m. EST    73W38 40N45
AA: CSH quotes B.C. (Leonard Alfred Schneider)
**Bryant, Anita**    March 25, 1940    Bamsdall, OK
Entertainer    3:10 p.m. CST    96W10 36N34
AA: *Constellations '77* quotes B.C. (Anita Jane Bryant)

**Byrd, Richard**     October 25, 1888     Winchester, VA
Admiral     11:30 a.m. EST     78W10 39N11
A: NAJ April 1933 quotes his mother (Richard Evelyn Byrd)
**Burton, Robert**     February 18, 1577 NS Lindley, England
Writer     8:56 a.m. LMT     1W00 52N30
A: BJA quotes his own chart, February 8 OS
**Busch, Adolphus**     July 10, 1839     Mainz-Kastel, Germany
Brewer     4:00 p.m. LMT     8E17 50N00
AA: B.C. in hand, ECS
**Cage, John**     September 5,1912     Los Angeles, CA
Composer     5:00 a.m. PST     118W15 34N04
AA: CSH quotes B.C. (John Milton Cage, Jr.)
**Carradine, David**     December 8,1936     Hollywood, CA
Actor     12:00 p.m. PST     118W21 34N06
AA: GBAC quotes B.C.
**Carson, Johnny**     October 23, 1925     Corning, IA
TV Host     7:15 a.m. CST     94W44 40N59
AA: CSH quotes B.C.
**Carter, Amy**     October 19, 1967     Plains, GA
Noted Family     00:26 a.m. CDT     84W24 32N02
A: *Dell Horoscope* October, 1977, quotes Mrs. Carter's press secretary
**Carter, Billy**     March 29, 1937     Americus, GA
Noted Family     00:30 a.m. CST     84W14 32N04
AA: Marine Taylor quotes B.C. in MH April 1979
**Catherine the Great**     May 2,1729 NS     Stettin, Germany
Empress of Russia     2:30 a.m. LMT     14E32 53N24
B: *Memoirs,* edited by Anthony, Lodon Knoppf, 1927, "in the morning at half past two o'clock," April 21 OS (Sophia Augusta Frederica of Anhalt-Zerbst)
**Cavell, Edith Louise**     December 4,1865     Swardeston, England
Nurse     2:30 a.m. LMT     1E15 52N34
A: M.A. March 1933, "data from family."
**Champion, Marge**     September 2, 1919     Los Angeles, CA
Dancer     9:35 a.m. PWT     118W15 34N04
AA: B.C. in hand, Wilson (Marjorie Celeste Belcher)
**Charles, Prince**     November 14, 1948     London, England
British Royalty     9:14 p.m. GMT     0W10 51N30
AA: AFA quotes official records (Charles Philip Arthur George Windsor)
**Chase, Kate**     August 13, 1840     Cincinnati, OH
Socialite     2:00 a.m. LMT     84W31 39N06
B: Beldon, So *Fell the Angels,* 1956
**Cher**     May 20, 1946     El Centro, CA
Entertainer     7:25 a.m. PST     115W34 32N48
AA: CAH quotes B.C. (Cherilyn Sarkesian)

**Chevalier, Maurice**   September 12, 1888   Paris, France
Actor, dancer   2:00 a.m. LMT   2E20 48N52
AA: Gauquelin Vol 5 #171

**Child, Julia**   August 15,1912   Pasadena, CA
Chef   11:30 p.m. PST   118W09 34N09
AA: CSH quotes B.C. (Julia McWilliams)

**Clark, Geneva**   August 9, 1948   Little Rock, AR
Homemaker   8:54AMCST   92W17 34N45
AA: LMR quotes her, B.C. (Geneva Diane Goss)

**Clark, Karen Lorraine**   April 20, 1971   Torrance, CA
Disabled   1:53 p.m. PST   118W19 33N50
AA: LMR quotes her mother, B.C.

**CLark, Kristy Lynn**   March 24,1972   Los Angeles, CA
Disabled   10:51 a.m. PST   118W.15 34N.04
AA: LMR quotes her, B.C.

**Cliburn, Van**   July 12,1934   Shreveport, LA
Pianist   11:45 a.m. CST   93W45 32N32
AA: CAH quotes B.C. (Harvey Lavan Cliburn, Jr.)

**Clinton, Bill**   August 19, 1946   Hope, AR
Politician   8:51 a.m. CST   93W35 33N40
A: Shelley Ackerman quotes his mother (William Jefferson Blythe IV)

**Collins, Judy**   May 1, 1939   Seattle, WA
Singer   11:55 a.m. PST   122W20 47N36
AA: CSH quotes B.C.

**Cooper, Alice**   February 4, 1948   Detroit, MI
Rock star   10:33 p.m. EST   83W03 42N20
AA: CSH quotes B.C. (Vincent Damon Furnier)

**Cousteau, Jacques Yves**   June 11, 1910   St.Andre Cubzac,
France
Oceanographer   1:15 p.m. Paris time   0W27 45N00
AA: Gauquelin Vol 3 #444

**Dahmer, Jeffrey**   May 21, 1960   Milwaukee, WI
Serial killer   4:34 p.m. CDT   87W54 43N02
AA: Steve Przybylowski quotes B.C.

**Daladier, Edouard**   June 18,1884   Carpentras, France
Politician   5:00 a.m. LMT   5E03 44N03
AA: Gauquelin Vol 5 #1437

**Davies, Marion**   January 3, 1897   Brooklyn, NY
Actress   6:00 a.m. EST   73W56 40N38
B: F.L. Guiles, *Marion Davies,* 1972 (Marion Cecilia Douros)

**Davis, Angela Yvonne**   January 26, 1944   Birmingham, AL
Educator   12:30 p.m. CWT   86W48 33N31
AA: ECS quotes Bob Garner, B.C.

**Day, Doris**  April 3, 1922  Cincinnati, OH
Actress  4:30 p.m. CST  84W31 39N06
AA: CSH quotes B.C. (Doris von Kappelhoff)

**Dederick, Charles** E.  March 22, 1913  Toledo, OH
Synanon founder  4:20 a.m. CST  83W33 41N39
AA: B.R. in hand, ECS

**De Sica, Vittorio**  July 7, 1901  Sora, Italy
Film director  11:00 a.m. MET  13E37 41N43
AA: Gauquelin Vol 5 #868

**Dickinson, Emily**  December 10, 1830  Amherst, MA
Poet  5:00 a.m. LMT  72W31 42N23
AA: Richard Sewall, *The Life of Emily Dickinson,* "recorded by her father

**Diller, Phyllis**  July 17, 1917  Lima, OH
Comedienne  1:00 a.m. CST  84W06 40N44
AA: CAH quotes B.C. (Phyllis Driver)

**Disraeli, Benjamin**  December 21,1804  London, England
Politician  5:30 a.m. LMT  0W10 50N30
AA: BJA May 1921, "recorded"

**Dobyns, Zipporah**  August 26, 1921  Chicago, IL
Astrologer  9:48 p.m. CST  87W38 41N53
A: LMR quotes her, 1978

**Dooley, Dr. Tom**  January 17, 1927  St. Louis, MO
Humanitarian  2:20 a.m. CST  90W12 38N37
AA: Doris Chase Doane quotes B.C. (Thomas Anthony Dooley III)

**Drago, Fred C.**  August 11, 1929  Mobile, AL
Lottery winner  5:30 a.m. CST  88W03 30N41
A: Isaac Armstrong quotes him in AA April, 1985

**Duke, David Ernest**  July 1, 1950  Tulsa, OK
Politician  11:37 a.m. CST  95W55 36N10
AA: B.C. in hand, Buell Huggins

**Edward, Duke of Windsor**  June 23,1894  Richmond, England
British Royalty  9:55 p.m. GMT  0W18 51N27
AA: Pagan quotes official news release

**Einstein, Albert**  March 14, 1879  Ulm, Germany
Physicist  11:30 a.m. LMT  10E00 48N24
AA: Ebertin quotes B.C.

**Elizabeth II, Queen**  April 21, 1926  London, England
British royalty  2:40 a.m. GDT  0W10 51N30
AA: Cyril Fagan quotes official records

**Elliot, David**  November 15, 1947  Los Angeles, CA
Bank employee  3:15 p.m. PST  118W15 34N04
AA: LMR quotes him, B.C.

**Falwell, Jerry**      August 11, 1933      Lynchburg, VA
Evangelist      12:00 p.m. EST      79W09 37N25
A: Edith Custer quotes his twin "about noon."

**Fermi, Enrico**      September 29, 1901      Rome, Italy
Scientist      7:00 p.m. MET      12E29 41N54
AA: Gauquelin Vol 2 #3027

**Fischer, Bobby**      March 9, 1943      Chicago, IL
Chessmaster      2:39 p.m. CWT      87W38 41N53
B: F. Brady, *Profile of a Prodigy,* p.2. (CWT confirmed by ECS from Michael Reese Hospital) (Robert James Fischer)

**Fitzgerald, F. Scott**      September 24, 1896      St. Paul, MN
Writer      3:30 p.m. LMT      93W06 44N57
B: Sara Mayfield, *Exiles from Paradise,* 1971 (Frances Scott Key Fitzgerald)

**Flynt, Larry**      November 1, 1942      Saylersville, KY
Publisher      9:10 p.m. EWT      83W.0437N.45
AA: Genivieve Wolfsohn quotes B.C. in AA January 1979

**Ford, Henry**      July 30, 1863      Dearborn, MI
Industrialist      7:00 a.m. LMT      83W.1142N.19
B: Allan Nevins, *Ford, the Times, the Man, the Company,* Charles Scribner's Sons, New York, 1954, p.22. On p. 592 the time is verified by George Holmes, son of the midwife who delivered the baby, taken from his mother's notes.

**Ford, Kathy**      February 11, 1940      Belding, MI
Model      5:30 a.m. EST      85W14 43N06
A: Penny Thornton quotes her in Sons *and Lovers*

**Ford, Susan**      July 6, 1957      Washington, DC
Noted family      3:53PMEDT      77W02 38N54
A: Ruth Dewey quotes Mrs. Ford's press secretary

**Fremont, John Charles**      January 21, 1813      Savannah, GA
Surveyor      11:00 p.m. LMT      81W06 32N05
A: Data from him quoted in *Constellations 1977*

**Freud, Sigmund**      May 6, 1856      Frieburg, Czech
Psychoanalysist      6:30 p.m. LMT      18E10 49N39
AA: Philip Lucas quotes his father's diary

**Friedan, Betty**      February 4,1921      Peoria, IL
Feminist writer      4:00 a.m. CST      89W35 40N42
AA: CAH quotes B.C. (Betty Naomi Goldstein)

**Frost, David**      April 7, 1939      Tenterden, England
TV host      10:30 a.m. GMT      0E42 51N05
A: Paul Rosner quotes Diahann Carrol, data from Frost (David Parradine Frost)

**Furstenberg, Diane von**   December 31, 1946   Brussels, Belgium
Designer                     3:00 a.m. MET      4E20 50N50
A: LMR quotes her letter, 1977 (Diane Simone Michelle Halfin)
**Gacy, John Wayne**         March 17, 1942     Chicago, IL
Serial killer                00:29 a.m. CST     87W38 41N53
AA: Edith Custer quotes hospital records in MH April 1979 (CST confirmed)
**Gale, Dr. Robert Peter**   October 11, 1945   Manhattan, NY
Physician                    8:50 p.m. EST      73W59 40N46
AA: B.C. in hand
**Gates, William Henry III**  October 28, 1955   Seattle, WA
Entrepreneur                 9:15 p.m. PST      122W20 47N36
B: James Wallace and Jim Erickson, *Hard Drive: Bill Gates and the Making of the Microsoft Empire,* John Wiley and Sons Inc, New York, 1992, p. 10
**Gauquelin, Michel**        November 13, 1928  Paris, France
Astrologer                   10:15 p.m. GMT     2E20 48N52
A: LMR quotes him, "10:15 to 10:20 PM" (Michel Roland Gauquelin)
**Gauguin, Paul**            June 7, 1848       Paris, France
Artist                       10:00 a.m. LMT     2E20 48N52
AA: Francoise Gauquelin quotes B.C. in correction of Vol 4 #439 (Eugene Henri Paul Gauguin)
**Gaylord, Mitch**           March 10, 1961     Hollywood, CA
Gymnast                      12:41 p.m. PST     118W21 34N06
AA: Marion March quotes his mother reading the B.C. over the phone
**Geller, Uri**              December 20,1946   Tel Aviv, Palestine
Telekinetic                  2:00 a.m. EET      34E46 32N04
A: Richard Nolle quotes him to Puharich
**Genet, Jean**              December 19, 1910  Paris, France
Writer                       7:45 p.m. LMT      2E20 48N52
AA: Gauquelin Vol 3 #1984
**Gershwin, George**         September 26,1898  Brooklyn, NY
Composer                     11:09 a.m. EST     73W56 40N38
A: M.E.Jones quotes Augusta Wiley, "verified." (Jacob Gershvin)
**Getty, Jean Paul**         December 15,1892   Minneapolis, MN
Entrepreneur                 8:43 a.m. LMT      93W16 44N59
B: Ralph Hewins, *The Richest American,* 1960, p.38, "father knew at 9:00 a.m. that Sarah was safely delivered of their son"
**Godzik, Gregory**          March 23, 1959     Chicago, IL
Homicide victim              3:54 p.m. CST      87W38 41N53
AA: B.R. quoted in MH April, 1979
**Goering, Hermann**         January 12, 1893   Rosenheim, Germany
Nazi military                4:00 a.m. MET      12E07 47N51
AA: Gauquelin Vol 3 #1881

**Goethe, Johann von**     August 28, 1749 NS
Writer     12:00 p.m. LMT
A: Ebertin quotes his autobiography, "born mid-day when the clock struck 12:00" (Johann Wolfgang von Goethe)

**Gogh, Vincent van**     March 30, 1853     Zundert, Neth.
Artist     11:00 a.m. LMT     4E40 51N28
AA: B.C. in hand, ECS (Vinqent Willem van Gogh)

**Grace, Princess**     November 12, 1929     Philadelphia, PA
Royalty of Monaco     5:31 a.m. EST     75W10 39N57
AA: B.C. in hand, ECS (Grace Patricia Kelly)

**Greene, Kenneth**     January 3, 1958     Seekonk, MA
Lottery winner     6:16 p.m. EST     71W20 41N49
AA: Frances McEvoy quotes B.C.

**Greer, Gennaine**     January 29, 1939     Melbourne, Australia
Feminist writer     6:00 a.m. ST-10     144E58 37S49
A: Tiffany Holmes quotes her

**Gretzky, Wayne**     January 26, 1961     Brantford, Ont, Canada
Hockey player     7:45 a.m. EST     80W16 43N08
AA: Brian Clark quotes him, hospital birth card

**Haggard, Henry Rider**     June 22, 1856     Bradenham, England
Writer     5:10 a.m. LMT     0W49 51N41
AA: M.A. June 1925 quotes family bible

**Haldeman, H. R.**     October 27, 1926     Los Angeles, CA
Govemment official     3:30 a.m. PST     118W15 34N04
AA: B.C. in hand (Harry Robbins Haldeman)

**Hall, Rex**     March 13, 1912     Nephi, UT
Engineer     8:30 a.m. MST     111W50 39N42
A: LMR quotes him, mother's statement

**Harlow, Jean**     March 3, 1911     Kansas City, MO
Actress     7:40 p.m. CST     94W35 39N06
AA: CL quotes B.C. (Harlean Carpenter)

**Hawes, Amy**     November 23, 1949     PaloAlto, CA
Musician     00:45 a.m. PST     122W09 37N27
AA: B.C. in hand (Amy Kae Rodden)

**Hawn, Goldie Jean**     November 21, 1945     Washington, DC
Actress     9:20 a.m. EST     77W02 38N54
AA: CAH quotes B.C.

**Hearst, Patricia C.**     February 20, 1954     San Francisco, CA
Heiress     6:01 PM PST     122W25 37N47
AA: CSH quotes B.C.

**Helmsley, Leona**     July 4, 1920     Marbeltown, NY
Entrepreneur     6:00 a.m. EDT     74W09 41N51
AA: B.C. quoted in AA June 1990 (Leona Mindy Rosenthal, Columbia County)

**Hepburn, Audrey**    May 4, 1929    Ixelles, Belgium
Actress    3:00 a.m. GDT    4E22 50N50
AA: Luc De Marre quotes B.R. (Audrey Hepburn-Ruston)
**Hendrix, Jimi**    November 27, 1942    Seattle, WA
Musician    10:15 AM PWT    122W20 47N36
AA: CSH quotes B.C. (Johnny Allen Hendrix)
**Hesse, Hermann**    July 2, 1877    Calw, Germany
Writer    6:30 p.m. LMT    8E44 48N43
AA: Zeiler, *Portrait of Hesse*, "time stated in his mother's diary"
**Hill, Benny**    January 21, 1924    Southampton, England
Comedian    8:15 a.m. GMT    1W25 50N55
A: Russell Grant quotes him in TV Times (Alfred Hawthorn Hill)
**Houston, Whitney**    August 9, 1963    Newark, NJ
Singer    8:55 p.m. EDT    74W10 40N44
AA: B.C. in hand from Kathryn Farmer (Whitney Elizabeth Houston)
**Hughes, Howard**    December 24, 1905    Houston, TX
Entrepreneur    10: UPMOST    95W22 29N46
A: His uncle, Rupert Hughes, to LeGros (Howard Robard Hughes, Jr.)
**Hutton, Barbara**    November 14, 1912    New York, NY
Actress    2:25 p.m. EST    73W57 40N45
AA: Blanca Holmes, "data from her baby book"
**Jackson, Glenda**    May 9, 1936    Birkinhead, England
Actress    8:00 a.m. GDT    3W02 53N24
A: R.H. Oliver quotes her, "about 8:00 AM"
**Jeffcoat, Hugh**    June 3,1934    Birmingham, AL
Gambler    12:04 p.m. CST    86W48 33N31
A: Him in MH Extra October 1983
**Joan of Arc**    January 15, 1412 NS    Domremy-la-Pucelle, FR
Maid of Orleans    4:30 p.m. LMT    5E41 48N27
DD: The Rev. Denis in his biog, 1919, quotes "sunset from actual records."
Another account refers to "church and family documents for one hour after
sunset" which would still give an Aries MC
**John, Elton**    March 25, 1947    Pinner, England
Singer    4:00 p.m. GDT    0W23 51N36
A: Ruth Dewey, "confirmed by him" (Reginald Kenneth Dwight)
**Jones, Jim**    May 13, 1931    Lynn, IN
Cult leader    10:00 p.m. CST    84W56 40N03
AA: ECS quotes B.R. in hand (James Warren Jones)
**Joplin, Janis**    January 19, 1943    Port Arthur, TX
Singer    9:45 a.m. CWT    93W56 29N54
AA: R.H. Oliver quotes B.C.

**Kars, Sylvia**  September 28, 1933 Kansas City, MO
Sex therapist  3:35 p.m. CST  94W35 39N06
A: Jim Eshelman quotes her
**Kennedy, Ethel**  April 11, 1928  Chicago, IL
Noted family  3:30 a.m. CST  87W.3941N.53
AA: B.C. in hand, Wilson (Ethel Skakel)
**Kennedy, Joan**  September 5, 1935 New York, NY
Noted family  6:10 a.m. EST  73W57 40N45
AA: B.C. in hand, Wilsons
**Kennedy, John F.**  May 29, 1917  Brookline, MA
Politician  3:00 p.m. EST  71W07 42N20
B: Doris Kearns Goodwin, *The Fitzgeralds and the Kennedys*, 1987, p. 274)
**Kepler, Johannes**  January 6, 1572 NS Weil Der Stadt, Ger.
Astronomer-astrologer 2:37 p.m. LMT  8E52 48N45
B: Given in his book, *Harmonics*
**Kerouac,Jack**  March 12, 1922  Lowell, MA
Writer  5:00 p.m. EST  71W19 42N38
B: Anne Charters, Kerouac (Jean-Louis le Bris de Kerouac)
**Kerrigan, Nancy**  October 13, 1969 Wobum.MA
Figure skater  5:17 p.m. EDT  71W09 42N29
AA: Frances McEvoy quotes B.C.
**King, Billie Jean**  November 22,1943 Long Beach, CA
Tennis player  11:45 a.m. PWT 118W11 33N46
AA: CAH quotes B.C. (Billie Jean Moffitt)
**King, Stephen**  September 21, 1947 Portland, ME
Writer  1:30 a.m. EDT  70W15 43N40
A: D.Jo and M.J. Wagner quotes him in MH January 1981
**Kinman, Donald**  May 31, 1923  Petersburg, IN
Homicide  1:45 p.m. CST  87W17 38N30
AA: T.P. Davis quotes B.C.
**Knievel, Evel**  October 17, 1938 Butte, MT
Daredevil  2:40 p.m. MST  112W32 46N00
AA: CSH quotes B.C. (Robert Craig Knievel)
**lang, k.d.**  November 9, 1961 Edmonton, Alb, Can
Singer  2:03 a.m. MST  113W28 53N33
A: Marion March quotes her to Robin Bulla (Kathy Dawn Lang)
**Lawrence, Mary Wells** May 25, 1928  Youngstown, OH
Ad executive  11:30 a.m. EST  80W39 41N06
AA: CSH quotes B.C. (Mary Georgene Berg)
**Leary, Dr. Timothy** October 22, 1920 Springfield, MA
Psychedelicist  10:45 AM EDT  72W35 42N06
AA: ECS quotes Bob Garner for B.R. (Timothy Francis Leary)

**Lee, Bruce**          November 27, 1940    San Francisco, CA
Martial arts actor       7:12 a.m. PST      122W25 37N47
AA: Robert Paige quotes B.C. (Li Jun Fan)

**Leigh, Vivien**         November 5, 1913     Darjeeling, India
Actress               5:16 p.m. LMT      88E16 27N02
B: Cottrell, Lawrence and Oliuier, 1975, "sunset" (Vivien Mary Hartley)

**Leonardo da Vinci**     April 23, 1452 NS     Vinci, Italy
Artist                9:40PMLMT         10E55 43N47
B: Biography, "Grandson born April 15, Saturday, 3:00 o'clock at night" (Florentine time)

**Leopold, Nathan**       November 19, 1904    Chicago, IL
Homicide             3:55 PM CST       87W38 41N53
AA: T.Pat Davis quotes his wife for family records

**Levant, Oscar**         December 27, 1906    Pittsburgh, PA
Pianist, composer, actor  11:45 p.m. EST     80W00 40N26
AA: Lockhart quotes B.C.

**Levine, Mimi Donner**   March 18,1927       Brooklyn, NY
Astrologer            00:24 a.m. EST     73W56 40N38
A: Her in *Geocosmic News* Vol 9 #3/4

**Lincoln, Abraham**     February 12,1809     Hodgenvitle, KY
Politician             6:54 a.m. LMT      85W44 37N34
B: William Barton, *Women Lincoln Loved*, 1927, p.81-85, "sunup"

**Lippert, George W.**     May 9,1849        Aschaffenburg, Ger
Three-legged man      8:32 p.m. LMT      9E09 49N59
A: Signs of the Times February, 1885 quotes him

**London, Jack**          January 12, 1876      San Francisco, CA
Writer                2:00 p.m. LMT      122W25 37N47
B: Biography by his wife (John Griffith Chaney)

**Love, Michael**         March 15, 1941      Los Angeles, CA
Musician             10:55 a.m. PST    118W15 34N04
AA: LMR quotes him, B.C.

**Luther, Martin**        November 19, 1483 NS Eisleben, Germany
Reformationist        11:00 PM LAT      11E32 51N31
AA: B.R. in hand from ECS (November 10 OS)

**Machiavelli, Nicolo**    May 11, 1469 NS     Florence, Italy
Politician             11:07 p.m. LMT     11E15 43N46
B: Blackwell quotes Vita de Nicolo Machiavelli for "May 3 at 4 o'clock" (Florentine time)

**Madonna**              August 16, 1958      Bay City, MI
Singer                7:05 a.m. EST      83W53 43N36
A: Tashi Grady quotes her father for B.C. (Madonna Louise Veronica Ciccone)

**Maharaj-Ji** December 10, 1957 Bandrinath, India
Guru 2:30 a.m. IST 79E30 30N44
A: Ruth Dewey quotes his mother to colleagues
**Maimonides** April 6, 1135 NS Cordoba, Spain
Linguist 1:00 p.m. LAT 4W46 37N53
B: Macrison and Hubler, Trial and Triumph (March 30 OS) (Moses ben
Maimon ben Joseph)
**Marconi, Guglieimo** April 25, 1874 Bologna, Italy
Inventor 9:15 a.m. Rome time 11E20 44N29
AA: Gauquelin Vol 2 #3071 (Guglieimo Marchese Marconi)
**Margaret Rose, Princess** August 21, 1930 Glamis Castle, Scotland
British royalty 9:22 p.m. GDT 3W01 56N37
AA: Joanne Clancy quotes B.R.
**Marx, Harpo** November 23, 1888 New York, NY
Comedian 2:30 a.m. EST 73W57 40N45
A: C.Harvey quotes him to S. Michaud (Adolph Arthur Marx)
**Marx, Karl Heinrich** May 5, 1818 Trier, Germany
Socialist 2:00 a.m. LMT 6 E38 49N45
AA: Wemyss FN #157 "recorded"
**Mayfair Boy** September 13,1916 St-Johns Wood, Eng.
Jewel thief 4:15 a.m. GDT 0Wll 51N31
A: Autobiography, *Mayfair Boy*
**McLaughlin, James** December 31, 1954 Boston, MA
Carpenter 00:52 a.m. EST 71W04 42N22
AA: (Frances McEvoy quotes B.C.)
**McLaughlin, Kathleen** February 17,1957 Boston, MA
Lottery winner 6:35 a.m. EST 71W04 42N22
AA: Frances McEvoy quotes B.C.
**Medici, Catherine de** April 23, 1519 NS Florence, Italy
Queen of France 5:04 a.m. LMT 11E15 43N46
AA: Fagan quotes records for " sunrise"
**Mehta, Zubin** April 29,1936 Bombay, India
Conductor 2:50 a.m. IST 72E50 18N58
B: Brookspan and Yockey, *The Zubin Mehta Story*, p.5
**Merton, Thomas** January 31,1915 Prades, France
Ecclesiastic 9:00 a.m. GMT 2E26 42N37
AA: B.R. in hand, ECS (Monica Furlong gives 9:30 p.m. in *Merton, A Bi-
ography*
**Michelangelo** March 15, 1475 NS Caprese, Italy
Artist 1:45 AM LMT 11E59 43N39
B: J.A. Symonds, *The Life ofMichaelangelo*, "father's notebook, four or
five hours before daybreak, March 6 OS" (Michelangelo di Lodivico
Buonarroti Simoni)

**Miller, Henry Valentine**   December 26, 189   Brooklyn, NY
Wrter                         12:30 p.m. EST   73W56 40N38
B: My Friend Henry Miller (The biography, *Always Merry and Bright*
gives 12:17 PM)

**Mitchell, John Newton**   September 5, 1913   Detroit, MI
Attorney                    3:30 a.m. CST      83W03 42N20
AA: CSH quotes B.C.

**Monroe, Marilyn**   June 1, 1926      Los Angeles, CA
Actress              9:30 a.m. PST     118W15 34N04
AA: B.C. in hand, ECS (Norma Jean Mortenson)

**Montessori, Maria**   August 31, 1870       Chiaravalle, Italy
Educator                3:30 a.m. Rome time   13E19 43N36
AA: Gauquelin Vol 2 #1509

**Moore, Marcia**   May 22,1928      Cambridge, MA
Astrologer          9:10 a.m. EDT    71W06 42N22
A: LMR quotes her, 1972

**Moricand, Conrad**      January 17, 1887   Paris, France
Occultist, pomographer   7:08 p.m. LMT      2E20 48N52
B: Dana Holliday quotes Henry Miller, A *Devil in Paradise*

**Morrison, James D.**   December 8, 1943   Melbourne, FL
Musician                 11:55 a.m. EWT     80W37 28N05
AA: B.C. in hand, ECS

**Moses, Grandma** *see Anna Mary Robertson*

**Murphy, George Arthur**   May 25, 1932   San Francisco, CA
Accountant                 3:57 p.m. PST   122W25 37N47
AA: B.C. from him

**Murray, Anne**   June 20, 1945      Springhill, N.S. Canada
Singer              10:40 a.m. AWT     64W03 45N39
B: Brian dark quotes D. Livingstone, *The Story So Far*

**Mussolini, Benito**   July 29, 1883           Dovia il Predappio, Italy
Dictator               2:00 p.m. Rome time   12E02 44N13
AA: Gauquelin Vol 5 #1745

**Neff, Hildegard**   December 28, 1925   Ulm, Germany
Actress, writer      5:15 a.m. MET       10E00 48N34
AA: Gauquelin Vol 5 #1157

**Nelson, Willie**   April 30, 1933    Abbott, TX
Singer              12:30 p.m. CST   97W04 31N53
AA: GBAC quotes B.C. (William Hugh Nelson)

**Nicholson, Jack**   April 22, 1937    Neptune, NJ
Actor                11:20 a.m. EST   74W04 40N15
A: Linda Clark quotes him; same from Frederick Davies

**Nietzsche, Friedrich** October 15, 1844 Rocken, Germany
Philosopher 10:00 a.m. LMT 12E08 51N15
B: M.A. November 1914 quotes biography (Friedrich Wilhehn Nietzsche)
**Nilsen, Dennis Andrew** November 23,1945 Fraserburgh, Scotland
Serial killer 4:00 a.m. GMT 2W00 57N42
AA: Paul Wright quotes B.C.
**Nin, Anais** February 21, 1903 Paris, France
Writer 8:25 p.m. LMT 2E20 48N52
AA: ECS quotes B.C. in hand (Rose Jean Anais Edelmina Antolina Nin)
**Nobile, Umberto** January 21, 1885 Lauro, Italy
Military 3:15 p.m. Rome time 14E38 40N52
AA: Gauquelin Vol 3 #3089
**O'Hair, Madalyn Murray** April 13, 1919 Pittsburgh, PA
Attorney 9:00 a.m. EWT 80W00 40N26
AA: CSH quotes B.C. (Madalyn Mays Murray)
**Onassis, Christina** December 11, 1950 New York, NY
Heiress 3:00 p.m. EST 73W57 40N45
AA: Ruth Dewey quotes hospital records
**O'Neal, Tatum** November 5, 1963 Los Angeles, CA
Actress 3:38a.m. PST 118W15 34N04
AA: B.C. in hand, Wilson (Tatum Beatrice O'Neal)
**Packard, Vance Oakley** May 22, 1914 Granville, PA
Writer 5:30 a.m. EST 77W38 40N33
AA: CSH quotes B.C.
**Pahlavi, Prince Reza** October 31, 1960 Teheran, Iran Ali Reza
Pahlavi of Iran 11:55 a.m. ST -3.5 51E26 35N40
AA: AQ Winter 1960 "official"
**Parker, Mary Alice** June 8, 1928 Riverside, CA
Pharmacist 12:50 p.m. PST 117W22 33N59
AA: LMR quotes her, B.C. (Mary Alice Pearson)
**Parker, Webster John** August 18, 1926 McKeesport, PA
Pharmacist 3:50 p.m. EST 79W51 40N21
AA: LMR quotes him, B.C.
**Pasteur, Louis** December 27, 1822 Dole, France
Scientist 2:00 a.m. LMT 5E30 47N06
AA: Gauquelin Vol 2 #555
**Peckinpah, Sam** February 21, 1925 Fresno, CA
Film director 2:15 p.m. PST 119W46 36N45
AA: B.R. in hand, ECS (David Samuel Peckinpah)
**Perot, Henry Ross** June 27, 1930 Texarkana, TX
Entrepreneur 5:34 a.m. CST 94W03 33N25
AA: GBAC quotes B.C.

**Philip, Prince**      June 10, 1921      Corfu, Greece
British royalty      9:46 p.m. EET      19E42 39N40
AA: Luc De Marre quotes official bulletin (Philippos Schleswig-Holstein
Sonderburg Glucksberg)
**Phoenix, River**      August 23, 1970      Madras, OR
Actor      12:10 p.m. PDT      121W08 44N38
A: John Woodsmall quotes him to colleague Marie Yates
**Piaf, Edith**      December 19, 1915      Paris, France
Singer      5:00 a.m. GMT      2E20 48N52
AA: Gauquelin Vol 4 #628 (Edith Giovanna Cassion)
**Piccard, Auguste**      January 28, 1884      Basel, Switzerland
Scientist      11:00 p.m. LMT      7E35 47N33
AA: Wemyss FN# 143, "recorded"
**Piccard, Jean Felix**      January 28, 1884      Basel, Switzerland
Scientist      10:45 p.m. LMT      7E35 47N33
AA: Wemyss FN #143 "recorded"
**Presley, Elvis Aaron**      January 8, 1935      Tupelo, MS
Singer      4:35 a.m. CST      88W42 34N15
AA: B.C. in hand, Eugene Moore
**Proust, Marcel**      July 10,1871      Paris, France
Writer      11:30PMLMT      2E20 48N52
AA: Gauquelin Vol 6 #658
**Rajneesh, Bhagwan Shree**  December 11, 1931      Kutchwada, India
Guru      5:13 p.m. IST      77E23 23N15
A: ECS quotes his ashram, "from mother's memory"
**Raphael of Urbino**      April 5, 1483 NS      Urbino, Italy
Artist      9:30 p.m. LMT      12E38 43N43
A: Fagan quotes Varsi c. 1511, "3:00 o'clock into the night on Good Fri-
day" (March 28: Florentine time) (Raffaelo Sanzio)
**RamDas**      April 6, 1931      Boston, MA
Guru      10:40 a.m. EST      71W04 42N22
B: Autobiography, *The Only Dance There Is* (Richard Alpert)
**Ray, James Earl**      March 10, 1928      Alton, IL
Assassin, Thief      3:00 p.m. CST      90W11 38N53
AA: Penny Bertucelli quotes B.C. in M.H. July 1978
**Reagan, Ronald Jr.**      May 20, 1958      Los Angeles, CA
Noted Family      8:46 a.m. PDT      118W15 34N04
AA: B.C. in hand, Wilson
**Renay, Liz**      April 14, 1926      Chandler, AZ
ExoticDancer      11:30 a.m. MST      111W50 33N18
A: LMR quotes her, 1974 (Pearl Elizabeth Dobbins)

**Renoir, Pierre-August**    February 25, 1841    Limoges, France
Artist    6:00 a.m. LMT    1E16 45N50
AA: Gauquelin Vol 4 #946

**Robertson, Anna Mary**    September 7, 1860    Greenwich, NY
Artist    3:58 p.m. LMT    73W30 43N05
A: Tucker's *Research Quarterly* quotes her

**Rodden, Dana Roerich**    July 3, 1957    Castro Valley, CA
Musician    5:11 p.m.PDT    122W05 37N42
AA: B.C. in hand

**Rodden, Jonathan David**    October 26, 1960    Covina, CA
Military    4:53 a.m.PST    117W52 34N05
AA: B.C. in hand

**Rodden, Lynn Andrea**    March 14, 1951    PaloAlto, CA
Shen practioner    11:11 p.m. PST    122W10 37N27
AA: B.C. in hand

**Rommel, Erwin**    November 15, 1891    Heidenheim, Germany
Military    12:00 p.m. Munich time 10E08 48N40
AA: Gauquelin Vol 3 #2098 (Erwin Johannes Eugin Rommel)

**Rooney, Mickey**    September 23, 1920    Brooklyn, NY
Entertainer    11:55 a.m. EDT    73W56 40N38
A: *I.E. An Autobiography* (Joe Yule, Jr.)

**Roussel, Athina Helene**    January 29, 1985    Neuilly sur Seine, FR
Heiress    2:50 a.m. GMT    2E16 48N53
AA: B.C. in hand, ECS

**Ruskin, John**    February 8, 1819    London, England
Writer    7:30 a.m. LMT    0W10 51N30
B: W.G. Collingwood quotes him in *Life and Works*

**Russell, Jane**    June 21, 1921    Bemidji, MN
Actress    6:15 a.m. CST    94W53 47N28
AA: CSH quotes B.C. (Ernestine Jane Geraldine Russell)

**Sagan, Francoise**    June 21, 1935    Carjoc France
Writer    11:00 a.m. GDT    1E50 44N30
AA: Gauquelin Vol 6 #716 (Francoise Quoirez)

**St. Denis, Ruth**    January 20, 1878    Newark, NY
Dancer    00:05 a.m. LMT    74W10 40N44
A: Rudhyar quotes her for "a few minutes past midnight"

**Sarandon, Susan**    October 4, 1946    New York, NY
Actress    2:25 p.m. EST    73W57 40N45
A: F. Davies quotes her in *Signs of the Stars,* 1988 (Susan Tomalin)

**Schwarzkopf, H. Norman**    August 22, 1934    Trenton, NJ
Military    4:45 a.m. EDT    74W45 40N13
AA: B.C. in hand (Herbert Norman Schwarzkopf, Jr.)

**Schweitzer, Albert**    January 14, 1875    Kayserburg, Alsace
Humanitarian    11:50 p.m. LMT    7E15 48N08
AA: Bruno Huber quotes B.C.

**Sells, Betsy**    May 7, 1952    Palo Alto, CA
Artist    4:42 a.m. PDT    122W10 37N27
AA: B.C. in hand (Betsy Alison Rodden)

**Seiznick, David O.**    May 10, 1902    Pittsburgh, PA
Film producer    10:00 a.m. EST    80W00 40N26
A: C.L. quotes him to Tobey in 1932 (David Oliver Seiznick)

**Sharif, Omar**    April 10, 1932    Alexandria, Egypt
Actor    5:30 p.m. EET    29E54 31N11
B: Autobiography, *The Eternal Male* (Michael Shalhoub)

**Shelley, Mary**    August 30, 1797    London, England
Writer    11:20 p.m. LMT    0W10 51N30
AA: MS Magazine quotes father's diary (Mary Wollstonecraft Godwin)

**Shields, Brooke**    May 31, 1965    Manhattan, NY
Actress    1:45 p.m. EDT    74W.01 40N.48
B: Autobiography *The Brooke Book* (Brooke Christa Shields)

**Shore, Dinah**    February 29, 1916    Winchester, TN
Entertainer    11:45 a.m. CST    86W07 35N11
AA: CSH quotes B.C. (Frances Rose Shore)

**Simpson, O.J.**    July 9, 1947    San Francisco, CA
Football player    8:08 a.m. PST    122W25 37N47
AA: CSH quotes B.C. (Orenthal James Simpson)

**Sinclair, Upton Beall Jr.**    September 20, 1878    Baltimore, MD
Writer    9:00 a.m. LMT    76W37 39N17
A: Lockhart quotes him in AFA Data Exchange

**Speer, Albert**    March 19, 1905    Mannheim, Germany
Nazi architect    11:15 a.m. MET    8E29 49N29
AA: B.C. in hand, ECS

**Spielberg, Max Samuel**    June 13, 1985    Los Angeles, CA
Heir    L52PMPDT    118W15 34N04
A: Beth Koch quotes studio publicity department

**Spielberg, Steven**    December 18,1946    Cincinnati, OH
Film producer    6:16 p.m. EST    84W31 39N06
AA: B.C. in hand from Joan Negus, obtained by Linda Lineaveuer

**Starr, Ringo**    July 7, 1940    Liverpool, England
Drummer    00:05 a.m. GDT    2W57 53N23
B: F. Davies, *The Beatles,* "just after midnight" (Richard Starkey)

**Steinem, Gloria**    March 25, 1934    Toledo, OH
Feminist writer    10:00 p.m. EST    83W33 41N39
AA: B.R. in hand, ECS

**Stokowski, Leopold**    April 18, 1882    London, England
Conductor    4:00 a.m. GMT    0W10 51N30
A: C.L. quotes him personally (Leopold Anthony Stokowski)
**Strauss, Richard**    June 11, 1864    Munich, Germany
Composer    6:00 a.m. LMT    11E34 48N08
AA: Ernst Krause quotes father's diary in *Richard Strauss, the Man and his Work*
**Streep, Meryl**    June 22, 1949    Summit, NJ
Actress    8:05 a.m. EDT    74W22 40N43
AA: B.R. in hand, ECS (Mary Louise Streep)
**Strieber, Louis Whitney**    June 13, 1945    San Antonio, TX
Writer    4:45 a.m. CWT    98W30 29N25
AA: David Dozier quotes B.C. in hand
**Streisand, Barbra**    April 24, 1942    Brooklyn, NY
Singer, actress    5:08 a.m. EWT    73W56 40N38
AA: ECS quotes her to a mutual friend, B.C. (Barbara Joan Streisand)
**Struthers, Sally**    July 28, 1947    Portland, OR
Actress    10:30 a.m. PST    122W41 45N32
A: John Hanson quotes her
**Tate, Sharon**    January 24, 1943    Dallas, TX
Actress    5:47 p.m. CWT    96W48 32N47
AA: Lockhart quotes B.C.
**Tesia, Nikola**    July 10, 1856    Smiljan, Yugoslavia
Inventor    00:00 LMT    15E19 44N35
B: Biography, "the stroke of midnight of July 9/10"
**Therese de Lisieux**    January 2, 1873    Alencon, France
Saint    11:30 p.m. LMT    0E05 48N26
AA: T.Pat Davis quotes B.R. (Marie Francoise Therese Martin)
8:50 a.m. ESTSeptember 2, 1937 12:42 p.m. CST
**Tomlin, Lily**    September 1, 1939    Highland Park, MI
Comedienne    1:45 a.m. EST    83W06 42N24
AA: ECS quotes her, B.C. (Mary Jean Tomlin)
**Toulouse-Lautrec, Henri de**    November 24, 1864    Aibi, France
Artist    6:00 a.m. LMT    2E09 43N56
AA: Gauquelin Vol 4 #1078
**Tracy, Harry**    October 23, 1875    Minong, WI
Rustler    9:45 p.m. LMT    91W49 46N06
A: AFA December 1938 quotes his mother
**Trump, Donald John**    June 14, 1946    Queens, NY
Entrepreneur    9:51 a.m. EDT    73W52 40N43
A: LMR quotes his mother to a mutual friend

**Turner, Robert Edward**  November 19, 1938  Cincinnati, OH
Entrepreneur  8:50 a.m. EST  84W31 39N06
AA: GBAC quotes B.C.
**Ueberroth, Peter Victor**  September 2, 1937  Chicago, IL
Entrepreneur  12:42 p.m. CST  87W38 41N53
AA: B.C. in hand, Wilson
**Uston, Ken**  January 12, 1935  New York, NY
Gambler  3:00 a.m. EST  73W57 40N45
A: LMR quotes him, 1979, data from his mother
**Vanderbilt, Gloria**  February 20, 1924  New York, NY
Designer  9:55 a.m. EST  73W57 40N45
A: Dana Holliday quotes her personally
**Verne, Jules**  February 8, 1828  Nantes, France
Writer  12:00 p.m. LMT  1W33 47N13
AA: Gauquelin Vol 6 #794
**Walker, Robert Hudson Jr.**April 15, 1940  Queens, NY
Noted family  6:08 a.m. EST  73W54 40N45
AA: B.C. in hand, Wilson
**Walker, Michael Ross**  March 17, 1941  Queens, NY
Noted family  8:13 a.m. EST  73 W54 40N45
AA: B.C. in hand, Wilson
**Wallace, George Corley**  August 25,1919  Clio, AL
Politician  3:30 a.m. CWT  85W37 31N43
A: Marion March quotes his mother to Elizabeth Mayo (George Corley
Wallace)
**Watson, Charles "Tex"**  December 2, 1945  Dallas, TX
Homicide  9:15 p.m. CST  96W48 32N47
AA: Lockhart quotes B.C.
**Watts, Alan Wilson**  January 6, 1915  Chislehurst, England
Writer  6:20 a.m. GMT  0E04 51N25
B: Autobiography, *In My Own Way,* 1972, p. 10
**West, Mae**  August 17, 1892  Brooklyn, NY
Actress  10:30 p.m. EST  73W56 40N38
A: Marianne Dunn quotes Paul Noval, West's companion for 20 years
(Mary Jane West)
**Wilde, Oscar**  October 16, 1854  Dublin, Ireland
Writer  3:00 a.m. Dunsink time  6W15 53N20
AA: Pagan quotes B.R. in *American Astrology* September, 1963 (Oscar
Fingal O'Flahertie)
**Yeats, William Butler**  June 13, 1865  Sandymount, Ireland
Writer  10:40 p.m. Dublin tm  6W10 53N16
AA: His neighbor, Sheila Lindsay, quotes his family bible

**Yoakum, Ellen**    August 2, 1903    Hillsboro,TX
Healer    1:20 a.m. CST    97W08 32N01
A: C.L. quotes her acquaintance Elbert Wheeler
**Yogananda, Paramhansa**  January 5, 1893    Gorakhpur, India
Mystic    8:38 p.m. LMT    83E22 26N46
A: MH July 1976 quotes the SRI (Mukanda Lal Ghosh)
**Young, Loretta**    January 6, 1913    Salt Lake City, UT
Actress    3:30 p.m. MST    111W53 40N46
AA: CAH quotes B.C. (Gretchen Michaela Young)
**Young, Sean**    November 20, 1959  Louisville, KY
Actress    10:46 a.m. CST    85W46 38N15
AA: B.C. in hand, Kathryn Farmer (Mary Sean Young)
**Zappa, Dweezil**    September 5, 1969  Los Angeles, CA
Musician    8:05 a.m. PDT    118W15 34N04
A: ECS quotes him to Jean Berlow

**Source abbreviations:**
AA: *American Astrology*
AFA: American Federation of Astrologers, *Today's Astrologer*
AQ: *Astrological Quarterly*
BJA: *British Journal of Astrology*
Blackwell: Arthur Blackwell
Bordoni: Grazia Bordoni, *Data Di Nascita Interessanti,* six Vol.
CAH: *Contemporary American Horoscopes*
CL: Church of Light
CSH: *Contemporary Sidereal Horoscopes*
Ebertin: Reinhold Ebertin
ECS: Edwin C. Steinbrecher
Fagan: Cyril Fagan
GBAC: *Gauquelin Book of American Charts*
LMR: Lois M. Rodden
Lockhart: Gene Lockhart
MA: *Modern Astrology*
MH: *Mercury Hour*
NAJ: *National Astrology Journal*
Rudhyar: Dane Rudhyar
Wilson: Thelma and Tom Wilson

Printed in the United States
91166LV00002B/161/A

9 780866 905640